The State of Play

Ex Machina: Law, Technology, and Society

General Editors: Jack M. Balkin *and* Beth Simone Noveck

The Digital Person: Technology and Privacy in the Information Age
Daniel J. Solove

The State of Play: Law, Games, and Virtual Worlds
Edited by Jack M. Balkin and Beth Simone Noveck

The State of Play

Law, Games, and Virtual Worlds

EDITED BY

Jack M. Balkin and Beth Simone Noveck

New York University Press

NEW YORK AND LONDON

NEW YORK UNIVERSITY PRESS
New York and London
www.nyupress.org

Library of Congress Cataloging-in-Publication Data
The state of play : law, games, and virtual worlds / edited by Jack M. Balkin
and Beth Simone Noveck.
p. cm. — (Ex machina)
Includes bibliographical references and index.
ISBN-13: 978-0-8147-9971-0 (cloth : alk. paper)
ISBN-10: 0-8147-9971-X (cloth : alk. paper)
ISBN-13: 978-0-8147-9972-7 (pbk. : alk. paper)
ISBN-10: 0-8147-9972-8 (pbk. : alk. paper)
1. Computer games—Law and legislation. 2. Virtual reality. I. Balkin, J.
M. II. Noveck, Beth Simone.
K3705.V53S73   2006
343.09'944—dc22   2006018394

New York University Press books are printed on acid-free paper, and their
binding materials are chosen for strength and durability.

Manufactured in the United States of America
c 10 9 8 7 6 5 4 3 2 1
p 10 9 8 7 6 5 4 3 2 1

To the participants at the State of Play conferences,
and to all the avatars we have loved and known.

Contents

Introduction

1

Introduction

Jack M. Balkin and Beth Simone Noveck

In his 1992 novel *Snow Crash,* science fiction writer Neal Stephenson imagined the Metaverse. The Metaverse was a virtual world—a three-dimensional simulation of reality in cyberspace—where people lived, worked, and socialized. Since then programmers have used increasingly sophisticated graphical interfaces to create their own versions of the Metaverse. Although the development of these virtual worlds has been driven by the game industry, by now these worlds are used for far more than play, and soon they will be widely adopted as spaces for research, education, politics, and work. In the years to come our gateway to the Internet will probably look more like a video game and less like a book. Thus anyone who wants to understand the future of the Internet needs to understand virtual worlds.

Millions of people around the globe now play in these virtual or synthetic worlds. In fact, many of the 20 to 30 million regular participants now spend more time in virtual environments than they do at their real-world jobs or engaged with their real-world communities; according to one recent estimate, the average number of hours played is almost twenty-two per week. People who do not vote or engage in politics in real space eagerly do so in virtual spaces, drawn by the promise of new adventures, new identities, and the possibility of building new social universes.

People go to virtual spaces like Britannia or Norrath or Second Life to create characters, swap stories, build things, solve problems, pay taxes, enact rules, and break them. Some play in military virtual worlds like *America's Army;* in fact, the U.S. military now uses virtual worlds to simulate military situations and train and recruit real soldiers for battle. Virtual worlds have become active sites for commerce, where players trade in virtual goods and services. On any given day between ten and twenty thousand virtual-world items are for sale on eBay. Participants go to virtual churches, join virtual societies, and engage in social activism and political protest.

The rich, persistent, interactive and graphical interfaces of virtual worlds stimulate social experimentation and encourage people to create new lives and to build vibrant economies and cultures. Virtual worlds are full of social cooperation and social conflict; they present all the problems of social order we find in real space and some that we do not. No wonder, then, that legal scholars have increasingly been drawn to study these worlds, both for the legal problems arising within them and for what these worlds might tell us about law and social order in real space.

This book brings together essays by some of the most important thinkers on law and virtual worlds. It grows out of the first annual State of Play Conference, held at New York Law School from November 13 to 15, 2003. The State of Play was organized by the Institute for Information Law and Policy at New York Law School and the Information Society Project at Yale Law School; it brought together leading legal scholars, game designers, and software industry professionals, as well as cognitive psychologists, communications experts, computer scientists, visual artists, and game players to explore the next frontier of cyberspace: the virtual world.

Greg Lastowka and Dan Hunter's introductory essay explains the basic terminology of virtual worlds and gives a brief history. They trace the origins of today's virtual worlds from the early text-based adventure games called MUDs (standing for either "multiuser dungeon" or "multiuser dimension") and MOOs ("MUD object oriented"—a reference to the style of programming used) to much larger and more interactive games with elaborate graphical interfaces. These games are sometimes called MORPGs (multiplayer online role-playing games) or MMORPGs (massively multiplayer online role-playing games).

The second section of the book, "Game Gods and Game Players," describes the basic conflicts that arise in virtual worlds between the players, the game owners, and the state. Private companies build and control virtual worlds for the entertainment of their subscribers. Players sign end-user license agreements (EULAs) that give them the right to play in the space in return for agreeing to the game owner's terms. As these games evolve into online societies, the question naturally arises whether and when real-world law should step in to protect the players from arbitrary decisions by the "game gods" and from allegedly unfair features of EULAs.

Should the law leave the regulation of virtual worlds largely to the market and to the artistic decisions and programming expertise of game owners or should legislatures and courts create new legal rules to constrain game owners?

The authors in this section take contrasting positions about the appropriate balance of rights between the players, game owners, and the state. Richard Bartle, one of the earliest virtual-world designers and cocreator of the first MUD, argues strongly for the rights of game designers in the virtual world. Playing a game means agreeing to abide by the rules the game designers set down. Designers, Bartle points out, have natural incentives to create worlds that people will want to play in, and so they should be given wide discretion in the way they organize a virtual world. Designers crucially maintain order in the game world, disciplining and even expelling players who make the game worse for everyone. Without the ability to recode the rules as the game designer chooses, a virtual world is "greatly diminished if not mortally wounded," and the game designer's incentives to design are skewed. Adminstrators of virtual worlds (often called "admins") can and sometimes do willingly surrender their powers over the game to the players, Bartle explains, but "I am not happy for them to be taken away through ignorance by external forces."

An opposing view comes from Raph Koster, creative director of Sony On-Line Entertainment, and the designer of *Star Wars Galaxies* and many other of the most popular massively multiplayer games. Koster argues that players deserve respect from the game designers and administrators as well as basic regulatory protections. Koster's contribution to this volume is an expanded version of his famous essay "A Declaration of the Rights of Avatars," a manifesto for the age of virtual worlds loosely based on the 1789 Declaration of the Rights of Man. Game administrators, Koster argues, should bind themselves to basic standards of decency and conduct, not only because it makes good business sense but because avatars are not merely fictional characters, but represent real people and their identities. "Some day," Koster predicts, "there won't be any [game] admin[istrator]s. Some day it's gonna be your bank records and your grocery list and your credit report. . . . Some day it's gonna be *Snow Crash* and *Neuromancer* and *Otherland* all wrapped up into one, and it may be a little harder to write to Customer Service." "On the day that happens, I bet we'll all wish we had a few more rights in the face of a very large, distributed server, anarchic, virtual world where it might be very *hard* to move to a different service provider."

Ted Castronova is one of the first social scientists to have taken virtual-worlds seriously; he pioneered the study of virtual world economies, demonstrating that the GDP of Norrath, part of the virtual world *EverQuest,* was larger than that of several developing countries. Although Castronova gained fame by studying how players made real-world money from virtual economies, he argues that game spaces should be reserved for play and not for commodification. The point of virtual worlds, Castronova argues, is to allow the players to engage in fantasy. The law should safeguard the "Magic Circle" that allows them to do this. Castronova worries that the buying and selling of virtual goods using real-world money has turned virtual worlds into real-world economic zones, destroying the distinction between the play space and ordinary life. To prevent this, Castronova proposes the idea of "interration." Just as the law has statutes of incorporation that allow for the creation of corporations—fictional legal persons with certain rights and obligations—the law should have special legal charters that he calls "statutes of interration." These would recognize game spaces as fictional worlds with their own independent powers of regulation. Interrated worlds would be "closed" worlds. Goods and services may not be traded for real-world currency in these closed worlds and players who attempt to do so can be excluded from the game. In addition, closed worlds would be separate jurisdictions with rules of their own, into which real-world law would not enter: "Once a world is interrated under th[e] law whatever rights or obligations its internal government decrees (again, assuming they do not violate the terms of the charter itself) are sacrosanct there, and no user has a right to redress under any outside authority."

By contrast, Jack Balkin argues that the law cannot be kept out of virtual worlds. As more and more people spend increasing amounts of time and energy there, they will inevitably call upon the state to protect their interests, and legislatures, administrative agencies, and courts will inevitably respond. Balkin believes that commercialization and commodification are the root causes of this trend. Because both game owners and players seek property protection for goods created in virtual worlds, they are effectively inviting the law in.

Balkin argues that the players' freedom to play and the designers' freedom to design are related to but not identical with the First Amendment rights of freedom of speech and association. He emphasizes the importance of protecting the free speech rights of both players and game designers from the state and balancing the free speech interests of players and designers. Building on Castronova's notion of interration, he argues that interration statutes should allow game designers to choose among different kinds of regulatory schemes for virtual worlds, some which protect property rights and some which do not, some which secure public spaces for unfettered dissent and protest, and some which protect the free association rights of game designers. Whereas Castronova suggests that statutes of interration should be used to keep the real law out, Balkin believes that the real point of statutes of interration is to bring law in to protect free speech property and privacy rights.

Property rights are one of the most hotly debated topics about virtual worlds. Many view property as essential to the existence not only of virtual worlds, but of society more generally. The next section of essays, entitled "Property and Creativity in Virtual Worlds," asks about the proper role of real-world law in regulating property in virtual worlds. The very idea of property in virtual worlds raises a host of questions: Can there be crime or theft of property? What kind of governance of property should apply in virtual worlds? How should property protections be reshaped to serve the larger purposes of promoting social interaction and creativity in different kinds of virtual worlds? Although nominally about property, the essays in this section reflect a broader philosophical debate about the role of the law in producing social order and shaping social life.

Greg Lastowka and Dan Hunter's essay "Virtual Crime" considers whether the law should penalize the theft of virtual property that people invest time and energy in creating. What complicates the issue is that crime sometimes takes place in the context of the game, and may or may not be part of the game. Thus, Lastowka and Hunter worry that courts and legislatures will misunderstand the setting in which disputes about theft of virtual goods arise. They argue that the issue of virtual crime should be resolved by the EULA. "By concentrating the legal control of and rules regarding virtual property in their own hands, game owners and designers may essentially disarm many of the difficult legal issues stemming from inter-avatar property crime." "Some degree of confusion and category mistake would almost inevitably result from judicial attempts to interpret traditional criminal laws in order to police player behaviors in virtual worlds. Ironically, if we wish to preserve the benefits of virtual worlds as free and independent social experiments, it may be best if we keep the criminal law at a safe distance."

Julian Dibbell is a journalist of cyberspace, and the author of a famous *Village Voice* article, "A Rape in Cyberspace," that described a rape in a virtual world and introduced many people to the special characteristics of these worlds. In his essay, "Owned!" Dibbell tells the story of Black Snow Interactive, a fly-by-night organization which hired Mexican nationals in Tijuana to play Mythic Entertainment's *Dark Age of Camelot* around the clock to produce game currency that could be exchanged for dollars.

The best way to deal with property rights in virtual worlds, Dibbell argues, is to allow the game designer to control the rules of play and the existence or nonexistence of real-world property. When faced with exploits like Black Snow's, Dibbell contends, "the end-user license agreement—that egregious tool of corporate tyranny over the defenseless, voiceless customer (or so I had painted it)—starts to look more like the place where a complicated give and take between designers and players is finally ratified, transformed from a murky power struggle into the legally binding rules of the game. The EULA starts to look less like a contract of adhesion, in other words, than like a social contract." Indeed, Dibbell argues, "the feedback loop" between game players and game designers "is at best a crude approximation of democratic government—and for the sake of whatever fun inheres in these games is probably better left that way."

While Dibbell hopes that the EULA might serve as an imperfect social contract that guarantees some decree of democratic accountability between players and game gods, James Grimmelmann views this social contract in far more Hobbesian terms. Grimmelmann sees disputes in virtual worlds as the rough and tumble of politics. "Every debate over the rules and every change to the software is political," he explains. "When players talk about the rules, they are practicing politics." Grimmelmann argues that there is no logical distinction between what he calls an "exploit," taking advantage of a loophole in the game's coding to contravene the spirit, if not the rules of the game, and a "feature" of the game that players discover and use to make the game more fun and to secure a competitive advantage. Grimmelmann believes the distinction between exploits and features will be decided, if at all, through the political negotiation between the various players and the game gods. Hence, Grimmelmann concludes that virtual worlds present many of the same problems that we see in real-world politics, including international politics. "Any difference [between real and virtual worlds] is illusory; these worlds may be virtual, but their politics are wholly real."

Cory Ondrejka is one of the designers of *Second Life*, a popular virtual world that encourages its inhabitants to build and create new items. Inspired by Neal Stephenson's vision of the Metaverse in *Snow Crash*,

Ondrejka argues in his contribution, "Escaping the Guilded Cage: User-Created Content and Building the Metaverse," that today's technology finally allows people, for the first time, to construct the Metaverse for themselves. But Ondrejka argues that the Metaverse cannot succeed without players owning property rights in their own creations.

To this end, Ondrejka's company, Linden Lab, has declined to exercise exclusive property rights in the digital works that players create in *Second Life*. Ondrejka argues that if players own rights to their own works, they will be more likely to create things, and by creating, become attached to the place that gives them tools to build their own creations. The Metaverse can happen if we let the players build it themselves rather than have game owners design it for them. By safeguarding players' intellectual property rights and giving them the right to make money from their creations, game companies foster genuine creativity and the production of new objects and institutions, rather than mere crafting or tinkering. Give the players the ability to collaborate creatively, and let them make money from their efforts, Ondrejka argues, and they will homestead a new virtual frontier.

Yochai Benkler's "There Is No Spoon" takes its title from a line from the movie *The Matrix*, in which the hero learns that everything that appears real is actually a computer simulation. Benkler argues that talk about property rights conceals a larger set of issues. The question is not whether players and game gods have rights or even whether virtual objects are property. Rather, the question is what kind of social relations a virtual world is trying to achieve. Property rights are only a means to realizing a particular set of social ends. For Benkler, "the interesting questions are, which approach will better foster creativity on this platform, give users greater creative autonomy, and create a more effective social network." Benkler argues that the graphical rendering of virtual worlds is largely irrelevant to these questions because the graphical interface says little about the kind of social relations that the space is designed to achieve. For example, some virtual worlds will be largely for entertainment purposes or for buying and selling items. Others will be much closer to systems for the peer-production of knowledge like Wikipedia, an online collaboratively produced encyclopedia. To decide whether a virtual world like *Second Life* should adopt a particular set of intellectual property rights for players, Benkler argues, the designers must ask what kind of virtual world they want to be and what kinds of social relations they wish to foster.

Benkler's argument raises a key issue implicit in many of the other essays in this book. Is there something about the rich graphical and interactive interfaces of virtual worlds that makes them importantly different from other forms of Internet activity? Do these interfaces help explain the sort of behavior we are likely to find within them? Or can virtual worlds produce any sort of social behavior and social ordering, depending on the designs of the game gods?

A key feature of virtual worlds is their flexibility about identity: They allow players to assume multiple identities and take on new social roles. Multiple identities and role playing are hardly unique to virtual worlds. Nevertheless, the graphical representation of avatars is one of virtual worlds' most salient characteristics, and it creates a wide range of interesting problems about identity and personal privacy. Virtual spaces encourage people to adopt new and multiple identities, which are often very different from their real-world identity. The rules of the space, controlled by the game gods, regulate what kinds of identities people can adopt, and whether they can keep their real-world identity hidden and separate from their online identities. The essays in the next section, "Privacy and Identity in Virtual Worlds" are concerned with these issues.

Tracy Spaight's essay, "Who Killed Miss Norway?" tells the fascinating story of a beauty pageant contestant who became a central part of the lives of her virtual-world friends until she was mysteriously killed in an automobile accident. Or was she? Spaight's story demonstrates vividly how virtual-world identities become as important to people as their real-world identities. Behind identity is the problem of trust; the players sympathized with Miss Norway because they trusted that she was who she said she was. The flip side of trust, however, is the possibility of deception and even betrayal, and virtual spaces make such deception particularly easy to accomplish. Not only do participants take on specially constructed identities in these virtual spaces, but the spaces themselves are generally understood to be places for play and make-believe. Nevertheless, play itself requires some degree of trust between the players, and that trust may often blossom into friendship, which players may regard as quite genuine and every bit as important to them as their friendships in real space. Spaight's compelling tale illuminates how virtual worlds generate and even require friendship and trust because of their complex social interactions, while at the same time undermining the consistency and authenticity of players' identities.

Susan Crawford's essay, "Who's in Charge of Who I Am?" focuses on how technology shapes the construction of human identity. Identity is central to human autonomy and self-fulfillment, but in virtual spaces players may have multiple identities. These identities are subject to the ultimate authority of the game owner, who can limit the forms of identity that players can inhabit and who can even eliminate particular characters at will. Crawford argues that the law, which generally conceives of identity as unitary, is a poor instrument for regulating virtual worlds in which multiple identities coexist simultaneously. At the same time, she points out that in one respect identity in virtual worlds is not so different from everyday experience: In the real world people belong to multiple social groups and therefore inhabit multiple social roles that define their various identities. In the same fashion, Crawford argues, social groups can and should regulate player identities in virtual worlds. Social groups, Crawford argues, can often perform this task better than either game owners or real-world law.

Tal Zarsky's contribution points out that virtual worlds create special problems of privacy. Players not only may want to keep their online identities (and activities) secret in the real world, but they may also want to keep their real-world identities secret in their online communities, where they also have reputations built up over time. Game gods are omniscient; they can trace everything that avatars do inside the virtual world as well as collate this information with information about players' real-world identities. This allows game owners to violate players' privacy in both directions. Equally important, it allows them to create digital dossiers on players' preferences much more efficiently than in other Internet interactions that are spread over many different sites not controlled by a single entity. This, in turn, enables game owners to manipulate players more effectively in order to sell them goods and services.

The essays in the last section, "Virtual Worlds and Real-World Power" consider how virtual spaces can change the law and affect social relations in the real world. Caroline Bradley and Michael Froomkin argue that social scientists can use virtual spaces as test-beds to experiment with different sets of social and legal rules. Because virtual worlds feature complex social relationships, they are good platforms for trying out different legal rules and testing their consequences over time. In effect, virtual worlds allow a kind of cyberfederalism in which different communities can experiment with different rule sets. And because virtual worlds exist largely apart from real-world law, they can test legal rules prior to implementing them in real space.

David Johnson extends the theme of decentralization and experimentation. He argues that the graphical technologies originally developed for virtual worlds allow new groups and new legal arrangements to be realized in the real world. For example, business organizations can exploit virtual-world interfaces to create new corporate forms. By exploiting the unique attributes of the computer interface, people can come together spontaneously to buy, sell, and distribute assets without incurring the costs of traditional corporate organization. Johnson believes that graphical interfaces offer increasing flexibility for forming and organizing social and business relationships. Instead of creating relatively permanent organizational structures, groups can form and organize themselves for specific purposes and then disband when their tasks are accomplished.

Beth Simone Noveck's essay "Democracy—The Video Game," also focuses on the special features of virtual-world technology. She agrees with Yochai Benkler that technology's impact on social relations is the key question, but in contrast to Benkler, she emphasizes that the tools through which people experience the Metaverse help determine what kind of social relations are possible there. Noveck argues that virtual-world interfaces, which render persons as avatars inhabiting simulated locales, allow people to form loosely knit social organizations and groups that can effectively wield power together. Unlike the first generation of World Wide Web technologies, virtual worlds reintroduce location, place, and space to Internet interactions; they allow participants to visualize themselves in embodied relationships to the communities to which they belong. By making it easier for people to see the groups to which they belong, virtual worlds make it easier for them to speak and act as a group. For this reason, virtual worlds, unlike the web-based Internet that preceded them, have a different and more powerful impact on collective action that can enhance the prospects for self-governance. Drawing repeated distinctions between older text-based cyberspace and new graphical virtual worlds, she argues that the latter have enormous untapped potential to shape real-world power and foster real-world democracy.

2

Virtual Worlds

A Primer

F. Gregory Lastowka and Dan Hunter

A snow-capped mountain range stretches over the town's northern border and tapers down to a southward-facing, concave bay embracing a small archipelago of glittering islands. Homes are clustered in predictable locations: on the islands, against the seaside, and close to the mountains. This is the community of Blazing Falls, a town with over 25,000 inhabitants— roughly the size of Timbuktu or Poughkeepsie. Its young and attractive twenty-something inhabitants can be found chatting and working together in their eclectically furnished dwellings. Most live with roommates, with whom they share both rights of ownership and the duties of taking out the garbage, washing the dishes, and paying for parties and furniture. In their leisure time, they chat with neighbors, attend shows, dance at nightclubs, work out, and visit local attractions. Undoubtedly, many Blazing Falls residents are engaged in such activities at this very moment. As you are reading this, they are eating, sleeping, or resting on comfortable couches in front of television sets while they discuss politics and the latest movies with their roommates.

All manner of social groups exist in Blazing Falls—Christians, Wiccans, Goths, Punks, and poets. Many professional types are represented: Some work as telemarketers; others work as repairmen; some are aspiring musicians; and there are even people who manufacture lawn gnomes for a living. Most people do business honestly, but there is a shady side to Blazing Falls. Some Blazing Falls residents are confidence men, preying on gullible newcomers. There are even a few brothels and strip clubs, though the legality of these establishments is dubious.

All this seems familiar. Yet there is much about Blazing Falls that is decidedly unfamiliar. A casual visitor might at first be nonplussed by the common social practices in the community. Homeowners in Blazing Falls generally encourage strangers to enter their property, lie in their beds, eat their food, use their bathrooms, and monopolize their possessions. When these visitors break their pinball machines and exercise equipment, the owners may complain a bit, but for the most part they cheerfully repair the items and let the visitors have a go at them again.

Other aspects of Blazing Falls are harder to explain. No one there has ever been ill. And though marriages occur often enough, no children have ever been seen. Strangely for a town of 25,000, even if one of the nubile and newly married residents were to become pregnant, she would find no hospital where a child might be delivered. Most importantly (for the purposes of the legal scholar) there are no courts, no halls of Congress, and not even a visible police force—yet not one murder has ever been reported.

If you ask the average resident of Blazing Falls what she thinks about the absence of familiar legal institutions, however, she will generally seem more intrigued than alarmed. In Blazing Falls, she will ask, is all that messy business of law and government truly necessary? After all, none of this is real.

Blazing Falls, as you have probably guessed, is a virtual world. Using less lofty language, you might call it a computer game. Blazing Falls is just one town in the larger environment of *The Sims Online,* a popular game with reportedly over 100,000 subscribers.[1] Other contemporary virtual worlds include the tropical beaches of Tiki (There.com's *There*), the fantasy world of Norrath (Sony's *EverQuest*), the interstellar expanses of the Milky Way (Electronic Art's *Earth & Beyond*), and even a galaxy far, far away (Sony's *Star Wars Galaxies*). In Blazing Falls and these other places, millions of people with Internet connections are currently living large portions of their lives, forming friendships with others, building and acquiring virtual property, and forming social organizations.[2] In South Korea, the game *Lineage* is currently more popular than television, with some 4 million registered participants.[3] In the United States, *EverQuest's* Norrath is the most popular virtual world, with over 440,000 subscribers at last count. *Ultima Online* and *Dark Age of Camelot* are serious competitors, having 250,000 and 200,000 participants, respectively.[4]

This is obviously a new concept in games, if it is even properly characterized as a game at all. Non-networked computer games resemble the mental world of a two-year-old: everything revolves around you and nothing happens when you are not present. Virtual worlds are different. *The Sims Online,* like all virtual worlds, is both persistent and dynamic. Even when you are not in Blazing Falls, the environment continues to exist and changes over time. While you sleep in real life, other people's representations may be eating and dancing in your home in Blazing Falls; your neighbors' virtual houses will be remodeled and redecorated while you commute to work; virtual weddings will take place while you chat at the physical world water cooler; and new social structures will emerge while you have dinner. By the time you get back to Blazing Falls in the evening, you may find that the entire infrastructure and character of your neighborhood has changed.

Of course, all these changes occur in a represented reality, and the inhabitants of Blazing Falls know each other through representational proxies that may or may not reflect the physical attributes of their controllers. Representational proxies in these virtual spaces are known as "avatars," a word of Hindu religious origin.[5] Avatars, unlike prior video game alter egos, can be richly customized and are designed primarily for social interaction. Currently, the avatars of virtual worlds speak with each other through either textual chat windows or "speech bubbles" that float over their heads. Avatars express themselves through appearance as well. You can choose the face, clothes, and body shape of your avatar and communicate with others through body language. For instance, in *The Sims Online,* avatars yawn, clap, shout, shake their fists, cry, hug, kiss, dance, and perform hundreds of other ordinary human actions to let others know how they're feeling.

Perhaps because virtual worlds support this kind of rich social interaction, many of those who have chosen to visit virtual worlds remain residents of them. The average *EverQuest* player and Norrath avatar, for instance, spends about twenty hours a week within the virtual world.[6] Virtual-world participants design costumes, furniture, and houses for their avatars, and sell their creations to others. They buy and barter virtual chattels on eBay.[7] They form clubs and organizations devoted to mutual aid and protection. They pressure their roommates and organizational members to spend more time in the virtual world in order to foster the common good.

Virtual worlds are unreal: They are artificial, fictitious, imaginary, intangible, and invented. Yet virtual worlds are real, as well. All things artificial or invented do not fall entirely outside the ambit of reality. If they did, we would need to banish from reality all manner of human actions and creations, including buildings, languages, and—most important for our purposes—laws. As Jack Balkin and Julian Dibbell have noted, while laws may be invented and intangible, they are hardly insignificant.[8]

We suggest that the laws of virtual worlds are significant for three primary reasons. First, virtual worlds are attracting an ever-increasing population of participants who believe that the social interactions that occur within these environments are important.

When economics professor Edward Castronova undertook a study of the economics of *EverQuest,* he was challenged by the impression that others within his field might have thought he was wasting his time on something lacking in real-world relevance. His explanation for why this "silly game" really mattered was as follows:

> Economists believe that it is the practical actions of people, and not abstract arguments, that determine the social value of things. One does not study the labor market because work is holy and ethical; one does it because the conditions of work mean a great deal to a large number of ordinary people. By the same reasoning, economists and other social scientists will become more interested in Norrath and similar virtual worlds as they realize that such places have begun to mean a great deal to large numbers of ordinary people.[9]

Castronova is right. Millions of people spend a large portion of their waking lives in virtual worlds. A significant number of users even claim primary citizenship in virtual worlds. In Castronova's study, 20 percent of participants in a large survey of *EverQuest*'s users attested to living their lives mostly in *EverQuest*'s Norrath, 22 percent expressed the desire to spend all their time there, and 40 percent indicated that if a sufficient wage were available in Norrath they would quit their job or studies on earth.[10]

A second reason why virtual worlds are worthy of consideration is that the economic boundaries between the real and the virtual world are not as distinct as they might appear. If you're going on a virtual date with a new acquaintance you met in the online game *There,* you'll probably want to dress to impress. So perhaps you'll pick up some baggy Levi's jeans, a Nike sweatshirt, or maybe a snazzy new hoverboard for your avatar. You may even want to fine-tune your avatar's face and haircut. All these virtual chattels and services will set you back a tidy sum of Therebucks at the *There*-controlled rate of 1,787 Therebucks to the U.S. dollar. Your nonvirtual credit card will be charged for these purchases. Nike and Levi Strauss seem to be intrigued by a market for virtual "goods" which requires no costly physical inputs.[11]

Even where the creator of the virtual world does not facilitate markets for virtual goods, the residents may take it upon themselves to do so. For instance, if one spends enough time in virtual worlds, one can accumulate property that other people value: virtual castles, swords, silk sashes, and even one's own avatar. By listing a well-developed avatar and its virtual castle on eBay, you can convert your virtual asset from a virtual value to real U.S. dollars.[12] In fact, these transfers happen so often that one can calculate an exchange rate between virtual- and real-world currencies.[13]

Simply put, the real and the virtual overlap from an economic perspective. For better or for worse, it is now possible to work in a fantasy world to pay rent in reality.[14] The process differs little from, say, a Filipino overseas contract worker who works in another country for a period and sends money back to the Philippines. The implication is that some day people will walk their well-dressed avatars to virtual offices, where they, through their avatars, will labor to convince other avatars to cough up real cash for virtual goods. One obvious question that emerges from these transactions is how to deal with the jurisdictional issues presented by the disputes that will inevitably arise over virtual assets and transactions. It is unclear how existing property rules apply to such virtual rights and properties.

A third reason for exploring the laws of virtual worlds is that they provide a parallel alternative to existing legal systems, where new forms of social regulation can be explored. This point was made several years ago by Professor Jennifer Mnookin in her discussion of the virtual world of LambdaMOO. As Mnookin observed in regard to LambdaMOO's emerging legal system, "Virtual communities like LambdaMOO, odd hybrids between games and worlds, simulations and society, may prove to be spaces for institutional reimagining, for questioning and reshaping conceptions of self, politics, and law."[15] The same arguments Mnookin applied to LambdaMOO apply to the far more prevalent phenomenon of today's virtual worlds, which have progressed far beyond the small communities and textual interface of early virtual worlds like LambdaMOO. The laws of virtual worlds, where hundreds of thousands of individuals interact and form social bonds, can provide researchers with interesting insights into the emergence of law within new societies that exist purely through the medium of computer software.[16]

How did virtual worlds come to be? The original virtual worlds were created in fiction. Fictional geographies, often lovingly detailed, are frequently an important part of imagined literary worlds. The most important twentieth-century popularizer of virtual worlds, J. R. R. Tolkien, created comprehensive maps of Middle-Earth and its Shire, the imaginary places where *The Hobbit* and *The Lord of the Rings* trilogy take place. One of the distinct pleasures of reading Tolkien stems from the richness of his imaginary topography, expressed through his hand-drawn maps. One can trace the movement of the protagonists across a landscape of forests, mountains, and marshes, and wonder at the nature of those regions that his text does not explore. Perhaps because of the richness of Tolkien's world-building, his works have had an enormous and varied influence on contemporary fantasy novels and, arguably, have given birth to the fantasy-literature genre as it exists today.

Those who designed the precursors of today's virtual worlds were not immune to this influence. Among Tolkien's earliest devotees were medievalists, some of whom enjoyed the hobby of staging battles involving miniature lead soldiers. In 1974, two medievalist war-gamers, Gary Gygax and Dave Arneson, transformed Tolkien's richly imagined world into a game called Dungeons & Dragons (D&D). While billed as a wargame, D&D was a far cry from traditional historical reenactment. The D&D game simulated the adventures of individual dwarves, elves, hobbits, and humans. The players of the game identified with their individual avatars rather than controlling armies of game pieces, leading to the description of D&D as a "role-playing" game.[17]

In the game, a "dungeon master" creates opponents and obstacles for the players and describes them verbally. These challenges usually consist of hostile monsters such as dragons and orcs, as well as deadly puzzles. After defeating a certain number of obstacles according to the game's rules, a player's avatar increases in power. This process is known as "leveling"—a beginner starts as a weak level 1 avatar, progresses to become a more powerful level 2 avatar, and so on.

The Byzantine rules and imagination-taxing quality of the game prevented D&D from ever achieving the popularity of Monopoly. However, for the niche market of computer programmers, Byzantine rules and unreal environments were par for the course. Perhaps as a result, Tolkien and D&D ended up playing a crucial role in the development of computer-based virtual worlds.[18] The process began in 1976, when Will Crowther, a Tolkien and D&D aficionado, wrote a computer game called ADVENT.[19] The game, which Crowther wrote to amuse his children, presented a navigable textual database based on the real-world Mammoth

Cave in Kentucky, spiced up with D&D elements to make it more interesting. The game emulated the conversational style of a D&D dungeon master: "You are standing at the end of a road before a small brick building. Around you is a forest. A small stream flows out of the building and down a gulley."[20] Nothing further would occur in the game unless the player typed a textual command. For instance, if the player typed the word "enter," thus ordering the avatar to enter the building, the computer would respond by displaying the sentences: "You are inside a building, a well house for a large spring. There are some keys on the ground here." Like a D&D game, Crowther's program was replete with complicated puzzles requiring players to perform certain tasks with specific objects to avoid death and to progress in the game.[21]

The weak point of ADVENT and similar games was that they were not social. Only one avatar could exist within the textual space. In 1979, Roy Trubshaw and Richard Bartle created the first social textual world, MUD1, at Essex University in England.[22] In MUD1 and its derivatives, avatars could talk with others in the same "room" via simple text commands. If an avatar named Alice was in the same room as another avatar named Gulliver, the computer would alert Alice and Gulliver to each other's presence. If Alice wanted to speak, she would type "Gulliver hi," and Gulliver would then see the words "Alice tells you 'hi'" appear on his terminal. This feature had substantial appeal simply as an early instant messaging system.[23]

MUD1 and the other original MUDs, however, were not primarily friendly chat rooms. The primary game goal of MUD1 was navigating the textual environment while killing opponents and gathering treasures to score points and level up. The ultimate goal of the game was to reach the level of "wizard," at which one became an all-powerful entity within the game environment. When choosing targets, perhaps the most interesting way to score points was by killing other players. If Alice decided to kill Gulliver, she would simply type "Kill Gulliver" rather than "Gulliver hi." Gulliver would then need to type either "retaliate" or "flee." If Alice killed Gulliver (which would depend mainly on her avatar's skill and weaponry) she would gain points, and Gulliver would need to start his virtual life anew.[24]

Through the 1980s, Trubshaw and Bartle's original MUD1 spawned hundreds of derivative MUD-type environments, known variously as MOOs, MUSHes, and MUCKs, on university computer systems.[25] Some MUDs actually made money: When commercially released in the United States on CompuServe, MUD1 cost $12.50 an hour to play. Probably the most interesting development in MUD history occurred in 1989, when James Aspnes wrested MUDs away from their D&D roots by writing a short and easily portable MUD program known as TinyMUD. TinyMUD deemphasized traditional D&D elements, such as killing for points. Instead, the program gave avatars greater abilities to describe themselves and invent objects. In the multiple TinyMUDs that were quickly established, avatars did not kill each other quite so often. Rather, they spent a lot of time simply hanging out, chatting, and amusing each other with new virtual objects. This dimension, of course, appealed to a whole different social set, and TinyMUDs quickly branched out from Tolkienesque settings to encompass more diverse themes. Some were based on *Star Trek;* some were set within specific novels; and some were even set in real-world locations such as a virtual California.

Perhaps the most widely known social MUD is LambdaMOO, initially created in 1990 by Pavel Curtis of the Xerox Palo Alto Research Center. LambdaMOO still has over a thousand active participants, of whom one or two hundred are active at any given moment. The first virtual spaces of LambdaMOO were based on Curtis's home in California, although the environment has since greatly expanded. LambdaMOO is not a remarkable MUD in any way, except that it can be altered by its participants and it has served as a focal point for research of virtual space. Its popularity has led its community to post an unusual disclaimer on the welcome page: "Notice for Journalists and Researchers: The citizens of LambdaMOO request that you ask for permission from all direct participants before quoting any material collected here."[26]

Each avatar in LambdaMOO has the power to create a set of rooms and unique programmed objects. Members of the community have programmed interactive textual gardens, robots, Frisbees, butlers, toys, helicopters, puzzles, and fireworks in order to amuse and impress other participants. In the living room of the LambdaMOO mansion (the de facto social hub), there is a cockatoo programmed to repeat random lines of overheard dialogue at regular intervals; a fireplace that will burn or toast objects placed inside; a large couch, which one can reupholster in garish patterns and which consumes objects from one's pockets. Objects such as a blender and a black hole allow avatars entering them to commit "MOOicide," or virtual suicide—destroying their avatar existence in order to force the players to return to their "real" lives.[27]

Yet MUDs, for all their liveliness and social complexity, are not the most popular virtual worlds today. MUDs are like poetry compared to television. While MUDs offer what is perhaps a more valuable and rewarding medium for those who participate in them, people seem to be drawn to visual spectacle. Indeed, while most MUDs are free, millions of individuals pay to interact with visual virtual worlds. A picture, it seems, is worth a thousand words—and quite a few dollars as well.

Until recently, one could not commingle visual representation with interaction. When this technology arrived, its most popular embodiment was, perhaps unsurprisingly, amusement. Thus, the history of interactive visual virtual worlds has been largely a history of video games. This is not to say that Internet chat rooms, business teleconferencing, flight simulation, and other instances of nongame computer-mediated virtual environments are not important. However, from a historical point of view, video games have been on the cutting edge of socially significant visually interactive technology.

Despite their increasingly sophisticated graphics, arcade games lacked a world that could persist over time. Once the "GAME OVER" message appeared, a player's investment in the virtual world was set back to zero. Only with the introduction of personal computers could designers explore the possibilities of persistent visual virtual worlds. Persistence through local data storage led to a new breed of immersive games. For instance, *King's Quest: The Quest for the Crown,* introduced in 1984, popularized visual virtual worlds as much as ADVENT had text-based worlds. *King's Quest* let users pilot a tiny but vivid-enough avatar (you could see the feather in Prince Graham's cap) across the screen of the first IBM PC in order to solve puzzles in the virtual world of Daventry. King's Quest was immensely successful and spawned seven subsequent titles.[28]

Prince Graham, like the solo ADVENT player, was alone in Daventry. Only a year after *King's Quest* was released, however, and only a few years after MUD1 created a networked version of the ADVENT-type game, Lucasfilm created a persistent visual virtual world called *Habitat*. *Habitat's* graphics were crude and cartoonish by today's standards, in part because it was designed for the primitive Commodore 64 personal computer. *Habitat* players customized their avatars mainly by selecting among a variety of fanciful heads for avatar bodies. As in *The Sims Online,* avatars communicated through speech bubbles appearing above their heads. The environment was built to accommodate as many as 20,000 avatars present simultaneously.[29]

Like TinyMUD, *Habitat* didn't emphasize leveling up so much as hanging out virtually. Two of its lead designers, Chip Morningstar and F. Randall Farmer, explained that the greatest challenge for *Habitat*'s creators was simply figuring out what all the avatars were supposed to do. Originally, the planners had intended to organize group events for the whole community, but the first attempts at central planning were disastrous. As a result, the *Habitat* team "shifted into a style of operations in which [the designers] let the players themselves drive the direction of the design."[30]

The *Habitat* experiment ended with the obsolescence of the Commodore personal computer for which it was designed. Since the demise of *Habitat*, connection speeds have increased and computers have become more powerful; as a result, visual virtual worlds have become larger, more finely detailed, and populated with an increasing number of avatars.[31] The most popular worlds are profit-driven. A prospective avatar can generally sign up for about $40, with an extra $10 monthly subscription fee.

Sony's Norrath (*EverQuest*) is the most popular virtual world among U.S. citizens, with over 420,000 monthly subscribers. *EverQuest* fits squarely within the tradition of D&D-based virtual worlds. Participants begin the game by selecting a "shard," or game server, a subset of *EverQuest*'s virtual world containing several thousand participants. After selecting a shard, the new player chooses an avatar. The game begins when the player presses a button labeled "Enter World" and views on the computer display a real-time three-dimensional image of the virtual world. The player sees other avatars nearby and "hears" their conversations in a chat window. The other visible avatars may be "bots" or "nonplayer characters," meaning that they are controlled by a computer program and not another human. Generally, one can ascertain whether an avatar is a bot by simple observation: real avatars move erratically and generally don't speak medieval English.[32]

The *EverQuest* "Level 1" avatar is penniless, carries a flimsy weapon, and lacks any significant skills or abilities. He or she starts in a "beginner's section" of the *EverQuest* world that has a nearby area conveniently overrun with computer-generated killing fodder such as rats, bugs, or snakes. Prior to reaching Level 5, which may take a day or a week, depending on one's level of commitment, an avatar will generally be too frail to venture outside this area. Most players, however, quickly get down to the business of increasing the power of their avatars, or "leveling," as it is more commonly known. This does not mean that players do not interact. Indeed, the game encourages avatars to group together to accomplish an objective. Avatars that combine their skills in teams or guilds are more effective at defeating enemies and, therefore, can "level" more quickly. The most intimate interactions usually occur during the lulls in combat, while avatars are waiting for their bodies to "heal." During this down time, individuals often discuss their real-world lives and identities. The avatar bonds formed between individuals may extend to the formation of more elaborate *EverQuest* guilds with binding rules of membership and websites promoting social events. A close association with another avatar over a long period of time may even lead to an in-game *EverQuest* marriage, which may in turn lead to a real-world marriage—or the dissolution of one.

Other Tolkienesque leveling worlds such as *Ultima Online*'s Britannia and the three realms of *Dark Age of Camelot* operate in much the same manner as *EverQuest,* though each has some notable variations. *Ultima Online,* released two years before *EverQuest,* creates more significant opportunities for avatars to specialize in nonviolent skills, such as blacksmithing or baking bread. One interesting feature in *Ultima Online* is the possibility of home creation and ownership. A current advertising campaign for *Ultima Online* features the availability of new tools for the creation and customization of virtual castles. The more recent *Dark Age* is one of the most visually lush virtual worlds. *Dark Age* generally hews closely to the *EverQuest* and *Ultima Online* model of success, though it differs by coding into the environment an interesting factional system, where one must align one's avatar with one of three realms based on medieval British, Celtic, and Norse cultures.

Despite the socializing that takes place in these D&D-type worlds, the clear goal in each is to become a more powerful avatar. If one wishes to obtain the pinnacle of virtual success in Norrath or Britannia, such as becoming the powerful leader of a guild or a flashy and impressive wizard, one must (in theory) earn that status through hours and hours of "play" at killing things.

The Sims Online is the leading example of a nonleveling world. Most nonleveling worlds also abandon the trappings of fantasy: instead of choosing to become an elf or a hobbit, one customizes one's avatars by choosing from hundreds of doll-like physical components, including tuxedos, leather jackets, and T-shirts. If a goal exists in *The Sims Online,* it is never stated. However, most people seem interested in making money, and the primary means of making money is engaging in work activities. Increased skills can bring wealth to an avatar, as well as provide the avatar with improved capabilities, such as the ability to play a musical instrument.

A new avatar generally arrives on the sidewalks of Blazing Falls (or one of the other towns in *The Sims Online*) with a modest amount of cash and few skills. The owner of the lot where the avatar arrives normally offers the newcomer a friendly greeting, inviting him or her to enter, get something to eat, and take a look around. Unlike *EverQuest, The Sims Online* has no death-dealing mobs of rodents—so there is little risk in exploring all the homes in the environment. Given the lack of any clearly defined goals, most avatars in *The Sims Online* seem content just finding interesting places and people with whom to chat.

As these examples indicate, each virtual world is different, making categorical statements about virtual worlds suspect. Still, the lines drawn between worlds might not be as bright as they seem at first. For instance, while *The Sims Online* does not involve gaining power and wealth through leveling, prestige and affluence are motivating forces for many participants. And while leveling worlds such as *Ultima Online* often force players to engage in repetitive killing exercises, what makes this bearable seems to be the social bonds formed among players, who may find more fulfillment in being virtual seamstresses, alchemists, and blacksmiths.

As this virtual-world primer has shown, current virtual worlds are the end products of a long tradition of interactive representational environments, and this history helps illuminate both the social practices found in today's virtual spaces and the likely potential of future environments.

NOTES

1. Bruce Sterling Woodcock, An Analysis of MMOG Subscription Growth—Version 7.0, *at* http://pw1.netcom.com/<diff>sirbruce/Subscriptions.html (last visited Oct. 7, 2003).

2. See Geoff Keighley, The Sorcerer of Sony, Business 2.0, Aug. 2002, at 48, *available at* http://www.business2.com/articles/mag/0,1640,42210,FF.html.

3. Lineage, *at* http://www.lineage-us.com (last visited Aug. 5, 2003). Brad King, Online Games Go Multicultural, Wired News, Jan. 30, 2002, *at* http://www.wired.com/news/games/0,2101,50000,00.html (last visited July 26, 2003).

4. Woodcock, An Analysis of MMOG Subscription Growth; Brad King, Gamers Click Home for Holidays, Wired News, Dec. 11, 2002, *at* http://www.wired.com/news/games/0,2101,56759,00.html; Edward Castronova, On Virtual Economies 2 n.1 (CESIfo Working Paper No. 752, July 2002), *available at* http://papers.ssrn.com/abstract=338500 (last visited Aug. 8, 2003); *Dark Age of Camelot* News, May 9, 2002, *at* http://www.darkageofcamelot.com/news/ (last visited Aug. 8, 2003).

5. *See* Castronova, On Virtual Economies, at 7. The term was adopted in the context of computer-generated games by the creators of Lucasfilm's *Habitat,* and later popularized by Neal Stephenson in his 1992 novel *Snow Crash.*

6. Edward Castronova, Virtual Worlds: A First-Hand Account of Market and Society on the Cyberian Frontier 25 tbl. 3 (CESIfo Working Paper No. 618, Dec. 2001), *available at* http://papers.ssrn.com/abstract=294828 (last visited Aug. 4, 2003); *see also* Nick Yee, The Norrathian Scrolls: Real-Life Demographics, *at* http://www.nickyee.com/eqt/demographics.html#3 (last visited Aug. 8, 2003); Nick Yee, Codename Blue: An Ongoing Study of MMORPG Players 3 (2002), *at* http://www.nickyee.com/codeblue/Report.PDF (last visited Aug. 8, 2003).

7. *See* Julian Dibbell, The Unreal Estate Boom, Wired, Jan. 2003, at 106, *at* http://www.wired.com/wired/archive/11.01/gaming.html (last visited Aug. 8, 2003); eBay Listings, Internet Games, *at* http://listings.ebay.com/pool2/listings/list/all/category4596/index.html (last visited Aug. 8, 2003).

8. *See* Julian Dibbell, My Tiny Life 74 (1998) ("[It may seem that] sociopolitical reality is not that different, finally, from the virtual kind, and that a human being never inhabits a physical landscape without also inhabiting its ghostly, abstract counterpart—the geography of language, law, and fantasy we overlay, collectively, on everything we look at."); Jack Balkin, The Proliferation of Legal Truth, 26 Harv. J. L. & Pub. Pol'y 5, 6 (2003) ("Law creates truth—it makes things true as a matter of law. It makes things true in the eyes of the law. And when law makes things true in its own eyes, this has important consequences in the world.").

9. Castronova, Virtual Worlds: A First-Hand Account of Market and Society on the Cyberian Frontier, at 3, 7.

10. *Id.* at 23.

11. Leslie Walker, Will Women Go There? Wash. Post, Jan. 12, 2003, at H7. Nike and Levi Strauss have reportedly entered into licensing agreements with *There.com* whereby the clothing companies promote their real products through the sale of virtual renditions of these items to *There*'s avatars. The virtual transactions for Nikes and Levis, however, are also sales for virtual equivalents which are transacted using Therebucks.

12. *See* eBay auction listings for in-world assets, *at* http://listings.ebay.com/pool2/listings/list/all/category1654/index.html?from=R11 (last visited July 26, 2003).

13. Castronova, *supra* note 9, at 2; Edward Castronova, Synthetic World Economic Data, *at* http://business.fullerton.edu/ecastronova/Synthetic%20Worlds%20Economic%20Data/economic_data.htm (last visited Aug. 8, 2003).

14. Julian Dibbell, the author of My Tiny Life, recently attempted to break into this profession. His weblog recounting his experiences can be found at http://www.juliandibbell.com/playmoney/ (last visited Aug. 1, 2003).

15. *See* Jennifer L. Mnookin, Virtual(ly) Law: The Emergence of Law in Lamb-

daMOO, 2 J. Computer-Mediated Comm. (1996), *available at* http://www
.ascusc.org/jcmc/vol2/issue1/lambda.html (last visited July 26, 2003).

16. *See* Dan Hunter & F. Gregory Lastowka, To Kill an Avatar, Legal Affairs,
July/Aug. 2003, at 21, 24.

17. *See* Benjamin E. Sones, Here There Be Dragons, Computer Games Magazine, Dec. 18, 2001, http://www.cgonline.com/features/011218-f1-f1.html (last visited Aug. 5, 2003); FAQ, Games Domain, http://www.gamesdomain.com/faqdir/
rec.games.frp.dnd-3.txt, at C9 (last visited Oct. 7, 2003). The use of "avatar" in this
sentence is an intentional misnomer. Gygax and Arneson actually used the term
"character" to describe the player's alter ego. Gary Gygax, Player's Handbook 9–10
(1978). The term "avatar" is generally used to describe a player's alter ego in visual
virtual worlds.

18. *See* Sherry Turkle, Lord of the Hackers, N.Y. Times, Mar. 7, 2002, at A31.

19. *See* Chris McGowan & Jim McCullaugh, Entertainment in the Cyber Zone
49–52 (1995).

20. Dibbell, My Tiny Life, at 56; Julian Dibbell, A Marketable Wonder:
Spelunking the American Imagination, Topic (Autumn 2002), *at* http://www.top-
icmag.com/articles/02/dibbell.html (last visited Aug. 5, 2003).

21. Rick Adams, Colossal Cave Adventure Page, *at*
http://www.rickadams.org/adventure/ (last visited Aug. 4, 2003). Adams's website
provides several variants of the original game in a "downloads" section.

22. *See* Infocom Timeline, *at* http://www.csd.uwo.ca/Infocom/Articles/time-
line.html (last visited Aug. 8, 2003); Lauren P. Burka, A Hypertext History of
Multi-User Dimensions (1993), *at* http://www.apocalypse.org/pub/u/lpb/mud-
dex/essay/ (last visited Aug. 8, 2003), McGowan & McCullaugh, Entertainment in
the Cyberzone, at 88. The original MUD1 developed by Trubshaw and Bartle has
been renamed British Legends, and is still in operation. MUD1 was an acronym
for Multi-User Dungeon 1, again a nod to D&D. Some MUDers believe the MUD
acronym now stands for "Multi-User Dimension," though apparently this is a
euphemistic variation. Trubshaw, the original MUD1 creator, acknowledged a
debt to an earlier Adventure-type program named "DUNGEN" and to D&D.
Dibbell, My Tiny Life, at 57–58.

23. *See* Sherry Turkle, Life on the Screen: Identity in the Age of the Internet
181, 183 (1995); Howard Rheingold, The Virtual Community: Homesteading on
the Electronic Frontier 161–64, 184 (rev. ed., MIT Press, 2000) (1993); Richard A.
Bartle, MUD Glorious Mud, *at* http://www.mud.co.uk/richard/gnome.htm (Jan.
31, 1999).

24. Rheingold, The Virtual Community, at 167–68; Bartle, MUD, Glorious
Mud; Turkle, Life on the Screen, at 181; Richard A. Bartle, Adventures on the
Magic Network, *at* http://www.mud.co.uk/richard/chfeb85.htm (last visited
Aug. 8, 2003). Bartle has posted a rough map of the original MUD1 world on

his website, http://www.mud.co.uk/richard/mud1map.gif (last visited Aug. 8, 2003).

25. Authoritatively describing the taxonomy and nomenclature of MUD derivatives is a daunting task. The Open Directory's attempt to do so can be found at http://dmoz.org/Games/Internet/MUDs/ (last visited July 26, 2003), and its explanation for its results can be located at http://dmoz.org/Games/Internet/ MUDs/desc.html (last visited July 26, 2003). See generally Lauren P. Burka, A Hypertext History of Multi-User Dimensions (1993), *at* http://www.apocalypse .org/pub/u/lpb/muddex/essay/ (last visited Aug. 8, 2003); Lauren P. Burka, The MUDdex (1993), *at* http://www.apocalypse.org/pub/u/lpb/muddex/ (last visited July 26, 2003).

Generally, the appellation "MOO" stands for "MUD Object-Oriented," denoting the programming methodology—object orientation—which was used to build the MUD. According to most participants, "MUSH" stands for "Multi-User Shared Hallucination" and is generally reserved for MUD environments with a strong and enforced role-playing convention. Exactly what "MUCK" stands for is subject to debate: some say it refers to muck (in other words, something like mud) while others argue it stands for "Multi-User Consensual Kingdom." In any event, MUCKs are generally much like MUSHes in their emphasis on role play, but place more emphasis on achieving goals.

26. See Welcome to LambdaMOO! *at* telnet://lambda.moo.mud.org:8888/ (last visited July 26, 2003), Dibbell, My Tiny Life; Turkle, Life on the Screen.

27. For an excellent account of the history and features of the various rooms in LamdbaMOO, *see* Elizabeth Hess, Yib's Guide to MOOing: Getting the Most from Virtual Communities on the Internet, ch. 7 (2003), *at* http://www.yibco.com/ygm/ygmpdf/Chapter7.pdf.

28. McGowan & McCullaugh, *supra* note 19, at 58, 86–87.

29. Chip Morningstar & F. Randall Farmer, The Lessons of Lucasfilm's *Habitat*, in Cyberspace: First Steps (Michael Benedikt ed., 1991), *available at* http://www.fudco.com/chip/lessons.html (last visited Aug. 9, 2003). *Habitat* lacked most of the features we expect of games, such as a goal and puzzles. It was much more like a social MUD in which the interactivity among avatars was a goal in itself.

30. Chip Morningstar & F. Randall Farmer, The Lessons of Lucasfilm's *Habitat*, at 189–92.

31. *See* Virtual Reality: Multi-User Systems, Open Directory Project, *at* http://dmoz.org/Computers/Virtual_Reality/Multi-User_Systems/ (last visited Aug. 9, 2003) (listing various virtual-world platforms).

32. Many avatars speak in leetspeak (a.k.a. "1337sp34k," "133+5pe4k," and so forth) and other chat room conventions that will mystify those not fluent. *See* Kris Axtman, "r u online?': the evolving lexicon of wired teens, Christian Sci.

Monitor, Dec. 12, 2002, at 01. For instance, "brb afk" means "I'll be right back; I'm going away from my keyboard." For those more comfortable with 1337 than English, Google actually offers a leetspeak hacker ("h4x0r") language version of its search engine. *See* http://www.google.com/intl/xx-hacker/ (last visited Aug. 8, 2003).

Game Gods and Game Players

3

Virtual Worldliness

Richard A. Bartle

Virtual worlds are persistent, computer-mediated environments in which a plurality of players can interact with the world and each other. From their humble beginnings, virtual worlds have evolved to become major hubs of entertainment, education, and community. With this growing real-world importance has, however, come greater scrutiny from real-world institutions. Virtual-world developers are now experiencing a degree of accountability to which most are unaccustomed and of which many are deeply wary. For their part, real-world institutions have discovered a large, shaggy animal in their yard that wasn't there yesterday and that doesn't behave quite the same as the usual beasts they encounter.

Designers of virtual worlds have a duty to understand the laws that apply to their creations, but the people who make and interpret these laws also have a duty: to understand virtual worlds. If they don't understand what they're regulating, how can they hope to regulate it?

At the moment, virtual worlds are regulated by a set of industry "standards" unilaterally imposed by their developers. In this essay, I describe what these standards are, why they came to be, and what would happen were they to be weakened. I make no argument for or against them on a legal basis: that is for experts in the law to debate. Instead, I merely state the way things work now, that such experts may be better informed in their deliberations.

If a judge were to make a ruling that led to the widespread closing down of virtual worlds, I'd prefer that the judge knew beforehand that this would happen, rather than be surprised by it.

History

Twenty-five years ago, in the days when mainframes had less computational power than today's digital watches,[1] I sat down with my friend and fellow undergraduate, Roy Trubshaw, to discuss the design of MUD.

MUD ("Multi-User Dungeon") was the world's first virtual world, although we didn't know that at the time. We knew it was an imaginary place that up to thirty-six people could visit simultaneously; we knew that players could freely interact with one another in the context of the world we were creating; we knew that the world was entirely defined by software, but that it only *lived* in the imaginations of the players. We also knew (although up until now we hadn't actually said it) that, despite the fact that we referred to it as a game, MUD was something else entirely. It was what we would now call a "virtual world."

So it was, in an out-of-the-way seminar room where we'd found a terminal so dumb it didn't know it wasn't supposed to let us use it, that the subject of content arose. Roy had spent much of his time up until then programming the underlying code needed to support the virtual world—an activity that both he and I regarded as fun. However, there wasn't much of a virtual world to support: a handful of rooms (to test the concept of "room"), a handful of objects (to test the concept of "object"), a handful of commands (to—oh, you get the picture), plus a full-blown system for adding new rooms, objects, and commands on-the-fly. Everything was now in place: So what was the world going to look like?

Roy had written MUD to be a game. He could have written it to be an educational model of the human body, or a travelogue of Venice, or some kind of textual map for blind people to read using Braille, but no, he'd written it to be a game. In part, this was because only a game would attract sufficient users in an era when computer time was at a premium; however, that wasn't the main reason. The main reason was that only the pretext of its being a game gave him free rein to create an entire world from his imagination.

Well, who wouldn't seize upon the chance to make their imagination real if it were offered them?

Roy deferred to me when it came to the game aspects of MUD, because of my relatively strong background in gaming.[2] I had a better appreciation than he of what would and wouldn't work in a game context; he joked that it was as if I had a game design manual hidden in my head where no one else could read it.

I found this observation of Roy's interesting. Up until that point, I hadn't really given the notion of content (i.e., what players, considered as consumers, consume) much thought. I'd pictured places that I wanted to construct and the objects and beings I wanted to put in them; I'd figured out what players would do there, and what would happen when they did it. However, it hadn't occurred to me that I was working to an implicit, nonobvious rule set born of experience. Now, I realized I was.

To illustrate his point, Roy thought up a puzzle—something to do with a castle and a lake shaped like a key. It was a good puzzle for a single-player adventure game, but I could immediately see it wouldn't work in MUD: While it was being solved, the puzzle would lock up a good deal of the world, thereby spoiling it for everyone else; it was linear, forcing players to run on rails and offering them little choice of how to solve it; it had no *replay value*—if it was solved once, it was solved forever; it required rooms of radically different conceptual sizes that would just feel *wrong* to the players. In all this flood of reactions, though, two thoughts came through that made the rest seem petty: *This isn't a game, it's a place!* and *I want to go there!* I suddenly felt as if I was the first human being on a new planet.

I described my views to Roy. MUD should be a place—a world—that let players *do* whatever they wanted to do (within the context of its physics), and *be* whatever they wanted to be (in the context of their own personality). The phrase I used was "open-ended." If people wanted to play it as a game, as most perhaps would, then to them it would be a game; if, however, they preferred to wander around enjoying the scenery or poking things with sticks, that was fine too. We would provide the world; the players could take from the experience of visiting it whatever they had use for.

Roy was persuaded, so we adjourned for a cup of hot chocolate from the vending machine (our preferred choice of drink because the coffee, ironically, tasted of mud).

The Vision

I always knew what virtual worlds promised: freedom. Freedom to do, to be, to realize.[3] I like this kind of freedom, it's a good thing; virtual worlds are a force for good. Furthermore, what we have at the moment is just a foretaste of the wonders that idealists like me believe are yet to come.

Of course, things are never quite that simple.

In designing MUD, Roy and I had made a number of assumptions that did not stand up when challenged by the players. In our defense, we did foresee most of these: We simply put off acting on them until forced to by circumstance. Nevertheless, eventually they became problems.[4]

I'm going to describe some of these problems now, and how (historically) they were resolved. As a result of their resolution, certain "industry standards" emerged. While these standards pertain, the problems are manageable. If something were to happen to remove the standards, the problems would return. If the problems were to return, then either a new solution must be sought or the vision of virtual worlds as places to indulge imaginations would be lost forever.

Those charged with making decisions which might strike down these standards must therefore balance the desirability of doing so against the desirability of not having virtual worlds disappear as a result.

The Game Conceit

When people play games, they agree to abide temporarily by a set of rules which limits their behavior (i.e., restricts their freedom), in exchange for which they gain whatever benefits the game offers. Game theorists refer to the boundary that separates the game world from the nongame world as *the magic circle,* from an early description of play spaces by Johan Huizinga.[5] Virtual worlds are not games, but they use the same conceit: that some freedoms must be willingly given up for a time in order that new freedoms can be experienced during that time.[6] For example, in the real world a young man may find it awkward talking to young women because he fears rejection. He is prepared to accept the rules of a virtual world in order to talk to young women (or at least to people presenting as young women) in a context where rejection doesn't matter so much—he gains a freedom that he doesn't have in the real world. He can then learn from his experience and apply it back in the real world. Joy for him.

What happens, though, when someone doesn't play by the rules?

Suppose you were one of three people playing the game *Clue,* and that you were close to winning. The person playing Mrs. White suddenly leans over to the player playing Colonel Mustard and says, "I'll give you $20 if you show me your cards." Colonel Mustard obliges, Mrs. White pays up, and promptly announces that Reverend Green did it in the ballroom with the candlestick.

I don't know about you, but I wouldn't be all that pleased if this happened to me. Although there are no *written* rules in *Clue* about bribery, nevertheless there are *unwritten* rules that say this kind of activity stops a game from being a game.[7] I would think twice about playing with Colonel Mustard again, and three times about playing with Mrs. White.

In a virtual world, what can I do if I suspect one player of bribing another or otherwise stepping outside the boundaries of "play"?

Well, I can stop playing with them. However, that would also mean stopping playing with perhaps several thousand other people, some of whom might be very good friends.

OK, well maybe my friends will stop playing too and we can all move to some other virtual world where the game conceit still holds. Unfortunately, there's no guarantee that the miscreants won't simply follow us there (anonymously or otherwise).

So: Either I have to grit my teeth and accept it, try to prevent the miscreants from playing (or at least repeating their scam), or quit entirely in disgust.

With MUD, I knew that people might break the unwritten rules that protected its virtual world from the real one. Some indeed did so. Individually, they were usually easy to deal with: I would speak to them explaining the problem, that it was unfair on the other players if they behaved however they were behaving, and please would they stop. Most saw the light and obliged. Those that didn't were reminded that I had my finger on the off switch for their character and that I could therefore obliterate them entirely if I so chose. Some very few, I did obliterate entirely.

How could I justify this? Well, it was quite simple. To discover why, we need to look at the rationalization commonly employed by the people who broke the unwritten rules.

Some of the "written rules" of board games aren't actually written— they're coded in by the physical universe: Your *Clue* character can't be in two rooms at the same time because reality doesn't work that way. The remaining written rules are not coded in: all that stops me from moving my token more than the dice roll says I can move it is the alertness of the other players. In contrast, virtual worlds have *all* their written rules coded into them: You don't get to teleport unless the code says you do.

Board games and virtual worlds alike have additional, unwritten rules that are not coded in. However, the subversive players claimed that the code *alone* defined MUD. They didn't recognize the existence of unwritten rules, i.e., of the game conceit. Their view was that if the code let them do it, they could, legitimately, do it. This was how regular computer games worked, and this was how MUD should work. If an activity is not permissible, why didn't the software simply stop them from doing it in the first place?

The answer is that there are some things that virtual-world developers simply can't stop, using software alone; trivially, they can't prevent people from swearing (although they can make it difficult).[8] Less trivially, should you be able to stand in a doorway, thereby blocking people from entering a room? Well yes, if your aim is to prevent a thief from entering and stealing all your wounded friend's equipment, but no, if your aim is to annoy the hell out of someone racing to help their friend inside who is being beaten to pulp by an ogre. Except maybe yes, if they bought the last magic sword yesterday even though they didn't need it, just to stop your character from getting it.

Without recourse to artificial intelligence techniques that have yet to be invented, a virtual world's code can't hope to trap this kind of antisocial behaviour—even though it arises *inside* the virtual world. The attitude of the antisocial players to this was simple: "Tough." They argued that in computer games it was the program, not the players, that defined the rules. Only the code could dictate what they did. Swearing at people was fine because it was allowed by the rules as defined by the code. If I didn't want people to swear, I could always take out the communication commands.

Taking out the communication commands would have ruined MUD. Instead, I added a command, FOD ("Finger of Death"). If people swore, I FODded them. Their characters disintegrated. Hey, the program *allowed* me to do it, so it was OK! It didn't allow anyone *else* to do it unless I set the flag on their character, but it allowed *me*.

Virtual worlds are played by rules. The rules are written (embodied in the code) and unwritten (embodied in the expectations of the players). People can deny the existence of unwritten rules, but they can't deny the existence of coded rules. If the code says that you can't walk through walls, you can't walk through walls. If the code says you can shoot arrows round corners, you can shoot arrows round corners. If the code says I can obliterate your character, I can obliterate your character. You may be able to pick and choose which cultural norms to obey, but you don't get to pick and choose which rules of the virtual world's physical universe to obey— and the administrator's authority in a virtual world is *embodied* in those rules. You don't swear, because if you do you're disintegrated. You don't do *anything* that the administrator doesn't want you to do, because if you do you're disintegrated.

Some things the administrators object to are understandable: A virtual world for counseling rape victims (and there are such places) might dismiss journalists who turn up faking having been raped in order to get a story. Other things are more ambiguous: A virtual world created for worshipers of religion X (and there are such places, for different values of X) might dismiss members of religion Y who turn up hoping to participate in a ritual or service. Some things are completely arbitrary: I don't like the cut of your jib. All these, however, are *part of the rules of the virtual world*. If you play, they're enforced with the same authority as any other rule.

Strictly speaking, then, the dissenters are correct. Anything the virtual world lets its players do, they can indeed do. Their decision as to whether they *do* do it or not is entirely moderated by what the virtual world lets its more powerful players do should they dislike it. For most virtual worlds, the administrators are rational (that is, consistent if not always correct). Those who are irrational tend not to have many players: If you don't like the rules, you choose not to play.

So here's the first point I want to make. Virtual-world administrators have absolute control over their world vested in the mechanics of that world. While this state of affairs pertains, they can protect the game conceit. If they were denied absolute control, then the game conceit must be protected in some other way; otherwise, the virtual world would be just another extension of the real world.

Evolution

Virtual worlds are continually evolving. New content is added, old content is updated, exploits are curtailed, bugs are removed (hopefully at a greater rate than they are introduced), game play is rebalanced. If virtual-world designers were unable to make changes to their virtual world, that world would become stale, dated, dominated by exploits, and its game play would be all out of whack. Now it's possible that a relatively stable state could be achieved, with few bugs and exploits remaining and enough player-generated content appearing for it to retain its freshness; this is the case with the original MUD, which hasn't had new content added to it since 1985 but continues to be played. It takes many years to get a virtual world into this position, though, and even then occasional changes will still be called for.

What happens when players object to a change?

One day, I added a rabbit to MUD. We had a player with a character called Rabbit at the time. Because of the way that objects in MUD are referred to by unique, case-insensitive nouns, the moment I created a rabbit the character named Rabbit was unable to play. I knew this, but I wanted a rabbit for a puzzle I had in mind. I offered the player a name change; he accepted (he went for Wabit).

If he hadn't accepted, I'd have added the rabbit anyway. Otherwise, players would have taken the names of likely new additions to the virtual world and sat on them. This (what might now be regarded as an example of "cybersquatting") had indeed happened in the past: A player, anticipating that I might want to put a vampire into the virtual world, created a character called Vampire to stop me from doing so until I "compensated" him. Needless to say, the ruse didn't work.

Changes to a virtual world affect different characters (and hence different players) in different ways. Suppose a virtual world has two classes of fighter, the warrior and the paladin, where the paladin is the same as the warrior except that he is more powerful against evil foes. After a time, the designer notices that there are many paladins and few warriors. Because there are many paladins, fewer evil creatures are around as they keep being slaughtered. The paladins could go and kill non-evil creatures, but this would be harder for them so they don't want to do it. Instead, they kick their heels and complain about how boring the virtual world is now; there should be more evil creatures about.

The designer can address this problem in many ways, of which adding more evil creatures is but one. Ultimately, the root cause is that there's an incentive for players to be paladins rather than warriors, but no disincentive. If more players were warriors (or fewer were paladins), the problem would go away. Thus, the designer decides to make a change such that paladins are weaker against non-evil foes. Paladins aren't attacking these anyway, so shouldn't care. Thus, players now have a choice to play as warriors (and be equally effective against all kinds of foe), or as paladins (and be more effective against evil foes but less effective against non-evil foes). The virtual world should be better as a result.

Why is it, then, that although most players of paladins are pleased with the change, some are unhappy about it? "You nerfed paladins!"[9] Well, it's because although they didn't ever attack non-evil foes before, they did have the *option* to do so. That option has now been removed from them. If they'd known they were going to have this option removed, perhaps they wouldn't have chosen to be a paladin three months ago when they started playing.

Also, some players of warriors are complaining. They don't know why, but this new patch to the virtual world has somehow reduced the number of killable things. Previously, they could walk into a field and it would be full of orc children they could slaughter with wild abandon, but now when they stroll along, sword in hand, the field is already half-empty. If they'd known this was going to happen, maybe they wouldn't have chosen to be a warrior three months ago when they started playing.

The warriors are complaining because whereas in the past there were few warriors, the change in the rules has persuaded more players to become warriors. Therefore there is more competition for warrior-specialty resources (e.g., orc children). In order to give the paladins more to kill, the warriors have been given less. Both, however, do now have enough.

In general, even the tiniest changes can have repercussions that ripple through a virtual world, affecting things not immediately connected to them. In-context economies (i.e., those designed-in to the virtual world, as opposed to those containing elements the software knows nothing about, such as U.S. dollars) are particularly good in this regard: A slight adjustment in the way that a nonplayer character computes the value of a sword would affect the price that it paid for swords, which in turn might have an impact on the amount a sword-smith could afford for raw materials, and so on, the consequences gradually propagating throughout the virtual world as supply and demand checks and balances react. Perhaps as a result of the new sword-valuation policy, there is a 0.01 percent fall in the price of pig iron in a distant market. This change wouldn't be noticed by most players, but it could seriously annoy the merchant who has 100,000 units of pig iron in a warehouse there. If this could be foreseen (which is possible, if perhaps unlikely), would it be a reason not to make the initial change to the way the nonplayer character values a sword?

Virtual-world designers have to take all these things into account when they decide whether or not to change their virtual world. Any alteration that gives something to one group of players will *by definition* take something away from another group: At the very least (to put it in trade union parlance), their differentials will have been eroded. The decisions are hard, and mistakes are often made, but ultimately they're for the designer alone to make. A wise designer will explain what's happening and why, thus preparing the players for the change while giving them the opportunity to voice objections. Ultimately, though, the designer must weigh up the odds in terms of what's best for the virtual world as a whole.

Here, then, is my second point. Virtual-world administrators can't please all their players all the time, no matter how fair they try to be. They must on occasion change the virtual world in ways that some—perhaps all—of the players find unpalatable. While this situation pertains, and designers are able to ride roughshod over players' opinions, the virtual world can continue to evolve and improve. Anything that served to limit this process would limit the virtual world's evolution.

Achievement

As I explain in my book[10] on the subject, many people play virtual worlds as a way to explore their identity. Virtual worlds do this by delivering to the players an experience amounting to a *hero's journey*.[11] Not all virtual worlds are set up for this (educational ones usually aren't, for example), but most are. Similarly, not every player plays for this reason, but most do (although few of them necessarily realize this).

In those (majority) virtual worlds set up to guide players along their hero's journey, critical to success is the notion of *achievement*. Players must feel that that they are advancing relative to one another and that the advancement is worthwhile. Most virtual worlds therefore have a mechanism that allows a quick comparison between characters—normally a system of *levels,* with higher-level characters being more advanced than lower-level ones. Although, strictly speaking, virtual worlds don't *have* to have something like this to facilitate a hero's journey, it certainly helps; furthermore, if they do have it then they're implicitly offering a hero's journey whether they want to or not (but in almost all cases they *do* want to offer it).

An important point to note here is that the character reflects the state of advancement of the player. In general, a player who is close to ending his or her hero's journey will play a character that is of a very high level, whereas a less experienced player will play a lower-level character. Players therefore use their character's status to establish their place in the social order: someone of a higher level is "better" than you, as you are "better" than someone of a lower level. Players undertake actions in the virtual world that cause their characters to go up levels, thereby showing to the rest of the world (but mainly to themselves) just how good a player they are becoming. It's in the interests of all players on a hero's journey to do this: If you don't accept a metric that says some players are better than you, you can't hope to use that same metric to judge the improvement in play of your future self over your current self.

Now this would all fall apart if there were not a strong correlation between a character's level and its player's experience. It doesn't matter so much that if you see a low-level character then it must have a low-experience player behind it; the critical deduction is that if you see a high-level character then it must have a high-experience player behind it. Otherwise, when you're a high-experience player, how will anyone (least of all you) recognize your quality?

Virtual-world designers implicitly understand this, and will ensure through the virtual world's design that only those characters belonging to players who genuinely *are* good at what they do reach the higher levels. This maintains the integrity of the hierarchy, underpinning the players' sense of advancement and reinforcing their growing feelings of self-actualization. A virtual world in which the lucky roll of a die could instantly turn a newbie into a mighty wizard would remove all pretense that rank meant anything. Unless the players of this world could find some other way to measure their relative progress, it would become a very disappointing and dispiriting place for those on a hero's journey. It's perceived as an issue of *fairness*.

Virtual-world administrators strive to protect the integrity of the level hierarchy. If they discover that someone is exploiting some unintended design feature that fast-tracks them to higher levels, they have not only to track the bug down and fix it, but also remove all benefit that the player has gained from it. In its purest form, this may mean busting them down several levels, but it can also include actions such as removing in-world property or in-world currency wrongfully acquired. The interesting thing here is the definition of "wrongfully acquired". Who decides it's wrongful? What makes some actions in the virtual world "exploits" when other, similar actions, aren't?

Virtual worlds are designed to be open-ended. Designers are usually very pleased when they discover that their virtual world reacts sensibly to a situation which they hadn't foreseen. Suppose that, in a patch, the designers of one virtual world were to improve their physics engine such that object collisions were better detected. To their delight, they discover that players can now use axes to chop down trees, whereas previously they couldn't. To their dismay, they discover that the Axe of Great Magic can chop down stone walls too. Players in possession of this rare item have been breaking into castle treasuries and availing themselves of their entire contents unmolested by guards.

In both these examples, the effects were unintended. The chopping down of trees is something that the designers were pleased with, yet the chopping down of walls is something they were not pleased with—it gave players a shortcut to wealth that they could use to purchase high-powered objects. The former would be regarded as a feature, the latter as an exploit. The designers would alter the virtual world's code so as to maintain the former while suppressing the latter.

From an abstract point of view, though, there is little to choose between a feature (easy logs) and an exploit (easy treasure). In some virtual worlds, perhaps the chopping down of trees would be the exploit and the chopping down of walls would be the feature. It's a judgment call, and one that only the virtual-world designers are in a position to make. If they don't get to decide what is or isn't an exploit, exploiters will prevail and the achievement structure will break down.

Note that not all exploits are in the code. Sometimes, the exploits occur where the code can't reach—in the real world. If players do something in the real world that gives them an advantage that the designers deem to be unfair (e.g., they hack the client software to reveal information to which they should not be privy), administrators should be able to take action in the virtual world to protect the level system. If this means disintegrating characters played through hacked clients, so be it.

This is the third and final point I want to make. Those virtual worlds that offer one or more explicit, sanctioned methods by which the relative experience of players may (through their characters) be judged, have an obligation to uphold the integrity of those methods. In order to do this, the administrators must have the freedom to remove what they perceive to be shortcuts and to undo the results of what they perceive to be aberrant behavior whenever these situations arise—even if they arise in the real world. While this standard pertains, they are able to preserve the basic honesty of the measuring system. If their powers to interfere as they see fit were removed, then either some other way of preserving the hierarchy must be found or some other hierarchy must be implemented, or the virtual world will cease to operate as an effective venue for identity exploration.

Discussion

I've made three primary points here. To recapitulate:

- The powers that virtual-world administrators wield are embedded in the coded rules of the virtual world, which the administrators themselves define. If this were not the case, they could not protect the game conceit.
- Virtual-world administrators have *carte blanche* to change the virtual world however they deem appropriate, regardless of the will of the players. If this were not the case, the virtual world could not evolve.
- Administrators of virtual worlds that feature achievement are able to change the coded rules of their virtual world retrospectively and without warning, under conditions they need only specify after the event. If this were not the case, the virtual world's ability to support identity exploration would be compromised.

The game conceit, freedom to evolve, support of a hero's journey: Without all three of these fundamental characteristics, a virtual world is greatly diminished if not mortally wounded. Although I am happy for administrators of individual worlds willingly to relinquish one or more of these characteristics if they so choose, I am not happy for them to be taken away through ignorance by external forces.

The three standards that I have described currently protect their respective characteristics. These may not be the only ways to protect them (indeed, they may not be the only characteristics that need protection), but if the current standards fail then other means to achieve the same ends must be installed instead. Otherwise, virtual worlds will never deliver the wonders they promise, or even continue to deliver those wonders they can manage at present.

I do not therefore intend to defend the current standards per se. I shall, however, point out what threatens them. There are several emerging attitudes toward virtual worlds that at first glance seem perfectly reasonable, yet which on closer inspection are more than suspect. I only need one of these to illustrate the general principles involved, so I shall select the most contentious: the commodification[12] of virtual worlds.

There's One Born Every Minute

Although in the early days of MUD I foresaw many of the changes that were (and are) to come to virtual worlds, I did not predict the extent to which they would become commodified. I didn't realize people could be so touchingly trusting.

Because they evolve, virtual worlds change the whole time. If I, as a designer, determine for obscure reasons of balance to add a thousand new Swords of Shininess, that's up to me. What if you bought a Sword of Shininess yesterday for $500, though? Its value has immediately dropped, because the supply of Swords of Shininess has increased. Or perhaps for even more obscure reasons of balance I decided that the best solution was to remove Swords of Shininess as a concept altogether—you'd be down the whole $500. A player in this situation might think it reasonable to go to a court of law to seek compensation for loss, or to get the designer's decision reversed. For whatever reason, a judge might agree with them and award damages and/or instruct that the latest patch be reverted. This would not be a good thing for virtual worlds.

Every change to a virtual world has *some* effect that will impact one player less advantageously than another. If that player can call upon the law for compensation, so can someone else for some other change (or even, conceivably, for the change required by the judge to undo the first change). The overall effect is to remove the designer's freedom to change his or her world however he or she sees fit. The result: Virtual worlds will not evolve.

OK, so let's throw in that word "reasonable." Players expect that designers will patch the virtual world every so often, and they accept a certain amount of "reasonable" change. When the designer makes an "unreasonable" change, then they call in the judge. Better?

No, not better. There's no way to measure the "reasonableness" of virtual-world design decisions any more than there's a way to measure the reasonableness of a portrait. Artists do what artists do.

Even if it were feasible, it's pointless. Here's the thing: Any utility inherent in a virtual-world object is only there because of the software that provides its context. When you buy a virtual object, you're gambling that the virtual world giving it meaning will not change in such a way that it reduces the amount that people will pay for that object. Securing your bet by calling on the law to undo changes of which you disapprove attacks the standard that permits designers to make whatever changes they deem necessary to help the virtual world evolve. Every change affects *somebody* adversely: therefore in this scenario every change can in theory be prevented by law. Thus, the virtual world does not evolve, which ultimately kills it. Killing it removes the entirety of your investment anyway. In other words, if players wishing to protect their investments in a virtual world can invoke the law to limit changes, *that very action* will change the virtual world in such a way that the investments will *not* retain their value.

There's a rejoinder to this. What I've effectively done here is to set up an edifice only to knock it down. Sure, the law *might* seek to protect investments from the effects of designers' whims, but then again it might not. I could just as easily have suggested that the law might seek to make all virtual worlds have names beginning with the letter P, then demolish that argument instead. What evidence is there to suggest that players would want to bring in the law if they lost money because of a change?

Well, the evidence is that they already try to do this by other means. Players are subservient to designers, because designers control the code. However, players can leave the virtual world if they so choose, which gives them leverage on the developer's marketing team. The marketing team, being on the business side of the company, can call on higher management to instruct the designers to do things they don't want to do. Thus, there's a rock/paper/scissors relationship: designers beat players, players beat marketers, marketers beat designers. Unsurprisingly, there have been many occasions in the past where players have used their influence on marketers to cause major changes to be made to a virtual world (for example, the removal of player-versus-player combat in *Ultima Online*).

This approach only works when large numbers of players are involved, though. Individuals—even rich individuals—have little influence on marketers. They do, however, have (through their lawyers) influence on judges. If their monetary loss from a change to the virtual world were great enough, there's every reason to suppose that a player or group of players might seek redress through the courts.[13]

Hopefully, by then the courts will be ready.

Meaning

Bill Gates could be the world champion high jumper if he wanted to be. All he has to do is go to the current world champion high jumper[14] and buy his world record off him. Hey, once he's got it, maybe he can persuade the courts to prevent other people from attempting to beat it because that would be like stealing.

Well, no. World records are awarded to individuals only under certain conditions. You can't buy a world record—they're nontransferable. So are tickets to international sporting events, so are bank accounts, and so (if you want to enable the hero's journey) are characters with virtual worlds.

There are four main reasons why people buy characters in virtual worlds:

- As an investment. They think they can sell the character or the objects that came with it for more than they paid.
- For group-play reasons. They haven't played for a while and their friends are ahead to an extent that they couldn't easily catch up. They buy a character of an appropriate level so they can play with their friends again. This category also includes those who might purchase a character in order to fill a perceived void in their group's makeup (in a party of adventurers with one-too-many mages and one-too-few healers, the player of one of the mages may sell their mage and buy a cleric, for example).
- To inflate their status. They buy a higher-level character so they can act like they're a higher-ability player. This would also cover the situation where a player wants access to high-level content without having to "waste time" playing through the low-level content to get there.
- They want to acquire an object legitimately, but find they can only get it by paying real money to people who have tied up the market.

The first and fourth of these reasons are dependent on the other two for their success, so if those disappear they do too. The second reason is understandable, although ideally it should be unnecessary: virtual worlds ought to be set up so as to make mixed-ability parties of players viable. The third reason is the problematic one.

It's fairly obvious that paying for a higher-status character in order to appear to be a higher-status player is ultimately self-defeating. If one player buys status, those who know that player will also be tempted to do it (so as to reestablish their place in the hierarchy relative to that player). The more that players trade up their characters, the less anybody will associate character level with player ability, and therefore the lower the value of level as a measure of ability. If too many people debase the currency, the currency becomes worthless.

This has a bad effect on players undertaking a hero's journey. What's the point in beating down hordes of bad guys, scrimping and saving gold pieces to buy the next grade of magic shield, bouncing back from your defeats, using your wits to ensure victory—what is the *point* of it if someone with a few dollars to spare can get where you are while knowing squat about the game?

As a virtual-world designer, I don't want my players to have their sense of achievement trashed like this. I therefore seek to prevent players from buying and selling in the real world characters and objects from my virtual world. If I can't protect the integrity of the measuring system, players will lose faith in it. This will cause them to abandon their hero's journey, depriving the virtual world of one of its unique selling points.

Some virtual worlds don't care about this, which is fine. Some virtual worlds do care about it, however, and they mustn't be treated the same way as the virtual worlds that don't care. There is a step change difference between the two. Virtual worlds are just about the *only* places where an average person today can undertake a hero's journey, but even without this feature they can still qualify as virtual worlds (in the same way that a story without a plot can still be a story, Chekhov-style). What's acceptable in a virtual world for which the designers have opted out of supporting the hero's journey is not necessarily acceptable in one for which they haven't, though.

One option open to virtual-world administrators wishing to stop the trade in characters and objects is to delete any character or object found to have been traded. While this may work for the sale of characters, players are generally opposed to the idea when applied to objects: they don't buy objects because they want an unfair advantage, they buy them because a real-life company specializing in object sales has tied up the source and this is the only way to get them. They want the sellers to be punished, not the buyers.

Thus, administrators will often close down entire accounts discovered to belong to dealers, but leave those belonging to the people the dealers exploit untouched. Because accounts are real-world entities, most commercial virtual worlds assume the authority to do this under an end-user license agreement (EULA) that defines the conditions under which a player is allowed to enter that virtual world; breach of this contract means that an account can be canceled with no redress.

In either situation (loss of characters or loss of accounts), the sellers are not going to be happy. They are losing trade because of the administrator's actions. There are laws and constitutions and things (you can tell I'm not a lawyer?) that protect a company's right to do business. EULAs and other restrictive practices can be struck down.[15] Perhaps they will be?

I shan't go into the various legal arguments for and against the actions of virtual object traffickers.[16] As I indicated earlier, my task here is to explain why the current standards exist and what would happen if they didn't; it is not my place to determine whether they should or shouldn't exist in the eyes of the law (although this is not to say I would necessarily be overjoyed with whatever decision was handed down to me).

Early virtual worlds didn't have the problem of people claiming real-life ownership of virtual objects. The reason for this was because these worlds would periodically *reset*— everything was returned to its starting position, leaving only the character records of the players untouched. This was for design reasons,[17] but one consequence was that players took it for granted that everything in the virtual world was transitory: the lord giveth and the lord taketh away.[18] It was only when virtual worlds began taking on more permanence that suddenly some players began to think that because their *character* owned something, that meant that they as *players* owned it.

If players are given (or if the courts decide they already have) the right to buy and sell any characters or objects they "own" in virtual worlds when this is against the wishes of the administrators and most of the other players of those worlds, that would invalidate the current standard employed by developers to protect their achievement hierarchy. Unless some other way to maintain it could be found, this in turn would lead to a fundamental change in the nature of virtual worlds. It would be like insisting that TV drama adhered to the same standards of truth as TV documentaries— bye-bye TV drama.

Playing by the Rules

My final example of how commodification affects virtual worlds concerns the way it breaches the game conceit.

Commodification brings reality into virtuality. Unfortunately, except in very narrow circumstances,[19] the game conceit evaporates upon contact with this much reality. For *no other reason that this,* virtual-world administrators with a game conceit to protect *must* have the ability to extinguish the threat. There are other things they can try first, of course (such as attempting to persuade an individual of the harm their activity does to the virtual world); for those that don't cooperate, though, only the extinction of their characters will ultimately stop them.

I'm saying something quite strong here. I'm saying that administrators should be allowed to obliterate traded characters—or even characters they suspect are being manufactured for trading—merely for *existing*.

It's not hard to see whence objections to this might come. If I pay $5,000 for a virtual house and you disintegrate it (or even if you merely auction it off), I'm going to be absolutely livid. As far as I'm concerned, you just burned $5,000 of my money. I don't care that you prohibit commerce: Although my local park prohibits commerce if I bought a dog from someone there, that wouldn't give the park warden the right to shoot it.

Well, no. That's because the existence of a bought dog in a park doesn't diminish that park's ability to function as a park. The existence of a bought character in a virtual world does diminish that virtual world's ability to function as a virtual world. It's one more grain of reality, one more player who regards the virtual world as little different from the real one.

There's a familiar paradox here. All virtual objects are defined by the virtual world's code. That's not just *one* piece of code, but the *sum* of the code, along with all the data it operates on: everything is so dependent on everything else that it's impossible to isolate a single few lines of program and say, "these are the Spear of Destiny" or "these are the Sword of Truth." Those same lines that "define" the Spear of Destiny *also* partly define the Sword of Truth—if the spear did not exist, the sword's influence on the virtual world would be ever so slightly different. The code is the DNA of the virtual world, and—here's the crucial bit—*the administrators are part of that DNA*. A judge can strike down an administrator's powers in a virtual world, but those powers are embodied in the code. To change the powers is to modify the code; to modify the code is to modify all virtual objects—including the one that caused the judge to order that the code be modified.

Put another way, a virtual object is only what it is because the designer makes it so. Take away the designer's ability to make it so, and it ceases to be what it was.

OK, so the out-of-context sale of one object isn't going to make a lot of difference in itself. It's a drop in the ocean, and its feedback into the virtual world's value system is lost in the noise of in-context transactions. The *accumulation* of out-of-context sales, however, does make a difference. Unchecked, eventually it tips the scales and the virtual world flips from being a hero's journey world to being a world with no hero's journey. The game conceit has gone.

Which is the more important: supporting explorations of identity or supporting the free market? Are they compatible, or mutually exclusive? If those who make and interpret laws break down the barrier that is the game conceit, they're taking away the ability of virtual worlds to deliver that which only they *can* deliver. Is it right to do that? Is it right *not* to do that?

The scene: a regular Saturday afternoon match in the Premier League (this is soccer; hey, I'm English, it was either that or cricket). The referee awards a penalty. The defending goalkeeper stands in front of his goal, while the attacking striker places a ball on a spot twelve yards in front of him. The striker is going to run up to the ball and try to kick it past the goalkeeper and into the goal. The goalkeeper is going to try prevent the ball from getting into the goal. Except this one isn't, because this one has been paid by a gambling syndicate to throw the match. When the police find out, he's going to go to prison.

One goalkeeper taking a bribe, one player selling a character. The law does protect some game conceits once it understands the consequences of not protecting them. Will it do so for virtual worlds?

Summary

I've described here three standards of action that virtual-world developers commonly employ to ensure their creations' uniqueness and survival.

In truth, these standards are not quite as formally distinct as I have made out. As an administrator, if I find you're using an exploit then I might decide to obliterate your character using the powers I gave myself to protect the game conceit. Alternatively, I might change the virtual world so that the fruits of your exploit are worthless—using powers only "needed" to guarantee the virtual world's evolution. Then again, I may just fine you a few levels using the specific powers I possess for maintaining the integrity of the achievement system.

Everything is intertwined. Optimistically, this means the system is robust: if one standard were invalidated, the others could cover for it. Pessimistically, this means the system is fragile: if one standard were invalidated, the others would be invalidated with it.

I tend toward the pessimistic view. If one standard is invalidated, this will be because it can do something that it shouldn't be able to do. If another standard can achieve the same ends, it will be invalidated for the same reason. If it can't achieve the same ends, whatever the standard was protecting will be unprotected: this will ultimately mean the end to virtual worlds as we know them (and, worse, as we might yet have known them).

Here's my take on all this.

I have nothing against commodification for virtual worlds that want it. Good luck to them! As far as I'm concerned, the more virtual worlds there are, the better. I don't want *all* virtual worlds to be commodified, though.

What worries me is that precedents established in dealing with the virtual worlds that want commodification are applied to the virtual worlds that don't want it. Not only is this unfair on those developers and players who don't want it, but it's self-defeating: as I have shown three times in the above discussion, uninvited commodification ultimately leads to its own strangulation (and invited commodification isn't exactly risk-free either).

When Roy and I created MUD, we knew that other people would write programs based on it—that the idea would evolve. We knew these (let's call them) "virtual worlds" would become commercial entities in themselves, i.e., that people would pay to play them. After thinking about it, we figured there was scope for advertising in them, but that this would spoil the players' feeling of immersion unless it made sense in context. For the same reason, we rejected the idea of selling stuff inside the virtual world using real-world money (although we did miss a trick, in that it's immersion-busting to buy a magic sword with dollars, but less so to buy gold pieces with dollars, then buy the sword with gold pieces). Besides, who'd want to pay for something that might be worth nothing the next day—ha ha!

Virtual worlds have evolved. There are myriads of them out there of all shapes and sizes, from tiny, textual, role-playing MUSHes to mighty, all-conquering graphical spectaculars with more players than some countries have citizens. Their amazing variety can only increase as new designers with new ideas seize their own chance to make their imaginations real. Yet through all these worlds run threads of similarity, the fundamental concepts about which they crystalized: the core characteristics that say, "this is a virtual world."

If virtual worlds are to continue to astound us, to fill us with wonder, to allow us to be who we really are, these threads of similarity must be protected—cherished, even.

They're not games, they're places.

And I still want to go there.

NOTES

This chapter greatly benefited from comments made by Ren Reynolds (http://www.ren-reynolds.com) on its first draft. Thanks, Ren!

1. I offer no evidence in support of this statement whatsoever. However, an essay about law wouldn't be an essay about law without an endnote in its first sentence. Furthermore, a book about law wouldn't be a book about law if it didn't reorganize material so that its original first sentence now appears elsewhere.

2. I'd run my own postal games magazine for two years, and had a game published as a result. R. A. Bartle, *The Solo Dungeon* (Birmingham, UK: Games Publications, 1978). It was a book version of what would now be classified as a hypertext game.

3. Strictly speaking, this should be "virtualize," as I mean it in the sense of making the imagination nonimaginary (i.e., "real" under normal circumstances, but "virtual" here). Designers want freedom in the designing of virtual worlds every bit as much as players want freedom in the playing.

4. Some assumptions have stayed the course and are only now being challenged. For example, we (well, I) used the excuse of "you don't have to play if you don't want to" to fob off people who complained about the way the virtual world was run, all the while knowing that, actually, if all your friends are in the virtual world then you may feel you do "have to" play even though you don't really "want to." In other words, I knew that (what would now be called) "social capital" existed, but dismissed its significance. The reason why I did this will shortly become apparent, but that isn't to say I necessarily *should* have done it.

5. J. Huizinga, *Homo Ludens* (Haarlem, the Netherlands: Tjeenk Willink, 1938).

6. The subject of giving up selected freedoms to gain greater freedoms has a long history in philosophy, stemming in the main from Thomas Hobbes's *Leviathan* (ch. 14). I shall not, however, discuss this here except to note that the debate exists; my purpose is descriptive, not normative.

7. Furthermore, there are an infinite number of them. K. Salen & E. Zimmerman, *Rules of Play,* 129 (Cambridge, MA: MIT Press, 2003).

8. There is a town in the U.K. called Scunthorpe. Do you ban all reference to its name (as AOL's ever-vigilant profanity-filters originally did when they saw the second-to-fifth letters) or do you allow reference to it in the full knowledge that people will then start using it as a profanity?

9. Nerf (nərf) *vb. (tr.)* to render less effective. [C20: from the Nerf™ brand of safe-play toys.]

10. R. A. Bartle, *Designing Virtual Worlds* (Indianapolis: New Riders, 2003) (ch. 5).

11. J. Campbell, *The Hero with a Thousand Faces* (Princeton: Princeton University Press, *Bollinger Series 17,* 1949). This is far too detailed to go into here, but

essentially there is a pattern followed by much of myth, ancient and modern, that takes an individual on a journey to a world of adventure (i.e., a *virtual world* in our case) where challenges are met, foes defeated, aspects of the self confronted, and identity asserted. As a result, the individual is a more complete person than he or she was before making the journey. In virtual worlds, the undertaking of a hero's journey is, for many players, the ultimate source of the fun they derive from playing.

12. *Commodification* is a term used to describe the transformation of previously noncommercial relationships into commercial relationships. In virtual worlds, this is generally taken to refer to the treatment of virtual objects (or currency or characters) as objects of real-world commerce. Its principal manifestation is the buying and selling of virtual goods for real money on auction sites such as eBay.

13. Celia Pearce reports that the parents of an *EverQuest* player who bought him a high-level character for his birthday tried to hold the developers accountable when he subsequently got it killed. It's not clear from her article the extent to which lawyers became involved, however, nor whether the anecdote is basically true or merely an urban legend. C. Pearce, *Emergent Authorship: The Next Interactive Revolution,* in *Computers & Graphics* vol. 6 (1), Elsevier, February 2002, http://www.cpandfriends.com/writing/pearceCAG.pdf.

14. The current holder of the outdoor world record for the high-jump (men) can be found at http://www.iaaf.org/statistics/records/gender=M/allrecords/discipline=HJ/index.html. It's not Bill Gates.

15. Although it may appear that once again I am building up an edifice just so I can bulldoze it, this one is constructed on stronger foundations. Mythic, the developer of *Dark Age of Camelot,* was sued by a virtual object trading company called Black Snow, after Mythic suspended Black Snow's accounts. Unfortunately (from our perspective) the case was never resolved, because Black Snow neglected to pay its lawyers.

16. For a summary of these, see R. Reynolds, *Hands Off MY Avatar: Issues with Claims of Virtual Property and Identity,* Proc. Digital Games Industry, University of Manchester, 2003, http://www.ren-reynolds.com/downloads/HandsOffMYavatar.doc.

17. You can give actions far more complicated consequences if you know that their effects will all be wiped out simultaneously. Otherwise, undoing the effects of one action might interfere with the continued ability to undertake some other action (e.g., the door someone burned down yesterday suddenly respawns and traps you in a dead-end room).

18. Job 1:21.

19. Playing poker for money involves making game-critical decisions based on foreseeable consequences occurring outside the game, i.e., can you afford to stay

with the betting? To do this, poker temporarily co-opts part of the nongame world into its magic circle. With careful design and planning, virtual worlds can do the same kind of thing in a limited way; this does not in general extend to the routine buying and selling of characters on auction sites, however.

4

Declaring the Rights of Players

Raph Koster

Do players of virtual worlds have rights?

One of those questions that I shouldn't write about. No matter what, any answer I give is bound to be wrong, either from the perspective of my employers or my customers. The pesky thing about rights is that they keep coming up. Players keep claiming that they have them. Of course, administrators of any virtual space are loathe to "grant players rights" because it curbs their ability to take action against people and holds them to standards they may not be able to live up to.

There's at least one theory of rights which says that rights aren't "granted" by anyone. They arise because the populace decides to grant them to themselves. The flip side of this is that unless you continually fight to make that claim true, it won't stick. The battleground is not a military one: It's a perception one; as long as everyone is convinced that people have rights, they do. And, of course, as long as they are enshrined in some sort of law. In other words, the guys in charge sign away a chunk of power, in writing, that the populace expects them to sign away.

There's another theory of rights which holds them to be intrinsic to people. Under this far more rigid standard, all those cultures which fail to grant them are benighted bastions of savagery. The harder part here is agreeing on what rights are intrinsic to all people everywhere.

Many MUD administrators (usually called "admins" for short) are of the belief that their MUDs are their private playgrounds. That they have discretion on who enters and who gets to stay. That they can choose to eject someone on any grounds whatsoever, can delete a character at whim, can play favorites and choose to grant administrative favors to their friends. Even in pay-for-play circles, it is always made very clear who owns the data, who has to sign Terms of Service, and so on.

It's pretty clear that there are some rights which leak over from the real world into the virtual. If your local pay-for-play MUD operator isn't providing adequate service, you can report him or her to the Better Business Bureau; there are probably laws that apply equally well in both kinds of space. But rights (and much less legislation) have not caught up to the notion of virtual spaces very well. Which makes for an interesting thought experiment.

What if we declared the rights of avatars?

I've based what follows on a couple of seminal documents: The Declaration of the Rights of Man and of the Citizen approved by the National Assembly of France on August 26, 1789; and the first ten amendments to the Constitution of the United States, perhaps better known as the Bill of Rights. This is, perhaps, not the best basis from which to begin a stab at this hypothetical exercise, given our multicultural world today; some have suggested that a better starting point might be the UN Charter of Rights and Freedoms. I admit that one reason for choosing the version I did was its language, not its content per se.

So let's give it a whirl. This is all still hypothetical, OK?

I. Declaration of the Rights of Avatars

When a time comes that new modes and venues exist for communities, and said modes are different enough from the existing ones that question arises as to the applicability of past custom and law; and when said venues have become a forum for interaction and society for the general public regardless of the intent of the creators of said venue; and at a time when said communities and spaces are rising in popularity and are now widely exploited for commercial gain; it behooves those involved in said communities and venues to affirm and declare the inalienable rights of the members of said communities. Therefore herein have been set forth those rights which are inalienable rights of the inhabitants of virtual spaces of all sorts, in their form henceforth referred to as avatars, in order that this declaration may continually remind those who hold power over virtual spaces and the avatars contained therein of their duties and responsibilities; in order that the forms of administration of a virtual space may be at any time compared to that of other virtual spaces; and in order that the grievances of players may hereafter be judged against the explicit rights set forth, to better govern the virtual space and improve the general welfare and happiness of all.

Therefore this document holds the following truths to be self-evident: That avatars are the manifestation of actual people in an online medium, and that their utterances, actions, thoughts, and emotions should be considered to be as valid as the utterances, actions, thoughts, and emotions of people in any other forum, venue, location, or space. That the well-established rights of man approved by the National Assembly of France on August 26th of 1789 do therefore apply to avatars in full measure saving only the aspects of said rights that do not pertain in a virtual space or which must be abrogated in order to ensure the continued existence of the space in question. That by the act of affirming membership in the community within the virtual space, the avatars form a social contract with the community, forming a populace which may and must self-affirm and self-impose rights and concomitant restrictions upon their behavior. That the nature of virtual spaces is such that there must, by physical law, always be a higher power or administrator who maintains the space and has complete power over all participants, but who is undeniably part of the community formed within the space and who must therefore take action in accord with that which benefits the space as well as the participants, and who therefore also has the rights of avatars and may have other rights as well. That the ease of moving between virtual spaces and the potential transience of the community do not limit or reduce the level of emotional and social involvement that avatars may have with the community, and that therefore the ease of moving between virtual spaces and the potential transience of the community do not in any way limit, curtail, or remove these rights from avatars on the alleged grounds that avatars can always simply leave.

Articles:

1. Avatars are created free and equal in rights. Special powers or privileges shall be founded solely on the common good, and not based on whim, favoritism, nepotism, or the caprice of those who hold power. Those who act as ordinary avatars within the space shall all have only the rights of normal avatars.
2. The aim of virtual communities is the common good of its citizenry, from which arise the rights of avatars. Foremost among these rights is the right to be treated as people and not as disembodied, mean-

ingless, soulless puppets. Inherent in this right are therefore the natural and inalienable rights of man. These rights are liberty, property, security, and resistance to oppression.

3. The principle of all sovereignty in a virtual space resides in the unalterable fact that somewhere there resides an individual who controls the hardware on which the virtual space is running, and the software with which it is created, and the database which makes up its existence. However, the body populace has the right to know and demand the enforcement of the standards by which this individual uses this power over the community, as authority must proceed from the community; a community that does not know the standards by which the administrators use their power is a community which permits its administrators to have no standards, and is therefore a community abetting in tyranny.

4. Liberty consists of the freedom to do anything which injures no one else including the weal of the community as a whole and as an entity instantiated on hardware and by software; the exercise of the natural rights of avatars are therefore limited solely by the rights of other avatars sharing the same space and participating in the same community. These limits can only be determined by a clear code of conduct.

5. The code of conduct can only prohibit those actions and utterances that are hurtful to society, inclusive of the harm that may be done to the fabric of the virtual space via hurt done to the hardware, software, or data; and likewise inclusive of the harm that may be done to the individual who maintains said hardware, software, or data, in that harm done to this individual may result in direct harm done to the community.

6. The code of conduct is the expression of the general will of the community and the will of the individual who maintains the hardware and software that makes up the virtual space. Every member of the community has the right to contribute either directly or via representatives in the shaping of the code of conduct as the culture of the virtual space evolves, particularly as it evolves in directions that the administrator did not predict; the ultimate right of the administrator to shape and define the code of conduct shall not be abrogated, but it is clear that the administrator therefore has the duty and responsibility to work with the community to arrive at a code of conduct that is shaped by the input of the community. As a member

of the community himself, the administrator would be damaging the community itself if he failed in this responsibility, for abrogation of this right of avatars could result in the loss of population and therefore damage to the common weal.

7. No avatar shall be accused, muzzled, toaded, jailed, banned, or otherwise punished except in the cases and according to the forms prescribed by the code of conduct. Any one soliciting, transmitting, executing, or causing to be executed, any arbitrary order, shall be punished, even if said individual is one who has been granted special powers or privileges within the virtual space. But any avatar summoned or arrested in virtue of the code of conduct shall submit without delay, as resistance constitutes an offense.

8. The code of conduct shall provide for such punishments only as are strictly and obviously necessary, and no one shall suffer punishment except it be legally inflicted according to the provisions of a code of conduct promulgated before the commission of the offense; save in the case where the offense endangered the continued existence of the virtual space by attacking the hardware or software that provide the physical existence of the space.

9. As all avatars are held innocent until they shall have been declared guilty, if detainment, temporary banning, jailing, gluing, freezing, or toading shall be deemed indispensable, all harshness not essential to the securing of the prisoner's person shall be severely repressed by the code of conduct.

10. No one shall be disquieted on account of his opinions, provided their manifestation does not disturb the public order established by the code of conduct.

11. The free communication of ideas and opinions is one of the most precious of the rights of man. Every avatar may, accordingly, speak, write, chat, post, and print with freedom, but shall be responsible for such abuses of this freedom as shall be defined by the code of conduct, most particularly the abuse of affecting the performance of the space or the performance of a given avatar's representation of the space.

12. The security of the rights of avatars requires the existence of avatars with special powers and privileges, who are empowered to enforce the provisions of the code of conduct. These powers and privileges are therefore granted for the good of all and not for the personal advantage of those to whom they shall be entrusted. These powers

and privileges are also therefore not an entitlement, and can and should be removed in any instance where they are no longer used for the good of all, even if the offense is merely inactivity.

13. A common contribution may, at the discretion of the individual who maintains the hardware, the software, and the data that make up the virtual space, be required in order to maintain the existence of avatars who enforce the code of conduct and to maintain the hardware and the software and the continued existence of the virtual space. Avatars have the right to know the nature and amount of the contribution in advance, and said required contribution should be equitably distributed among all the citizens without regard to their social position; special rights and privileges shall never pertain to the avatar who contributes more except insofar as the special powers and privileges require greater resources from the hardware, software, or data store, and would not be possible save for the resources obtainable with the contribution; and as long as any and all avatars are able to make this contribution and therefore gain the powers and privileges if they so choose; nor shall any articles of this declaration be contingent upon a contribution being made.

14. The community has the right to require of every administrator or individual with special powers and privileges granted for the purpose of administration, an account of his administration.

15. A virtual community in which the observance of the code of conduct is not assured and universal, nor the separation of powers defined, has no constitution at all.

16. Since property is an inviolable and sacred right, and the virtual equivalent is integrity and persistence of data, no one shall be deprived thereof except where public necessity, legally determined per the code of conduct, shall clearly demand it, and then only on condition that the avatar shall have been previously and equitably indemnified, saving only cases wherein the continued existence of the space is jeopardized by the existence or integrity of said data.

17. The administrators of the virtual space shall not abridge the freedom of assembly, save to preserve the performance and continued viability of the virtual space.

18. Avatars have the right to be secure in their persons, communications, designated private spaces, and effects, against unreasonable snooping, eavesdropping, searching and seizures; no activity pertaining thereto shall be undertaken by administrators save with

probable cause supported by affirmation, particularly describing the
goal of said investigations.

19. The enumeration in this document of rights shall not be construed
to deny or disparage others retained by avatars.

Lofty, eh? And I don't doubt that there's some folks out there right now
seizing on this as an important document. For all I know, maybe it is.

But there's also some other folks who think that this exercise is plain
dangerous. As an example, let me take a coworker of mine to whom I
showed an early draft. He pointed out that virtual-world servers run on
somebody's hardware. And that most declarations of rights give rights
over personal property. By declaring that avatars have rights, we're abro-
gating that administrator's right to personal property.

Others point out that it's superfluous. After all, if virtual worlds are just
extensions of the real world, then surely all the rights we already have
apply?

What about if the virtual space in question is a game? Doesn't it, by its
nature, obviate some of these rights?

And the biggie: What if you don't accept the basic premises in the
prefatory paragraphs?

And that's where it gets interesting: in the details. I posted the document to a mailing list with a collection of the smartest virtual-world
admins and designers I know. Here's some of the various comments from
admins who got to see the original draft of this document (names hidden
to protect the innocent, and remarks vastly paraphrased, because many of
the objections were hypothetical ones).

- Rights of *avatars?* Why not of "chess pieces"? Maybe the players have
  rights, but avatars are just representations.
- I have not signed any agreement to keep the MUD running, and I
  have no responsibility toward the players. In fact, I might have made
  them sign an agreement saying so!
- What if the players don't want to accept their rights?
- You could arguably consider online actions merely speech, and
  therefore bound by those standards.
- You've left all sorts of abuses available by justifying them as "necessary for the world's survival."
- I don't believe in the notion of a social contract. Rights are granted
  explicitly by those in power.

- "Why should the creator of an online community—especially one which is created explicitly for the purpose of entertainment—be bound to do certain things simply because others have chosen to make an emotional or social investment in his/her construct?" (A direct quote).
- You just defined "the aim of virtual communities." That's not liberating, that's severely limiting!
- Property, freedom from oppression—these are pretty Western rights, you know. Are we dragging Western ideology into primacy in the virtual setting here?
- The one real right players incontrovertibly have is the right to log off.
- What about the notion that anything an admin orders you to do is by definition, the law?
- This really curtails the freedom admins have to police things. I have better things to do than try to anticipate everything a player might do.
- What about games where arbitrary orders are part of the rules? As a simple example, what about "Simon Says"? Or where no freedom of speech, or a corrupt government (even one that players can take on significant roles in) is part of the fictional game setting?
- Doesn't this prevent a community from selectively appointing admins, coders, whatever, since it requires that anyone who can make the contribution be allowed to?
- Does this mean that the game admins cannot sell a superpowered item for cash money to players?
- And do these really apply to the guy with his finger on the power button? He is unbannable, after all.
- Bad players should have fewer rights than good ones!

A final comment, because it's priceless:

> If I were the United States Secretary of Virtual Worlds and I were shopping around for an administration policy for USMud I would start with something like this. If I were Joe Businessman, I might pay lip-service to this, but I sure as heck wouldn't put it in my user contract and leave myself open to lawsuits.

Perhaps the most interesting thing about all the admin commentary on the document is that the biggest concerns boil down to just a few things:

1. I don't want to surrender control. I hate the notion of "rights" for players.
2. I may not be making this sort of virtual world. Maybe it's a game. (Which is largely easily answered by saying, "These rights apply out of character, not in character, of course.")
3. By the way, I *really* don't want to surrender control.

The second is interesting. It raises the question of what a MUD is for, and what lifecycle it has. Common wisdom has it that "a MUD must grow, or stagnate and die." If so, then the common good means anything that works against increasing the population of a MUD. However, a MUD that grows into something which all its members despise is not developing toward the common good. So a better definition might be, the common good is that which increases the population of a mud without surrendering core social tenets or mores. But that word "stagnate" is in that bit o' common wisdom too. So it may be good for a MUD to evolve its core social tenets in order to adapt to the changing population.

When all is said and done, though, I am clearly defending something completely implausible on one key level:

- as a document for players, it's a waste of time. They may trumpet it, but who cares? They have zero power, and the document actually states that several times over.
- as a document for admins, however, it's pretty much all common sense. Whether or not you believe in *any* of the principles that lead to calling these articles rights, or whether or not you believe in rights at all, you probably subscribe to most of these out of sheer, ruthless practicality and business horse sense.

What happens if we remove the word rights, and in fact remove all the high-flown language?

II. Advice to Virtual-World Admins

MUD players are people. They don't stop being people when they log on. Therefore they deserve to be treated like people. This means they have the rights of people. By joining a MUD, they join a community of people. Rights arise from the community. But there's always someone with their finger on the power switch. But he's part of the community too, and should use his powers for the common good and the survival of the community. The fact that you can easily move to another MUD doesn't mean that these rights go away.

Articles:

1. All MUD players get the same rights. Special powers on the MUD are given out for the good of the MUD, not because some guy is the friend of a wizard.

2. MUD players are people, and therefore they have the rights of people: liberty, property, security, and freedom from oppression.

3. Somewhere, there's a guy with his finger on the power button. What he says ultimately goes. The MUD players have the right to know the code of conduct he is going to enforce over them, and what rules and standards he's going to use when he makes a decision. Otherwise, they are suckers and deserve what mistreatment they get.

4. You can do whatever you want as long as it doesn't hurt others. "Hurting others" needs to be defined in the code of conduct.

5. The code of conduct shouldn't be capricious and arbitrary. The rules should be based on what is good for the MUD (and for the good of the MUD's hardware, software, and data).

6. The code of conduct should evolve based on the way the MUD culture evolves, and players should get a say in how it evolves. The MUD admins get to write it however they want, but they have an obligation to listen or else the players might leave.

7. You can't punish someone for something that isn't in the code of conduct. Abusing your wiz powers is a serious crime. If you are caught in a violation of the code of conduct, fess up.

8. You can't punish someone in a way not in the code of conduct, and you the admin don't get to rewrite the code of conduct after the fact to make it legal. The only exception is action taken to keep the MUD from going "poof."

9. Players are innocent until proven guilty. Treat them decently until guilt is proven.

10. As long as they aren't spamming or breaking the code of conduct, players should be free to believe whatever they want.

11. As long as they aren't spamming or breaking the code of conduct, players should be free to yell, chat, gossip, post, or otherwise say whatever they want.

12. You're probably going to want admins. Admins get special powers for the good of the MUD, not to make them feel cool. They aren't an entitlement because the imp is your cousin, and if you're not using them for the good of all (which includes not using them at all and shirking your admin duties) they should get yanked.

13. Players might have to pay to keep the MUD running. They should know how much they will have to pay beforehand. You shouldn't have different pay scales for different players unless those other players actually involve more costs. If you do let people buy greater privileges, then you should allow *any* player to buy these privileges, and not bar some people from it because you don't like them. Also, payment doesn't mean they get to have godlike powers to fry other people with—they still have to respect these rights.

14. Players have a right to know why the admins did things the way they did, like why they playerwiped or moved an area or whatever. In particular, why a given immort banned one guy for spamming but let the other off the hook. (Note that given the circumstances, you may not be able to do so for legal reasons.)

15. No exceptions to the code of conduct—it applies to everyone.

16. Don't playerwipe/data wipe unless the MUD can't survive unless you do. If you do have to wipe someone, make it up to them somehow.

17. Let people hang out wherever they want with whoever they want in the MUD, unless it's causing MUD slowdowns or something.

18. Players have a right to privacy. Don't snoop on them or spy on them or rifle through their mail unless you are investigating a code of conduct violation.

19. There's probably stuff missing in this doc.

The interesting thing is that MUD admins find the second doc much more palatable. Phrased in this way, it's not an abrogation of their power. It's concrete advice that will help you retain your playerbase. In fact, some even said they'd be willing to sign to it as a "declaration" because it would make them look good as admins to adhere to such a standard. There are damn few justifiable reasons to deny any of the things in the above version—and if you did, likely you'd be considered a jerk for doing it—or a power-hungry admin with a god complex (is there a difference?).

If admins see themselves as above the community, do they have any responsibilities toward the community whatsoever?

If they do, can they be articulated?

If they can be articulated and generally agreed upon, are they players' rights or are they merely good ethics on the part of a MUD administrator?

The irony is that it's all probably moot. The reason why players hold admins to this standard is because they have assumed that this standard is what should be there regardless. In other words, the advice works because it's what players expect and say they want. Which is no different from self-affirmed rights. This is probably why players scream that their rights have been violated when one of the above articles is violated (even if the admins are not signatories to any such document).

So the real point of a document like this would be to see how many admins would sign, not how many players. As an admin, yes, I'd probably sign, in the sense that I'd agree that these are solid administrative principles *in terms of practical effect*.

The question then becomes, if we subscribe in terms of practical effect, and as long as there are sufficient loopholes present that we can exercise power when we need to, who *cares* whether players think these are rights, laws, doohickeys, or power fantasies? Why do you want the freedom to do things that are *bad* admin or business practice? Especially since "rights" in the real world already have zero power?

(Note that I am not suggesting that all the MUDs or commercial endeavors should run out and implement this list of "rights," nor am I suggesting that if they don't they are run by power-hungry maniacs. This is too complex an issue to reduce to that level.)

The last step that would be required to actually make such a document into a Bill of Rights for players would be for it to be codified into "law" (which would probably be a Code of Conduct or Terms of Service agreement signed by all players, account holders, and admins) and thus be something that admins would be bound to. Admins are, by and large, not going to do this, even though some of the commercial MMORPG companies *do* require their game masters to sign documents saying that they will behave in a manner surprisingly similar to what the document espouses. But there's an interesting forward-thinking pie-in-the-sky reason for admins to contemplate doing so someday.

Someday there won't *be* any admins. Someday it's gonna be your bank records and your grocery shopping and your credit report and yes, your virtual homepage with data that exists nowhere else. Someday it's gonna be *Snow Crash* and *Neuromancer* and *Otherland* all wrapped up into one, and it may be a little harder to write to Customer Service. Your avatar profile might be your credit record and your resume and your academic transcript, as well as your XP earned.

On the day that happens, I bet we'll all wish we had a few more rights in the face of a very large, distributed server, anarchic, virtual world where it might be very *hard* to move to a different service provider. The future is already almost here.

So in the end, all the Declaration of the Rights of Avatars is, is a useful tool for players and admins alike: admins who don't know what they are doing can use it as a blueprint, and players can use it to evaluate MUD administrations in search of one they like.

So yeah. I'm not seriously proposing that we declare the rights of avatars. The doc is, as has been shown, riddled with gotchas and logical holes. It's a hypothetical exercise.

For now.

5

The Right to Play

Edward Castronova

The virtual worlds now emerging on the Internet manifest themselves with two faces, one invoking fantasy and play, the other merely extending day-to-day existence into a more entertaining circumstance. In this essay I argue that the more daily-life aspects of virtual worlds have begun to dominate their fantasy status. This is unfortunate. Virtual worlds represent a new technology that allows deeper and richer access to the mental states invoked by play, fantasy, myth, and saga, states that have immense intrinsic value to the human person. Yet virtual worlds cannot provide these mental states if the *magic circle,* the boundary that distinguishes them as play spaces, is eroded. Therefore any threats to the magic circle are also threats to long-run human well-being. The magic circle, and the fantastical nature of life inside it, warrant protection by some means.

One means of protection might be the law. In the past, law has shown itself to be congenial to the erection of magic circles and fantasy creations, and vigorous in their defense. For example, the corporation is defined in law as a fictional person, a fantasy that has indeed been vigorously defended by courts and lawmakers. In this essay I will propose an analogous act of law, *interration.* Where incorporation creates a fantasy person, interration creates a fantasy *place.* Like a corporation, an interration has special rights, but it is also subject to special duties. The creation of fictional people is justified because this treatment has benefits for society. In this essay, I will try to justify acts of interration on the same grounds, arguing that without them something very valuable in the realms of virtual reality may well be lost forever.

In the following sections, I treat incorporation as a critical precedent (I), and then describe the current ambiguous legal status of virtual worlds as part play, part not-play (II). In sections III and IV, I argue that while the line between play and not-play has become increasingly difficult to draw, it has become increasingly important that we do so. Section V analyzes efforts to draw the line under current contract law through End User Licensing Agreements, and shows why these efforts are likely to fail. The essence of the argument is that the play-status of a virtual world is a common property resource, and is therefore subject to long-run erosion effects (the "Tragedy of the Commons"). Section VI explicitly proposes the notion of a right to access the common property resources of play in virtual worlds, and describes law that would instantiate that right. Section VII discusses some of the changes in virtual world management that such a law would require, and some of the legal and policy implications it would have. Section VIII concludes.

I. Precedent: Incorporation

incorporate: f. late L. *incorporat-*, ppl. stem of *incorporare* to embody, include, f. *in-* + *corporare* to form into a body.

The merchant companies of the early seventeenth century were formed solely to impose trade monopolies. In the Charter of the Dutch West India Company of 1621, for example, there is no reference to the concept of embodiment, no effort to persuade the reader that the new organization is a fictional person. Over time, however, these companies became known by the term *corporation*. The OED reveals that the first use of the word in this sense was by one Mr. Speed in his *History of Great Britain* of 1611: "If there be any, bee hee priuate person, or be he corporation." Speed apparently felt that these entities, which were able to enter into contracts in their own name and to swallow all liability for their own actions, were best thought of as *people*. Virtual people, perhaps, but people nonetheless, things whose pronoun was properly "he," not "them" or "it."

These incorporated fictional persons were invented by governmental fiat, by declaration of authorities under existing law. Fictional personhood did not just emerge, it was a new power asserted by governments. Once this power was accepted, it became subject to scrutiny, delineation, and due process. Today, all states and countries have a detailed set of laws regulating just who may become a fictional person in this way.

Why did incorporation happen? What motivated its appearance as something a state could do? Largely, it was just a better way of doing business; by keeping financial responsibility quarantined inside the companies, the state freed individuals to invest without fear of complete ruin. If I loan money to Smith for a trade voyage and Smith's ship sinks, I can sue him for everything he owns to get my money back. But if I loan money to Smith's corporation for the same purpose, and the corporation's ship sinks, I only have a right to grab whatever the corporation owns; I have no right to go after Smith's house. The events are exactly the same in both cases, but the financial consequences are different when the state says that Smith Incorporated is a person in his own right (adopting Speed's pronoun).

When the state certified the existence of Smith Incorporated, it got everyone to play a little game of pretend. Everyone had to pretend that Smith had nothing to do with Smith Inc., beyond the monies that he put into the make-believe person's hands. And that made Smith safe to put in more money than he might have otherwise. Indeed, it enabled everyone to invest with less fear of the consequences. Take some of the fear out of investing and you will get more investing; increase investing and you will get economic growth. Any meme that increases economic growth will, through the resources it generates, propagate itself more powerfully. Cultural evolution has thus embedded the notion of incorporation deeply into contemporary economic life.

There is no denying the economic usefulness of the corporate form of governance, but there is also no denying the fact that the practice of treating corporate organizations as fictional people is like playing a little game of make-believe. It is not a game we choose, of course; as of 1600, the law forces us to play. Not only that, we have to play a certain way. We must treat this fictional person according to the rules the state imposes; for example, we do not have the right to pursue the people who have loaned him money. And precisely because this game imposes restrictions on our behavior, our decisions, and our rights, it is a strictly delimited game. Not every collective entity is allowed to become a make-believe person. No, inventing a fantasy person is serious business. There are firm rules about it.

In short, there was a moment some four hundred years ago when this set of fantastical rules—defining who or what could be a make-believe person and how that make-believe person would be treated—seemed sensible to large numbers of serious people. And no one since (certainly not any serious person, anyway) has been troubled by this collective fantasy.

II. The Legal Status of Games

Games are hard to define, but game scholars such as Johan Huizinga and Roger Caillois identify them using the notion of irrelevance. For Huizinga, nothing can be a game if it involves moral consequence.[1] Whatever is happening, if it really matters in an ethical or moral sense, it cannot be a game. Rather, games are places where we only *act* as if something matters. And indeed, play-acting seriousness can be one of the most important functions in a given game. But if some consequence really does matter in the end, the game is over. In fact, the only act of moral consequence that can happen within a game is the act of ending the game, of denying its as-if character, of spoiling the fantasy, of breaking the collective illusion that the game matters.

Huzinga also says, without much emphasis, that the collective illusion happens in a specific place, an arena specifically intended to host the game. Games, he says, happen in designated spaces.

We find ourselves at a moment in time when the space in which games may occur has suddenly and unexpectedly expanded beyond any known arena, indeed beyond the Earth, beyond the Moon and Sun, beyond the stars and the galaxies, beyond time itself. Games can happen anywhere, and everywhere, and always. Right now there are people hunched over keyboards in Seattle and Seoul who have not seen the light of our Sun in days, weeks. Their world is the world of Borges's Babylonian Lottery. For them, gaming is living. They have become immersed in play spaces that are permanent and exhibit the physics of Earth and the object constancy to which we have all been accustomed since infancy. Not only that, but these play spaces are perpetually occupied by other people, sometimes in the dozens, often in the thousands. Serious thinkers now call these spaces *virtual worlds* (although I prefer *synthetic worlds*), a usage that reflects our collective judgment that they are not very different from the Earth at all. They are fantastic, yes, but only in the sense that they are fantastical extensions of the universe into which humanity was born. They are worlds much like our world. And our species is beginning to spend many, many hours in them, playing.

Or not? As people have come together in synthetic worlds, they have begun to behave like people who come together on Earth: they talk, make agreements, exchange goods, make friendships, have sex. They also cheat and steal and abuse. They laugh, cry, and yell at one another. It's real-existing humanity, merely transported to a fantastical domain.

Something seems to be getting lost in the translation, however: the status of these places as *arenas*, and the understanding that the activity within them is play. True, if asked, most players will assert, "I don't care, it is just a game." Many people are formally committed to the idea that the events that occur are only play, but in the case of large-scale spectator sport, games acquire real consequences as the result of a self-confirming social consensus: if all society says that the World Series matters, then it does. I may not care who wins or loses, but I do care about other people crying, throwing things, beating strangers or their partners, falling into depression, and driving drunk. When sport is shared across society, society validates the seriousness of the consequences of sport, just as it validates the worth of money. It's all meaningful because everyone thinks it's meaningful—indeed, *only* because everyone thinks it's meaningful.

It is fairly easy to create conditions under which games do or do not matter. It's a choice we make as a society. And the state is not entirely without powers; it can have a great deal of influence on whether a game matters or not. With synthetic worlds, society seems to have begun a feeling-out process along the dimension of significance. For every player who is content to view the virtual world as play, there is another who gleefully buys and sells the game's wands, armor, and gold pieces for U.S. currency on eBay. For every player who does not care if the world is hacked and accounts are robbed, there is another who views the breach as a computer crime of the highest order. For every player who sleeps soundly after being banished from a guild, there is another who thinks about committing suicide.

The state is not neutral in this exploration of potential significance. The Korean police actively prosecute people who hack into games, and they give more weight to cases in which valuable game items are destroyed or transferred. On the face of it, this makes eminent good sense. The items in the game are valuable. They take time to acquire; they are observably bought and sold for real money in real markets; their owners are clearly distressed at their loss. Lastowka and Hunter have given us definitive arguments that the items inside synthetic worlds are just as eligible, in principle, for property rights-based protections as those outside synthetic worlds.[2]

The theft or destruction of valuable items is normally seen as actionable in courts, with few exceptions. The exceptions, however, are significant: when Allen Iverson steals a basketball, his opponent cannot have him arrested. That theft is part of the game. Similarly, when Nicky the Thief steals a hundred gold pieces in a synthetic world, *that* theft is part of the game. Not actionable. The Government of Korea does nothing. Yet when Nicky's owner hacks the world's servers and steals a hundred gold pieces, the Government of Korea says it *is* actionable.

One suspects that most governments would do the same thing: prosecute theft outside the rules of the game, but not theft inside the rules of the game. One also suspects that most players would probably view this as a sensible distinction. Rules create play.

It would seem, then, that we are implicitly granting a unique legal status to synthetic world games.

III. Drawing Lines

There is a fairly serious problem with this policy, however. The difficulty is that the line between the synthetic world and our world is much less clear than the line between the basketball court and the street outside. It is very, very easy to tell the difference between a "steal" in a basketball game and a "steal" involving the transport of a basketball from Person A's garage to Person B's garage and its subsequent permanent storage there. It is much harder to distinguish between in-world and out-world crime involving synthetic worlds. Lastowka and Hunter (chapter 2) cite examples from MUDs and graphical virtual worlds to show that the putatively unreal, gamelike environment of a virtual world seems to produce very real emotional consequences within its users. In the real world, they remind us, the term "rape" has a specific definition in terms of actions. Yet in cases where those actions have been typed rather than done, in a virtual world environment, the victims seem to have truly suffered. Who then is to say that there is a difference between real rape and virtual rape? If there is a difference, what is it?

So much of the activity inside the worlds is directly analogous to activity outside the worlds. What if the primary activity of human beings were to run around in large grass fields while attempting to kick white balls into big nets? What if that's what humanity *was*? What if that's all we cared about? Then suppose some wiseacre came up with the idea of designating a certain field as a "play" field, where the results of the running and kicking were to be agreed upon by all as being irrelevant and unimportant. It would be just for practice, just to enjoy the activity without the heavy consequences that normally attend. While we can imagine the distinction in our minds, I believe that this odd society would have trouble keeping things clear. There would always be those players who forget or ignore the irrelevance of the activity in the play space. If goals matter outside the space, then how could they not matter inside it? How could one persuade all of society to pretend that the activities in the play space, which look exactly like the activities outside it, do not have any consequences?

These questions might acquire a great deal of relevance in just a few decades. Synthetic worlds are growing in importance and the activity taking place within them looks very much like the activity taking place outside them. If the issues involving their legal status are not handled properly, we face the possibility that a tremendous boon to humankind may be irrevocably lost. The boon in peril is our ability to find refuge from the oppressions of the Earth's economic system, inside worlds that artists build. It's a new ability, just a few years old. Yet it may be our only hope to escape from the predations of the work system that we imposed on ourselves in the Industrial Revolution. World designers have already managed to make places that millions of people prefer to Earth, at least for a time (and often for a great deal of time). At the moment, these new worlds are treated as distinct play spaces where the normal rules of economics and law and government do not apply. Their distinctiveness seems to be a large part of the appeal. You can go there and be more than a cog in some other person's machine. At the same time, however, even these young worlds have begun to experience a creeping encroachment of meaning, an encroachment that erodes their claim to special legal treatment, and may thereby eliminate their ability to ennoble and enrich their users.

Meaning has begun to bleed into synthetic worlds in several ways. When players first began buying and selling game items for dollars on eBay, the world owners were shocked, or amused, but in either case they opposed the practice. Now, worlds have come into existence where trading dollars for game items is part of the rules. And while most owners maintain strict rules against out-world trade in their user agreements, they also seem to accept this trade as an unavoidable consequence of the large time and value disparities in the player base. Heavy media attention has made worlds into forums for protest and has also highlighted the psychological significance of events there. Worlds that designers intended to involve medievalistic or futuristic role playing have decayed into places where the atmosphere is more like a middle American shopping mall than the market of Rheims or Space Station Zebra.

Ironically, by failing to make the distinction between game and life, the players of synthetic world games themselves regularly commit Huizinga's One Moral Act: they wreck the illusion that the game is all play. The eBayers, the protesters, the out-of-character shouters, all blur the lines between game and life. It is understandable, of course; keeping the lines clear requires quite a bit of mental discipline, especially when the in-world society seems to act and breathe and feel just like the out-world society. In many ways, the game is more fun when you can talk not only about the odd behavior of the orc you just fought but also about the odd behavior of voters in certain political jurisdictions on the west coast of certain continents. To play these games as games is considerably harder than to play them as games in which you can deploy any real-world resources and ideas that you want. It's easier to go ahead and treat rule breaking as a kind of metagame, and illusion breaking as a tool that helps you exploit this world and its society toward your own ends, whatever they might be. It's fun to treat these game worlds as real worlds.

That is, it is fun so long as those odd voters on Earth keep what *they* are doing, and its consequences, away from what *you* are doing in the game. So long as the Earthlings and their economic and political and legal systems stay safely away, on far-off Earth, it is fun to half-live and half-play a fantastical existence within the confines of a synthetic world that the Earthlings have not yet reached.

IV. The Dire Consequences of Ambiguous Gaming

As long as the Earthlings stay away, in fact, residents of synthetic worlds can indulge in their fantasies of being "really in" the synthetic world as much as they are "really in" Earth. They can freely blur the line between play and not-play.

But if the users can step across blurred lines, so can the Earthlings.

Earth governments can see equivalences between gold pieces and dollars too. The gold piece would lose much of its luster if it were taxed like the dollar. Would the cottage in Avalon seem so charming if it came with a property tax assessment? Why, after all, should the state deploy its officers to protect that house from theft and destruction when its owner makes no contribution to the state in relation to the house's value? Eventually, the state will make a move into these places.

In sum: As meaning seeps into these play spaces, their status as play spaces will erode. As their status as play spaces erodes, the laws, expectations, and norms of contemporary Earth society will increasingly dominate the atmosphere. When Earth's culture dominates, the play will be over; the fantasy will be punctured; the illusion will be ended for good. Taxes will be paid. The rich and poor will dance the same macabre dance of mutual mistrust that they do on Earth, with no relief, no rewriting of beginnings, no chance to opt out and start again. The art that once framed an immersive imaginary experience will be retracted back to the walls of the space, and the people will go back to looking at it rather than living it. Living *there* will no longer be any different from living *here,* and a great opportunity to play the game of human life under different rules will have been lost.[3]

V. Responses in Law

If blurred lines are a problem, perhaps we can look to the efforts of game companies to clearly delineate the spaces they create. Their principal tool is the end-user license agreement (EULA). Users must click through these to enter the game world. By clicking, the user waives a number of significant rights, rights to own the fruits of labor, rights to assemble, rights to free speech. It is not clear to anyone outside the legal system whether the EULAs, as currently written, will be robust enough to meet the challenges that surely will come. Were a social club to require all members to waive their right to be critical of the club's managers, what would be the legal defense? If Jones, Smith, and Miller get together in the club and write a poem using the club's stationery, and then sell it on the street corner outside for $10,000, on what grounds can the club enjoin against that practice and even claim ownership of the poem? I don't know what the legal answers are, but these are things that EULAs try to do. The legitimacy of these clauses seems open to question.

Lastowka and Hunter analyze a number of doctrines that might be thought to support EULAs, and find all of them suspect. The EULAs are perhaps not very robust. Only time will tell how robust EULAs are, but let's assume that courts strike all the EULAs down. Then if Jones, Smith, and Miller use World of Warcraft to make an uber magic wand, they are said to own the wand, free and clear. As owners, they have a right of free disposal. They can sell it. They can sell it for gold pieces in the game or for dollars outside the game. Regardless of the location or currency of trade, if they are U.S. citizens, their wand-related earnings generate a tax liability to the U.S. government. If the wand is a taxable asset to the government, however, its theft or destruction must also be treated as a substantive violation of the laws of the United States. Indeed, the wand must be treated like any other economic asset of the nation, and all such assets, in principle, may be admitted as potential national security concerns. Without EULAs, these "games" are not games at all, they are merely extensions of the territory of the Earth, territory that must, in fairness, be defended, regulated, taxed, and policed just like the Earth.

Therefore, to accept the EULAs while also accepting the real value and serious meaning of events inside synthetic worlds, is to consciously apply a double standard. In effect, this is where we stand now: It is apparent to increasing numbers of serious people that the events of synthetic worlds are significant, emotionally (of course) but also economically and now, in Korea, legally. Yet we do not treat the things and events in those worlds the way we treat events out here, on the Earth. And for no apparent reason, other than that there is this EULA that claims to prevent equal treatment. According to the doctrine of the EULA, we can and should have in-world theft without police action, asset accumulation with no taxes, and citizenry without speech rights or voting privileges. What's missing is a justification for the EULA. Why, and when, is this double standard acceptable? Under what argument?

Indeed, there seems to be an absence of law here: Synthetic worlds are being treated as special cases, but no law has defined when and how this special treatment should apply. In the absence of specific law, we might expect that this special treatment will not last. It is a temporary state of affairs. As the assets and happenings in synthetic worlds grow in importance, more and more people will begin to wonder why dollars are taxed and gold pieces are not. It will seem unfair. And things will change. Remember, memes that promote economic growth are the most powerful memes in the cultural evolutionary processes. Here the struggle for survival is between these two contestants:

- Meme 1: Virtual Worlds Are Play Spaces
- Meme 2: Virtual Worlds Are Extensions of the Earth

It seems fairly clear to me that Meme 2 will win in the long run. Trade by trade, markets will knit the virtual world and the real world together, gradually erasing any distinction between them.

The evolutionary weakness of Meme 1 stems from the fact that the play status of a world is a *commons,* a shared good, that is subject to the tragedy of gradual erosion first identified by H. Scott Gordon in 1954 and popularized by Garrett Hardin in 1968.[4] Huizinga pointed out that the game remains a game only as long as everyone maintains the mental assumption that the game is a game. When someone announces that they no longer believe, the illusion is ruptured. Maintaining play status thus requires the active cooperation of all players. In the case of a game like basketball, this is not a problem because every player has the incentive to maintain the illusion. No single player can make himself better off by acting against the rules. If you break the rules, you get booted or the game just ends. Synthetic worlds are different; in most contemporary worlds, if you act against the play spirit of the world, say by importing some of your Earth income, you do not get booted; the game does not end; indeed, you make yourself better off. The Tragedy of the Commons argument predicts that, in such circumstances, the play status of the worlds will eventually erode completely.

The argument that play status is a commons provides strong conceptual (but not yet legal) support for the game EULAs as currently written. EULAs can be thought of as contracts that restrict the ability of individuals to erode the playness of the space, for the good of all users. In other words, the proper EULA can make everyone better off. Under a utilitarian conception of legal policy, if current law does not support the EULA, new law should be written that does.

VI. Defending Play as Commons: The Right to Play

What's missing, then, is a general statement of law that play spaces are a unique form of commons, a unique collective good, whose value can only be sustained under certain restrictions on individual behavior. The EULA that attempts to make *Dark Age of Camelot* into a medieval world should have a distinct legal status as a document that instantiates a place of play. The critical point is that *Dark Age of Camelot* has *no unique value whatsoever* as a place of play unless the EULA is effective. Without the EULA, *Dark Age of Camelot* is not a play space; it is a suburb of Newark, a place that used to be swampland but now has houses and businesses and athletic fields, all of which are utterly indistinguishable under law from the house and businesses and athletic fields of Newark itself. Yet in current law, there is nothing said about such instantiations of play. No law declares when and how this can be done.[5]

EULAs are an assertion of a distinct power to create a play space, but this power does not currently exist. If it did exist, it would certainly not be the power of an individual or a private company. Any declaration that a space is a play space is simultaneously a declaration that many laws of the government do not apply there. It is a limitation of governmental sovereignty. In the past, individuals and companies who made such assertions unilaterally—"your law does not apply to me!"—usually have found themselves paying taxes again in short order (occasionally to some other government), or if not, then jailed or eventually dead.

To justify the powers asserted by EULAs, new law must appear: a specific Law of Interration that grants EULAs a legal status robust enough to allow them to preserve virtual worlds as play spaces. Virtual worlds created under the terms of interration law would be considered "closed" worlds, while those not created under its terms would be considered "open":

- Closed worlds: the border between the virtual world and the real world is considered impermeable. The interests and conditions of users are regulated by the terms of the EULA. Earth courts and legislatures have no powers there. Conflicts among users or between users and designers or owners are only actionable within the virtual world, or only through institutions and processes that are at the sole discretion of the owners to devise and implement.
- Open worlds: The border between the virtual world and the real world is considered completely porous. The interests and conditions of users are regulated by applicable real-world law in whatever jurisdiction the users and world-servers find themselves. Conflicts are actionable in any court or legislative venue with jurisdiction.
- The state intervenes in closed worlds only under conditions defined within interration law. To the extent that outside law applies in closed worlds, it should protect the freedoms of users.

The act of interration—the creation of play space—is properly an act of government. Governments now have both imminent cause and ancient precedent to consider how this act should be structured and defined.

The cause is humanity's fundamental right to play. The recent appearance of massively immersive play spaces, where the ordinary rules of Earth do not apply, is a tremendous gift to us all, a great moment of liberation, and a dramatically powerful reconnection between human beings and the artists who sustain us. This technology now exists. If deployed properly, it will spread joy and self-esteem across the planet. According to a positive theory of rights, we have a right to have access to that joy and that self-esteem.[6] The urge to play is buried very deeply in our psyches, well below rational thought, somewhat above the urge to eat and have sex. Mammals do not speak, but they play, and so should we—indeed, so *must* we. How many horrors of history happened only because urges that ordinarily would have been exorcised through healthy play instead were diverted into mass politics and war? What *is* volkisch Nationalism if not a horribly distorted game of make-believe? How unfortunate that our innate desire to be a good member of the team became the Battle of the Somme. *Quake Arena* might have made a difference, although Plato would have recommended something more erudite, such as *A Tale in the Desert*.[7] When we perceive new opportunities to play in our play-starved world, we have a right to take advantage of them. It is part of being human.

The cause is imminent because as quickly as these new opportunities to play have emerged, they have begun to erode. They need protection, and current law seems unlikely to provide it.

The precedent is the act of incorporation. Some four hundred years ago, governments began to realize that society would be better off with certain restrictions on individual behavior and rights, restrictions that invoked a tightly defined and circumscribed game of make-believe about the notion of personhood. It invented the idea of a fictional person to promote a specific form of human interaction. On its face, the law that instantiates the fictional person and forces everyone into the game of make-believe about him, is truly oppressive to living, breathing people. Smith can fritter away the assets of Smith Incorporated, yet I cannot hold Smith accountable for that; I just lose my investment when the corporation goes under and that is the end of the story. Yet once the law has its effects, all people, including those who are oppressed and denied rights by the face of the law, are better off.

The legal act of incorporation creates a fictional person and is performed when the creation of this person has net social benefits. The analogous legal act of interration would have a similar purpose: to create a fictional place. It would also be performed only when the creation of this fictional world would be socially beneficial. The terms of creation and the restrictions it imposes on everyone in society would, as with incorporation, be laid down in the synthetic world's Charter of Interration. The Charter would define where this place is and how people can go there. It would clarify the legal status of events that happen there and of assets that accumulate there. It would define the rights of people in various roles: developers, users, outsiders. The legal status of the interration would be elevated, in the sense that acts and assets inside it are exempt from most of the laws of the Earth. Earth law would in fact state that these protections are necessary for the interrated place to provide the benefits that it does. They are essential for its functioning, and that is why an Act of Interration even exists.

In return for its privileges, the chartered interration would be subject to strict rules. To be preserved as play space under the law, the synthetic world would have to conform to standards of construction and policy, much as corporations must conform to such standards in order to retain their special status. For example, an interration would have to maintain strict separation of its economy from the economy of the outside world. If players can regularly buy and sell assets from the synthetic world for real dollars, the world is no longer clearly distinct from the Earth's economy; it is no longer a play space, it is a tax haven. A tax haven has no right to special privileges under Earth law; its case for interration is weak. In general, interrations would be subject to scrutiny on these matters; lack of good faith efforts to maintain the space as a *play* space could lead to the revocation of the charter.[8]

Eventually a body of law would emerge that properly balances the rights and obligations of everyone involved with interrated spaces. Under this law, synthetic worlds would be protected from numerous legal and regulatory sanctions, in return for providing society with the benefits of otherworldly play.

VII. Managing an Interrated Landscape

Today, corporations are a popular form of economic organization, but they are not the only form of economic organization. Partnerships and private businesses continue to thrive; economic organization follows a certain rationality and emerges in different forms to serve different ends.

We can hope that interrations will emerge in similar fashion. When it makes sense to preserve a play space as a *play* space, it will be preserved, insulated, and protected from the predations of the economic machine that surrounds it (and us). When it does not make sense to seal off a synthetic world, however, it will not be sealed off. Worlds not protected by explicit acts of interration will be (quite literally) nothing more than mundane extensions of Earth territories and will be treated as such under law.

Such "open" worlds will provide all kinds of benefits. Even though they will not really be play spaces, they will still allow us to rewrite many of the rules of physical interaction (through the construction of avatars, for example). They will be incredibly useful forms of communication. They will provide exciting new arenas for social interaction. And, as open worlds, they will host events that really do matter. By definition, these will be places that are *not* play. As worlds that matter, these open worlds will deserve exactly the same legal treatment as the Earth receives. We can use ordinary economic techniques (such as shadow pricing or time valuation) to place a real-world value on what happens there. And courts can then use these valuations to render appropriate judgments. By such processes, the assets (and by extension, the activities) of people who participate in open worlds can attain the same status as assets and activities of people who do not participate there. With this legal treatment, the open worlds can provide society with the benefits that are unique to them as forms of communication.

"Closed" worlds, by contrast, are intended to provide a different portfolio of benefits, and are subject to a different set of laws, as reflected in the charters that interrate them. Under these charters, the methods of asset valuation given above simply do not apply. These are play spaces. Nothing matters there. Assets there have no value. Losses there are unimportant. Crimes there create no claims of redress. Lost hours are simply lost. No act is actionable. The complete lack of consequence is, in fact, a declaration and imposition of the state. Indeed, it is the closed world's *raison d'être*.

VIII. A Declaration: This Is Not a Declaration

In 1996, John Perry Barlow famously (or infamously) proclaimed the sovereignty of Internet communities in his "Declaration of the Independence of Cyberspace."[9] Barlow was reacting to the first widespread attempt by government to regulate the Net's content. In retrospect, it has become increasingly evident that the Net has always been something that would be easy to regulate if anyone took the time. And, indeed, no three humans come together without soon wishing there were some overarching authority to take care of matters that are clearly communal in nature. The Net would not work without some kind of governance. The only issues are who and what and how.

More recently, Raph Koster somewhat playfully constructed a "Declaration of the Rights of Avatars" (a version appears in Chapter 4).[10] The declaration expresses something important. It makes sure that we all understand that communities of people who interact on the Internet are, indeed, communities of people. Like all networked folk, they depend on the infrastructure to keep their community alive, and that means they exist in a relationship to network administrators that is similar to the relationship between citizens and government. As Lawrence Lessig has told us, code is law. Koster's declaration just reminds everyone that codes, like laws, really ought to promote the general well-being and respect the dignity of the human person to the greatest extent possible.

This essay has identified a right to play that all humans have, and it has argued that governments may want to lay some legal groundwork so that certain opportunities to play are preserved. These opportunities happen to be emerging on the Internet. As a result, the argument of this essay might perhaps be identified with either Barlow's or Koster's declarations. It might be said that a Right to Play is a right to escape into the Internet, where everyone can be free. Or it might be said that a Right to Play is a right that the community of gamers have vis-à-vis the developers and world owners.

But neither of these identifications is really appropriate. The right to play is just a right to do something enjoyable. When a fine new play space becomes available, it elevates the human person, adding to her dignity and allowing her to drink more deeply from the stream of human aesthetic creation. It is a good thing, and it should be preserved. As it happens, the glorious new play spaces we have recently discovered are becoming available on the Internet, and unfortunately they are getting mixed in with lots of other things that are becoming available on the Internet at the same time, such as new currencies, new markets, and new social, political, and academic hierarchies. With all this wonderful undergrowth springing up at once, the status of these spaces as *play spaces* has become ambiguous. As a result, they are in danger of disappearing, of being swallowed up in the turbulent rush of ordinary human affairs. It would be a good idea to prevent this from happening, by making an explicit body of law that identifies what a play space is, how a space can qualify for play status, and what rights and obligations this status confers.

Is a call for this kind of new law implicitly a declaration, à la Barlow, that all people who wish to do so, *must* be allowed to use these places to escape from the jurisdiction of the governments of Earth? No. On the contrary, we rely on the governments of the Earth to charter these spaces and develop rules of fair use for them.

Is it implicitly a declaration, à la Koster, that communities in synthetic worlds have certain rights with respect to the owners of the world? Well, yes and no. In the case of open worlds, yes—an open world is just an extension of the Earth, and all rights and obligations that people have on Earth carry over to cyberspace. A net admin who shuts off the server of an open world and destroys $300,000 of magic wands will face his day in court. The community of avatars has all kinds of rights of redress.

But in the case of closed worlds, the answer is no. The closed world's charter explicitly nullifies any putative Rights of Avatars. A closed world is not an extension of the Earth. It is a fictional place with rules of its own. Whatever rights its users have are the rights that the owners have decreed. Of course, the rules by which such a place receives its charter will (indeed, must) impose restrictions on the decrees of owners; no one can legally interrate a world that is designed to immiserate people or violate their dignity. But that is a matter of the rights of people, not the rights of avatars; it is resolved a priori, in the struggle between citizens and governments of Earth nations as they try to define a good interration law. Once that struggle is resolved, the law of interration is set in place; once a world is interrated under that law, whatever rights or obligations its internal government decrees (again, assuming they do not violate the terms of the charter itself) are sacrosanct there, and no user has a right to redress under any outside authority.

It may seem strange, but in a very short period of time we humans have been confronted with a tricky problem: how to design law about fantasy worlds. But we should not be too anxious about it; centuries ago, humans like us solved the tricky problem of designing law about fantasy persons. The benefits of having fantasy people around soon became apparent to everyone, and there were no real objections to the suspension of disbelief that the law required. The game of make-believe people was not exactly fun, especially to people who lost the money they gave to corporations. But it was useful; it helped most investors sleep better at night, and it thereby promoted economic growth. A legal game of make-believe places will also be rather un-fun. It will require numerous creditors, theft victims, tax collectors, protestors, defeated warriors, and impoverished wizards to simply go home empty-handed, unsatisfied, perhaps distraught. But it will allow everyone, all of us, to spend time in worlds where magic is real. Goodness, we haven't done anything like that in hundreds of years. We miss it.

NOTES

1. Johan Huizinga, *Homo Ludens* (Boston: Beacon Press, 1938/1950), p. 210.

2. F. Gregory Lastowka and Dan Hunter, The Laws of the Virtual Worlds, 92 *Cal. L. Rev.* 1 (2004).

3. The argument here mirrors Lawrence Lessig's lamentations in *Code and Other Laws of Cyberspace* (New York: Basic Books, 1999). Hunter and Lastowka, note 2, supra at 95, also foresee problems.

4. H. Scott Gordon, The Economic Theory of a Common Property Resource: The Fishery, 62 *J. Pol. Econ.* 124 (1954); Garrett Hardin, The Tragedy of the Commons, 162 *Science* 1243 (1968).

5. David R. Johnson and David Post, Law and Borders: The Rise of Law in Cyberspace, 48 *Stan. L. Rev.* 1367 (1996) argue generally for unique legal treatment of cyberspace.

6. The right to play can be motivated from two articles of the Universal Declaration of Human Rights. Article 27 states, "Everyone has the right freely to participate in the cultural life of the community, to enjoy the arts and to share in scientific advancement and its benefits." Moments of play, especially in the case of synthetic worlds, are the result of a fortuitous collusion of science and art, and the article asserts that their benefits should be denied to no one. Article 24 asserts that "Everyone has the right to rest and leisure." Play represents a temporary exclusion, a rest, from the ordinary world and its penalty and reward system; the article asserts a right to this rest.

7. "Man is made God's plaything, and that is the best part of him. Therefore every man and woman should live life accordingly, and play the noblest games. . . . Life must be lived as play, playing certain games, making sacrifices, singing and dancing." Plato, *The Laws*.

8. In other words, an interration law would be a support for EULAs, but only for a certain kind of EULA: One that makes *more* effort, not less, to make the fantasy world into a legitimate fantasy.

9. *See* chapter 2 of Peter Ludlow (ed.), *Crypto Anarchy, Cyberstates, and Pirate Utopias* (Cambridge: MIT Press, 2001).

10. *See* http://www.legendmud.org/raph/gaming/index.html.

6

Law and Liberty in Virtual Worlds

Jack M. Balkin

As increasing numbers of people flock to virtual worlds and invest their time and resources there, the law will surely follow. How should we balance the interests of law and liberty in virtual worlds? I argue that both contract law and free speech law will play central roles.

Three Kinds of Virtual Liberty

There are three kinds of freedom in virtual worlds. The first is the freedom of the players to participate in the virtual world and interact with each other through their in-game representations, or avatars. This is the *freedom to play*.[1] The second is the freedom of the game designer or platform owner[2] to plan, construct, and maintain the virtual world. This is the *freedom to design*. The third kind of freedom is the collective right of the designers and players to build and enhance the game space. We might call this the *freedom to design together.*

Platform owners control virtual worlds through two basic devices—code and contract. Platform owners can write (or rewrite) the software that shapes the physics and ontology of the game space and sets parameters about what people can do there. Game designers can also regulate the game through contract. Usually players must sign an agreement to participate in the virtual world. The contract is normally called the Terms of Service (ToS) or the end-user license agreement (EULA). In most cases, the EULA covers rules about proper play, appropriate behavior, and decorum in the virtual space that the platform owner cannot easily impose through code. The platform owner can discipline players who violate the EULA, take away their privileges and powers, or even kick them out of the game space and eliminate their avatars.

The platform owner's freedom to design and the players' freedom to play are often synergistic. The code and the EULA create the architecture and social contract of the virtual world; they allow people to play within it. To a very considerable extent the players' freedom to play is the freedom to play within the rules the platform owners have created. Imagine, for example, that a designer creates a game called *The Gulag Online,* which simulates a Soviet-era prison camp in Siberia. The right to play in *The Gulag Online* is the right to experience—and to be subjected to—all that can happen in that space. Some of these experiences will be quite unpleasant, but that is the point of the game. The right to play in a particular virtual space depends in large part on what kind of space it is and what kind of game the platform owner is trying to create. Players who take on the role of political prisoners in *The Gulag Online* can hardly complain if their avatars cannot order virtual room service in their prison barracks. They can, however, strategize among themselves and revolt against their Soviet oppressors to the extent that the rules permit it.

Platform owners, particularly those who are in the business of making money from selling licenses to play in game spaces, are usually eager to keep the players happy so that they stay and bring even more people into the game space. Hence they often seek out the opinions of the player community about how to make the game more fun to play, how different features can be tweaked, how loopholes can be eliminated, and how previously unanticipated forms of player behavior which other players think unfair or not in the spirit of the game can be prevented through code or prohibited by the EULA. The platform owner usually cannot make everyone happy because suggestions may run in very different directions; some people may want to have a certain behavior prohibited, while others want it to become a legitimate part of the game. Nevertheless, the interaction between the platform owner and the player community assists both the freedom to design and the freedom to play; it is one aspect—although certainly not the only one—of the freedom to design together.

Even so, the interests and desires of players and platform owners can also conflict. Although the freedom to play generally exists within the rules of the game, platform owners may run their spaces in ways that players believe are unfair or tyrannical. As a result, claims about the platform owner's freedom to design may clash with players' claims about the freedom to play, and the law may have to arbitrate between them. For example, players may complain that platform owners have defrauded or misled them, stolen their intellectual property, or invaded their privacy. The enormous power that platform owners wield over events in the game space, and their ability to see everything that is going on in that space, means that they have abundant opportunity to abuse their authority. The fact that players have signed an agreement with the platform owner and can voluntarily exit from the space does not necessarily settle the matter. Although players make the initial choice of where to play, over time they often invest considerable time and energy in the game world and in their in-world identities.[3] Investment in game spaces and the desire to maintain social connections within the game space may make exit difficult, and it may be unfair to insist that exit is a player's only legal remedy.

Conversely, some players may behave in ways that the platform owners—and other players—think is inappropriate, undermines the rules of the game, or makes it less fun for everyone else. The platform owner may rewrite the code, change the EULA, or kick the offending players out. When this happens, these players may also argue—although with somewhat less justification—that the platform owner has abridged their right to play by behaving arbitrarily or illegally. Inevitably, the law will have to settle some of these disputes. Many of the most important legal problems in virtual worlds arise out of the potential conflicts between platform owners' assertions of the right to design and players' opposing assertions of the right to play.

Virtual Liberty and the First Amendment

The rights to design and play in virtual worlds overlap in important respects with the constitutional rights of freedom of speech, expression, and association. However, free speech law fails to protect important features of the rights to design and play because the First Amendment generally protects individuals only from abridgments by the state, and not by private parties.

When the state regulates virtual spaces because of disapproval of the ideas expressed by the activities of the players and the designers, the free speech principle is surely implicated. But that is true of almost any activity, even if it has nothing to do with speech: if the government punishes only arsonists who are critical of the government, this violates the First Amendment notwithstanding the fact that the government may make arson a crime. The more important question is whether design and play in virtual spaces are themselves protected forms of speech, like dance, charitable solicitation, picketing, leafleting, playing a musical instrument, or using a printing press to publish a newspaper.

Protected expression under the First Amendment is a historically contingent category, whose contours change with time as new conventions and technologies emerge. The key question is whether a particular activity serves as a medium for the communication of ideas.[4] A medium of communication combines technologies, conventions, and social practices. Motion pictures are a good example. This medium includes both the technologies for making and exhibiting movies, and social practices and conventions for expression using those technologies. In 1915, the Supreme Court did not consider motion pictures protected speech—that is, it did not regard movies as a medium for the communication of ideas. Instead, it saw movies as a form of mere "entertainment" like baseball or hockey.[5] Today it seems obvious to us that motion pictures, and the conventions and practices of telling stories within motion picture technology, are very much a medium for the communication of ideas, and, not surprisingly, the Supreme Court eventually came around to that assessment as well.[6]

Are the developing technologies and social practices of designing and playing games a new medium for the communication of ideas? Courts already recognize much simpler games—so-called first person shooter games—as artistic creations entitled to First Amendment protection.[7] If anything, the arguments for treating the design and play of massively multiplayer online games or virtual worlds as artistic creations or forms of expression are even stronger.

Designers purposefully create new worlds in which communities can form and stories can be told, and players, in turn, use the game platform to create identities, have adventures, and tell their own stories. The technologies for producing animated motion pictures and programming virtual worlds have been merging for some time. The design of movies and virtual worlds features are now quite similar in many respects, except that virtual worlds allow for interactivity. This interactivity makes virtual worlds even more of a medium for the communication and exchange of ideas than motion pictures, for not only can the platform owner exercise his or her imagination in the creation of new worlds, but so too can the players.[8] Motion pictures allow images to be viewed by a mass audience. But multiplayer online games convert that mass audience into active participants and storytellers. Virtual spaces allow players to add new features to the worlds they inhabit. Virtual worlds permit contingent events, path dependencies, and cumulative effects. In short, they permit the development of histories. They allow the players to make new meanings, to have new adventures, to take on new personas, to form new communities, and to express themselves and interact with and communicate with others in ever new ways.

We might make a useful, if imperfect, analogy between virtual worlds and improvisational theater. Just as the platform owner can determine who gets to participate in the virtual space, but cannot fully control the players' actions, the director of an improvisational troupe has control over who participates in the improvisation, but does not have complete control over the scene as it develops. Improvisational theater is a combination of freedom and constraint that enlists the participation and the creativity of the actors to produce new works that none of the participants could have created on their own. In the same way, game platforms enlist the participation and creativity of the players to create new characters and new stories that could not otherwise have been produced.

For this reason, both platform owners and players can assert First Amendment rights against state interference with rights to design and play. I predict that both game designers and players will regularly invoke the First Amendment in future years to challenge legal regulation of virtual worlds, much as telecommunications companies and media corporations regularly invoke the First Amendment to avoid regulation of their businesses.[9] As the analogy to telecommunications regulation suggests, some of the platform owners' and players' activities should be protected by the free speech principle, while others—like violations of consumer protection laws—should not. If the state dislikes the theme and design of the game, or dislikes the ideas that players and programmers communicate in the game space because these ideas are violent, offensive, or indecent, the state may not restrict the content of the design or the activities of the players under the First Amendment any more than it could ban books or movies because of the ideas expressed in them. The major exceptions to this principle are the same that apply to books and movies: the state may ban obscene expression, and it may protect children from exposure to indecency. Concerns about indecency, however, are best dealt with not by restricting the speech of adults in virtual spaces, but by restricting access to minors, or zoning the virtual space so that minors cannot enter certain areas of the virtual space.

Regulating the Game Space—
Torts and Crimes in Virtual Worlds

The First Amendment does not make virtual spaces regulation-free zones. The boundaries between the game space and real space are permeable. What happens to people (or their avatars) in the game space may have real-world effects on them and on third parties who are not part of the game.

Generally speaking the destruction of virtual property or the killing of one avatar by another raises no problem that would require special state regulation, as long as it occurs within the rules of the game. The ability to destroy or steal another's virtual possessions, or exterminate another character is part of what it means to participate in the medium. To the extent that these actions are within the rules, they are presumptively protected by the First Amendment. To return to the previous example of *The Gulag Online,* the platform owner has a First Amendment right to create a space in which some avatars (guards) imprison other avatars (prisoners) and shoot them if they try to escape. Accordingly, the players have a First Amendment right, as long as they are playing within the rules, to imprison, shoot, and attempt to escape.

To be sure, what falls within the rules is sometimes disputed. Players are enormously creative, and often come up with new strategies and devices that the platform owners could not have foreseen. As a result, internal norms arise in many virtual worlds to regulate what players may do in the spaces; people can shun or punish people who misbehave and some players have created in-world tribunals to adjudicate disputes.[10] The platform owner can also regulate behavior in the game space by altering the code or the EULA. The platform owner can sanction or expel players who hack into the game to give themselves special abilities, or who otherwise violate the rules or the spirit of the game. When platform owners do this, they are invoking their real-world contractual rights. To this extent, state regulation is always involved in the governance of the game space.

Apart from contact breaches, in-world behavior can have real-world effects that states may have reason to regulate or prevent. Most of these situations involve communications torts—a category of legal causes of action in which people are harmed by speech acts that are not otherwise protected by the First Amendment. Communications torts are likely to be a central feature of the legal regulation of game spaces for a simple reason.

All activity in virtual worlds must begin as a form of speech. When people injure each other in virtual worlds in ways that the law will recognize, they are almost always committing some form of communications tort.

Among the most important examples of communications torts that can apply in virtual worlds are violations of intellectual property protections like copyright and trademark. (Although these are statutory schemes instead of common law causes of action, I include them in the category of communications torts because people legally injure each other through communication). Reproducing copyrighted material in a virtual space may violate copyright, and creating virtual items with company logos may violate trademark rights. Because many virtual worlds encourage the creation and design of virtual items, the possibilities for infringement are endless. If the platform owner allows the players to hold copyrights in their own designs, the game owner is inviting the law into the game space, and the problems of enforcing intellectual property rights are greatly multiplied. For example, people may have intellectual property interests in the designs of virtual items. Taking a screenshot of the game that displays these items makes a copy of the surface pattern, and thus may violate the owner's intellectual property rights. All of the emerging conflicts between freedom of expression and intellectual property law are present in virtual worlds. In fact, because so much activity in virtual spaces involves copying and building on existing elements, and because the entire space is a set of representations, the conflicts between freedom of speech and intellectual property are further heightened; in some respects, virtual worlds constitute a perfect storm.

Defamation can also occur in virtual spaces. People can defame other people's real-world identities in cyberspace, just as they can in real space. People can also defame players' in-world identities, or avatars, for example by falsely claiming that a particular character has cheated. Speech is defamatory when it harms one's reputation in one's community,[11] and in theory this should include virtual communities as well. Although leaving the virtual community for a new one or creating a new identity are technically available options, they may not be a sufficient remedy if people invest a great deal of time and energy in creating their in-world personas, and value their participation in the virtual community highly. In general, the more important virtual worlds become to people and the more time and effort they invest in them, the more likely it becomes that the law will take seriously injuries to their in-world reputation as well as their in-world possessions.

What about fraud and misrepresentation? These should not be actionable if the rules of the game allow players to trick and deceive each other, although platform owners are certainly not insulated from liability if they misrepresent the terms of the game or defraud their customers. The problem is that not all activities are clearly specified as being within the rules. Players are quite creative in devising new ways to take advantage of each other within the parameters permitted by the code. Although in-world dispute resolution may be helpful in some cases, when a great deal of money is at stake people may turn to the law where the code permits the maneuver and the EULA is silent.

It is likely that in the future virtual spaces will be used to create an entertaining space for people to shop online. That means that consumer protection laws will apply in these virtual spaces, including restrictions on false and misleading advertising. Nevertheless, the merger of collective storytelling and shopping may lead to difficult problems; is a certain maneuver or deception a form of false advertising, or is it just part of the game?

Finally, consider the tort of intentional infliction of emotional distress. Suppose one avatar rapes or tortures another, or a group of avatars gang tackle a player and make off with all of his or her virtual possessions. Can the victims argue that they suffered severe emotional distress because they were treated outrageously in ways that are inconsistent with civilized society? One might reject this claim on the ground that players assume the risk of bad things happening within the rules of the game, and that in any case norms and sanctions that develop within the game will serve as a sufficient deterrent and punishment for bad behavior. On the other hand, as people spend more of their lives in virtual worlds and their notions of self become increasingly bound up with these worlds, the argument for legal redress for outrageous behavior may become increasingly plausible.

Perhaps the best analogy would be to the way tort and criminal law deal with injuries in contact sports. Generally speaking, football players cannot sue other players who tackle them during the game even if the tackle results in lasting and permanent injury, and even if the tackle was ruled a foul. However, there is a limited exception for physical injuries that stem from egregious violations of the rules.[12] When players violate the rules with deliberate intent to injure or with reckless disregard of the consequences, a few courts have allowed the victims to sue for battery. Thus, although a linebacker is not liable for a rough tackle, he is liable for hitting a player on the kneecap with a pipe or taking out a pistol and shooting him.

In like fashion, suits for intentional infliction of emotional distress in virtual worlds would sometimes be appropriate, but the emotional injury would have to be severe and the behavior completely outside the bounds of the ordinary forms of mistreatment that players regularly inflict on each other in virtual worlds.[13] Most examples of what players call "griefing" are adequately addressed either by the EULA or by the players' internal norms and practices of dispute resolution and shunning that naturally spring up inside many virtual worlds. Courts and legislatures should be particularly wary of allowing suits for intentional infliction of emotional distress except in the most extreme cases, because these suits implicate the free speech concerns that underlie the right to design and the right to play in virtual worlds. Courts and legislatures should give virtual communities wide latitude to design their own rules and social norms to deal with misbehavior and leave plenty of room for the creativity of the people who design and play games.

Real-World Commodification and Its Consequences

The increasing commodification of virtual worlds will also lead to greater state regulation. Commodification occurs when things in the virtual world are subject to purchase and exchange. However, it is crucial to distinguish in-world commodification from real-world commodification. Lots of virtual spaces feature in-world commodification: people can barter items or buy and sell things using the game world's currency, and they can earn more in-world currency by performing various tasks. Real-world commodification goes further: It means the ability to buy and sell things in virtual worlds using real-world currency or in order to obtain real-world currency. For example, people now buy and sell weapons, magical powers, and even their characters on eBay. Game-world currency is increasingly easy to convert into real-world currency, and the Gaming Open Market now lets players buy and sell the currencies used in various popular game worlds.[14] In addition, businesses have sprung up that are entirely devoted to the sale of virtual items.[15]

In-world commodification generally presents no special problems that demand state regulation of virtual worlds, other than enforcing the contractual provisions of the EULA or Terms of Service agreement. Real-world commodification, on the other hand, breaches the barrier between the virtual and real worlds and creates new and difficult problems. When virtual worlds contain items of significant value to the players that are convertible into real-world property, governments will be increasingly interested in regulating what goes on in these virtual worlds. Suppose, for example, that a virtual world contains a casino in which players can win in-game currency. If the currency is freely transferable into dollars, the game offers an end-run around online gambling restrictions. In fact, virtual spaces present all of the same problems of crossing borders generally associated with the Internet. If players create and sell virtual Nazi memorabilia in the game space, this may run afoul of the laws in countries that prohibit the sale of such items.

If platform owners encourage real-world commodification of virtual worlds, encourage people in these worlds to treat virtual items like property, and allow the sale and purchase of these assets as if they were property, they should not be surprised if courts, legislatures, and administrative agencies begin to treat virtual items as property. Indeed, the more that activities in virtual worlds affect real-world commerce and real-world property interests, the more quickly virtual worlds will become targets of legal regulation.

Platform owners can attempt to head off this problem of real-world commodification through contract. They can write the EULA to state that players shall have no expectations of property rights in virtual items, that platform owners can remove or modify virtual items at will, and that players assume all risks of monetary loss when they play in the virtual world. The EULA can also state that players who attempt to sell virtual property in real space will be kicked out of the game and their virtual items destroyed. To the extent that the virtual space is designed to promote in-world storytelling and community formation—rather than real-world commerce—the EULA may be the best way to head off the problems caused by real-world commodification and to safeguard the virtual world from legal regulation. In addition, courts and legislatures should treat virtual worlds that resist or discourage real-world commodification differently from those that encourage it.

However, platform owners cannot have it both ways. They cannot simultaneously encourage the purchase and sale of virtual items and then write the EULA so that all virtual items remain the property of the platform owner. The EULA may not be enforceable in all cases, especially if courts—and more importantly, legislatures and administrative agencies— think that platform owners are taking advantage of players. Legislatures and administrative agencies like the Federal Trade Commission can modify the law to recognize and protect property rights in virtual worlds if players place sufficient political pressure on them to do so. As virtual worlds become larger and are inhabited by more players, as players spend more time and invest more of themselves in these virtual worlds, and as real-world markets emerge for the sale of virtual world items and the exchange of virtual world currencies, the pressure on legislatures and administrative agencies to recognize and protect the property rights of players in virtual worlds will become irresistible. In fact, one might even imagine a scenario in which a game goes bankrupt and the players petition a bankruptcy court to keep the game running, restructure the business, and/or sell it to another party so that the players' virtual property interests are not destroyed. (These assets would be like bailments in the care and keeping of the platform owner.) The argument might be even more compelling if virtual items could be transported to another game space.

Game designers will probably be particularly disturbed by the notion of a bankruptcy court taking over a game, because the one right that platform owners have always believed they possessed is the right to turn off the switch and end the simulation. However, when game designers encourage real-world commodification and propertization of their virtual worlds, they are inviting the law in, and when they do so, they will lose the degree of control over their worlds they had previously enjoyed.

Designers who wish to minimize legal interference with their worlds and maximize First Amendment protection must take care to structure their games to avoid or discourage real-world commodification and the legal problems that it brings. There is no problem with rules that allow in-world barter and in-world markets as long as the platform owner takes steps in the code and in the EULA to discourage the real-world commodification of virtual items. The First Amendment should protect the rights of designers to create and preserve spaces that are devoted to expression and the exercise of narrative imagination. But when designers create worlds that encourage real-world commodification and that focus on commerce and the acquisition and sale of items with real-world values, their First Amendment rights will not insulate them from consumer protection laws, whose purposes are unrelated to the supression of free expression. Treat the virtual space like a collective work of art, and it will receive artistic protection; treat the players as consumers and they will demand consumer protection.

Some real-world commodification of virtual spaces is probably unavoidable, especially as virtual spaces become increasingly popular.

Players will find ways to exchange virtual items for money, whether on eBay or through some other method. Platform owners may not be able to stamp out this practice entirely either through code or through enforcement of the EULA. Nevertheless, in designing legal regulation, the key issue should be the purposes of the virtual space and whether the platform owner encourages or discourages real-world commodification. Not all virtual spaces are alike, and the law should not treat them as if they were all the same. The law should afford special protection to designers who devote their spaces primarily to the exercise of freedom of speech and association; this helps preserve the free speech values that support the rights to design and to play. We should avoid making these rights hostage to behind-your-back sales of virtual items by a small number of players. Conversely, virtual spaces that are designed to be shopping malls and emporia for the purchase and sale of real and virtual goods should be treated as such, and should not be able to avoid consumer protection regulation by hiding behind the First Amendment.

Freedom of Design versus Freedom to Play

Although the freedom to design and the freedom to play can be synergistic, they can also conflict. When they conflict, current American free speech law is least helpful. First Amendment doctrine does not protect the interests of the game players against the actions of the platform owner or game designer because the platform owner is not a state actor. If anything, American free speech law will tend to reinforce the contractual and intellectual property rights of platform owners to control the structure of the game through the EULA, and to expel players for violating its terms.

Consider, as a recent example, the conflict between Peter Ludlow and Electronic Arts, owners of *The Sims Online*. Ludlow began a weblog called The Alphaville Herald,[16] in which he reported on the events that occurred in Alphaville, a virtual city in the game space of *The Sims Online*. According to Ludlow, these events included, among other things, thieves, scams, and an underage prostitution ring. Ludlow alleged that the virtual characters or avatars controlled by a group of underage players would offer to engage in sexual talk with other avatars in return for some of the game currency, called simoleans. Simoleans can be exchanged for U.S. dollars. As a result, Ludlow alleged, not only were minors engaged in indecent conversation with adults, but the adults were paying them money to do it.[17]

Ludlow repeatedly attacked the platform owners of *The Sims Online,* Electronic Arts, for allowing this and other misconduct to occur. In response, he says, Electronic Arts terminated his account, erasing his virtual property (including a virtual house) and his two virtual cats. Electronic Arts argued that Ludlow had violated the game's ToS: he had included a link on his personal profile to his Alphaville Herald site, and that site, in turn, included a link to sites that explained how to cheat at the game. Ludlow argued that this was a pretextual enforcement of a technical violation of the ToS not regularly applied against other players.[18]

If Electronic Arts were a real state and Alphaville a real city, Ludlow would have a colorable argument that his free speech rights had been violated—especially if he could show that the real reason for the termination was a desire to silence him. However, Electronic Arts is not a state actor and Alphaville is a virtual community. Ludlow's right to play conflicts with Electronic Arts's right to run its game. Moreover, Electronic Arts might regard Ludlow as someone who is spreading false reports about *The Sims Online* that are bad for its business. Electronic Arts would argue that it has the contractual right to refuse service to anyone who unreasonably disturbs the play of the game.

How can the right to play be protected from arbitrary decisions by the platform owner while still respecting the platform owner's right to design? One model of regulation would treat the platform owner like a company town.[19] In *Marsh v. Alabama,* the Supreme Court held that a town wholly owned by a company could not use its property rights to prevent people from distributing leaflets on its streets.[20] Because the company had assumed all of the major functions of a municipality, it had to obey First Amendment values.[21] Put in somewhat different terms, the streets of the company town formed a space in which people communicated, which the company fully controlled, and for which the company was ultimately responsible. The streets were important nodal points for communication and the exchange of ideas. As Justice Black explained, "Whether a corporation or a municipality owns or possesses the town the public in either case has an identical interest in the functioning of the community in such manner that the channels of communication remain free."[22] And as Justice Frankfurter pointed out, the central issue was not ownership of property but the "community aspects" of the company town[23]—the fact that the town operated as a community in which people exchanged ideas and opinions. When a business monopolizes control over the central modes of communication within a community, it must act as a fiduciary for the public interest and it must allow its property to be used for the free exchange of ideas. To be sure, the U.S. Supreme Court refused to extend the reasoning of *Marsh v. Alabama* to shopping malls on the ground that, unlike company towns, they did not take over the municipal functions of a city.[24] Thus, one could argue that shopping malls lack the community aspects that Justice Frankfurter identified. Nevertheless, several state supreme courts have held that large regional shopping malls are public spaces where people have free speech rights.[25]

Virtual worlds are like company towns in that the game owner forms the community, controls all of the space inside the community, and thus controls all avenues of communication within the community. Neither the free flow of ideas nor the formation of community can occur within a virtual world unless the designer permits it. Alphaville was a virtual city controlled by *The Sims Online* through its design of code and its ToS agreement. Although Electronic Arts does not take over "the full spectrum of municipal powers"[26] in real space, it does exercise all of those functions in the virtual world. If any private entity could be regarded as a company town, it would be a virtual world. This is especially so because the whole point of the virtual world is to create community (or communities), and action in the virtual world occurs through the exchange of ideas.

Nevertheless, one might object that people can always speak to each other outside the virtual world. For example, The Alphaville Herald (and its successor, The Second Life Herald), have been available to anyone on the World Wide Web, and nothing prevents the people behind the avatars from sending e-mails to each other. But if we treat *The Sims Online* as a virtual community, this objection is less compelling. It is important that communication among the participants occurs within the space of the community and between the avatars. In *Marsh,* it did not matter that people could listen to radio broadcasts and send mail in and out of the company town. That was simply not the same thing as speaking and organizing within the town itself. Keeping leafletters out of the company town prevented the free exchange of ideas. The same is true of Alphaville: Although Ludlow can still report on what goes on in Alphaville, excluding him from the community makes it far more difficult for him to do so.

Another objection to the company town analogy is that in *Marsh* people had to live in the company town in order to make a living. It was unfair to require them to give up their jobs in order to enjoy full free speech rights. By contrast, no one has to live in Alphaville, and if Ludlow does not like the way that Electronic Arts runs its world, he can go elsewhere to a virtual world that thinks more highly of virtual-world journalism. After all, one might insist, it's just a game. However, this objection fails to take seriously the notion of virtual worlds as communities. Some players already invest enormous amounts of time in these worlds; they make friends there and form attachments. As virtual worlds become more ubiquitous, and as they are employed for more and more functions—ranging from commerce to entertainment to education—it will not seem at all strange for people to spend considerable time in these worlds and to regard membership in a virtual community as part of their (multiple) social identities. Demanding exit as the price of free expression becomes less justified as people's social connections in these worlds become increasingly significant.

A third objection, I think, is far more powerful. Not all virtual worlds are alike, and they should not all be treated alike. For example, virtual worlds that are used for military simulations or for psychotherapy should not be regarded as company towns. They are created for specific uses, and treating them as open spaces for communication would defeat the purposes for which they are dedicated. But this argument, if accepted, actually strengthens the case for treating at least some virtual worlds as company towns. Military and therapeutic simulations are not designed to form communities or create channels for general public communication, and therefore they should be treated differently. That does not mean, however, that those virtual worlds which hold themselves open as general spaces for public communication and interaction should not be treated as company towns any more than Chickasaw, Alabama, could defend itself on the grounds that some business entities do not form communities that take over all municipal functions.

Although courts may ultimately not extend First Amendment privileges to players in virtual worlds, legislatures may well take these claims seriously and extend free speech rights by statute in order to recognize the speech rights of both players and platform owners. Two analogies come to mind. The first is that of private universities, which, although they are nominally private actors, understand themselves to be spaces for the free exchange of ideas. The second analogy is that of telecommunications law. In American telecommunications law, owners of communications networks such as cable companies are both conduits for the speech of cable programmers and speakers in their own right. Much of telecommunications law involves balancing the speech interests of owners of communications networks and independent speakers. To this end, federal cable regulations sometimes require that cable owners respect the free speech interests of independent programmers, for example, by providing public access channels. In like fashion, legislatures and administrative agencies may choose to balance the free speech interests of platform owners with those of the players.

Nevertheless, statutory protection of free speech rights by players may conflict with the platform owner's constitutional right to design. The objection is not simply based on the platform owner's property rights in the game space; rather, it is based on the platform owner's constitutional interest in creating and overseeing a collaborative work of art, somewhat like the First Amendment interests of a director of an improvisational theater. In assessing this conflict, everything depends on the nature of the virtual space that the platform owner has created. For example, if the game designer deliberately creates a totalitarian regime in which players are booted out for failing to conform, then the whole point of the game is that players not have free speech rights. Players may write letters and e-mails to the company asking for changes in the game, but the point of the simulation is that they will be dealt with harshly if they protest within the game space. *The Sims Online,* however, was not designed to be an artistic re-creation of a totalitarian state. It was designed as a general purpose simulation of real life similar to that in the contemporary United States. On the other hand, if someone creates *The Gulag Online* in order to appeal to players who want to know what it is like to live in a Soviet prison camp, legislatures should not interfere with this design choice. A one-size-fits-all solution to protecting players' rights in virtual worlds is untenable; rather, the question is what kind of virtual space is being designed.

A second way that legislatures might protect the right to play in virtual worlds is through the model of consumer protection law. Players in virtual worlds purchase a service from the platform owner, and the law should protect their reasonable expectations in the performance of that service. Consumer protection law may be a good way to protect reliance expectations in virtual property and to keep platform owners from violating the privacy rights of players. However, because the players also have free speech interests in virtual communities, consumer protection law may sometimes be the wrong paradigm for protecting the right to play.

In virtual worlds, the relationship between platform owners and players is not simply one between producers and consumers. Rather, it is often a relationship of governors to citizens. Virtual worlds form communities that grow and develop in ways that the platform owners do not foresee and cannot fully control. Virtual worlds quickly become joint projects between platform owners and players. The correct model is thus not the protection of the players' interests solely as consumers, but a model of joint governance.

This is true even in *The Gulag Online*. Although the virtual space is set up as a Soviet prison camp, things will happen in the space that the designers could not predict. As a result, the designers will probably encourage feedback from the players about how to improve the game, because players are consumers and platform owners want to keep them happy and make money. In fact, any multiplayer virtual world of sufficient complexity quickly becomes more than the creation of its designers. It becomes not so much a finished work of art or entertainment as an ongoing collective project. The players in these virtual worlds wear two hats: They are both competitors in the game, who subject themselves to its rules, whatever those rules may be, and also participants who have emotional, solidaristic, and artistic stakes in its growth and evolution over time. Similarly, platform owners wear two hats: They are both entrepreneurs providing a service to consumers and the governors and fiduciaries of a realm in which they must be responsive to the participants.

The dual roles of both players and platform owners suggest that their relations are always likely to be in flux and cannot fully be captured by the model of consumer protection. Platform owners do not merely provide a service to be consumed; they also act as governors of a community. Thus, we must augment the model of consumer protection with a model of political fairness, if not democracy. One can easily imagine a situation in which suitably disgruntled players gang up on the platform owners and, treating them like old King John, effectively require the platform owner to turn the EULA into a virtual Magna Carta that protects the rights of players from high-handed treatment. Indeed, *Second Life* has already experienced a "tax revolt" in which the players persuaded the platform owner to modify its code.[27]

In short, we need to think of virtual spaces as both forms of commerce and forms of governance. Raph Koster's Declaration of the Rights of Avatars reflects the basic idea that platform owners should treat players with a certain degree of respect.[28] However, the rights at stake are not really the rights of the avatars themselves. They are the rights of the players who take on particular (and possibly multiple) identities within virtual communities.

Here again the right to design and the right to play are likely to conflict. It is one thing for game designers voluntarily to assume such duties of respect. It is quite another for the state to require that all virtual worlds include such guarantees. That is because different games have different purposes, and the addition of some rights for players would effectively change the nature of the game. To the extent that the right to design has constitutional dimensions, the legislature may sometimes be forbidden from altering the relation between players and platform owners.

Platform owners will no doubt assert First Amendment defenses to legislative protections of player rights. In the Information Age, the First Amendment has become the first line of defense against almost every variety of government regulation of media enterprises.[29] Some of those First Amendment defenses should be taken seriously, but others should not. The First Amendment is misused if it allows platform owners to avoid what is essentially consumer protection regulation. In addition, because platform owners are conduits for the speech of others as well as speakers in their own right, we can imagine game spaces where regulating to protect the free speech interests of the players might be constitutional. But there is a great danger here: legislatures must understand that not all game spaces should be treated alike. A game space that is essentially a virtual Hyde Park should be treated like one. A game space that has different functions should be treated quite differently.

A third model of regulation treats the virtual space as a place of public accommodation.[30] Places of public accommodation are public venues—including inns, theaters, restaurants, transportation hubs, and, more recently, private clubs—that may not discriminate against their customers even though they may be privately owned. This model makes sense to the extent that the virtual world is heavily commercialized and bears many of the characteristics of a shopping mall or a place where real-world business and commerce are conducted. (Contrast this with a noncommodified world that engages only in barter exchanges and virtual commerce.) To the extent that players use virtual spaces to conduct real-world shopping and commerce, public accommodation laws should, in theory, protect them.[31]

Nevertheless, applying public accommodation laws to virtual spaces is likely to give players only modest protections. At most they would give players the right to join the virtual community and play according to its rules. Although the platform owner could not discriminate against, say,

African Americans who wanted to sign up for the game, the player would still be bound by the ToS or the EULA and could be excluded for breaching those agreements.

The model of public accommodations law raises many complicated problems, but one distinction is particularly important. We must distinguish cases where the platform owner discriminates against players on the basis of their race, sex, or religion, regardless of how they appear in the game, from the ability of the platform owner to discriminate by requiring that people appear in the game in particular ways. Consider, for example, a game in which the platform insists that all avatars in the game be white, male, or Christian. Although discrimination against players may be prohibited, discrimination against avatars is a different matter. Many games assign different characteristics and roles to different types of avatars. Ordinarily the rules of the game should allow discrimination among avatars as long as the player has the free choice to decide which role to assume.

Imagine a game that reenacts life on an antebellum Southern plantation. All the slave owner avatars are white, all the slave avatars are black, and players are given the choice about what kind of avatar they want to be, subject perhaps to a rule of first-come-first-served. Does the game violate public accommodation laws because it portrays the social supremacy of white avatars to black avatars, and portrays black avatars in a servile position? Clearly a play or motion picture telling the same story would be protected by the First Amendment, no matter how hateful or tasteless it might be. This might suggest that discrimination among avatars should ordinarily pose no problem for real-world antidiscrimination law. But the issue is far from clear. Imagine now a restaurant with the same Southern plantation theme, which features pictures of black slaves being whipped by their white owners prominently displayed on the walls, along with racist arguments justifying chattel slavery. Even if such a restaurant does not refuse service to blacks who walk through its doors, the decor might make blacks very likely to avoid it, and its policy might be in violation of public accommodation laws. In like fashion, African American consumers might well boycott a game that glorified the antebellum South's slaveocracy. The key question is whether the game space should be treated like a motion picture, in which case the platform owner has a First Amendment right to run the space however he or she likes, or as a place of public accommodation, in which case the platform owner may have created the equivalent of a hostile environment.

There can be no general answer to this question; it must depend on the nature and purposes of the game space, and its degree of commercialization. Noncommodified virtual spaces with themes that are blasphemous, racist, sexist, homophobic, or otherwise offensive should ordinarily be protected just like plays and motion pictures with similar themes. Not surprisingly, the difficult cases come when virtual spaces become like virtual shopping malls, an area for real-world commerce exercised in a virtual environment, or when they become spaces in which the players regularly attempt to make a living by trading in objects and items that have real-world values. The more the virtual world is a space for economic enterprise and the purchase and sale of goods, the more we must be concerned if the space attempts to discourage people of a certain race or religion from participating on an equal basis. Similarly, universities should not be immune from antidiscrimination laws simply because they provide educational services in virtual environments. Note, however, that a university might have legitimate educational reasons for reenacting a slave plantation in a virtual environment that would be very different from those that could be plausibly offered by a virtual shopping mall. Therefore the university should receive correspondingly greater protection on grounds of academic freedom.

Applying public accommodation models to virtual spaces will inevitably lead platform owners to respond by raising freedom of association claims to protect the way they run their spaces. Once again we will see the First Amendment used to combat state attempts to regulate game spaces, although in this case the freedom asserted will be the freedom of (virtual) association in virtual worlds.

The Supreme Court has rejected freedom of association claims made by the Rotary Club and the Jaycees on the grounds that sex discrimination was peripheral to their purposes of networking and forming business contacts.[32] In *Boy Scouts of America v. Dale,* however, the Supreme Court held that the Boy Scouts were not bound by a New Jersey public accommodation law that prohibited discrimination against homosexuals.[33] The Boy Scouts successfully argued that their moral objections to homosexuality were particularly important to the values of their association.[34] If legislatures attempt to regulate virtual spaces along the model of public accommodation laws, we may well see platform owners making *Dale*-in-cyberspace claims.

Some virtual worlds will be created for political and religious purposes, and reserved only for players who share a certain ideology or religious belief. These spaces should be protected by *Dale*. Once again much will turn on the commercial or noncommercial nature of the virtual space. For example, general purpose spaces like *The Sims Online, Second Life,* or *There* should not be able to claim that they are the cyberspace equivalent of the Boy Scouts or the Knights of Columbus.

Virtual worlds greatly raise the stakes in the conflict between freedom of speech and association and antidiscrimination norms. Antidiscrimination law and free speech law can live together amicably when we can easily settle on social conventions that will distinguish acts of speaking from acts of conduct, and can distinguish governmental purposes for regulation as being directed at speech or at conduct. The line between "speech" and "conduct" is a legal fiction that does not represent a natural division of the social world, but is rather largely conventional. Even so, in a wide variety of settings the categorization of certain activities as speech or conduct, or of government purposes as attempts to regulate conduct rather than speech, can become widely accepted.

When we move to virtual worlds, however, conventional agreements about what is speech and what is conduct quickly break down, because we have not yet developed understandings about what counts as "acting" versus "speaking" in a virtual environment. As I noted previously, torts that are actionable in virtual environments are, by and large, communications torts. They are activities where one person harms another through speaking or communicating. Virtual worlds blur the conventional boundaries between speech and conduct as we currently understand them precisely because all conduct in virtual worlds must begin as a form of speech.

This does not mean that the distinction between speech and conduct, or between permissible and impermissible government purposes for regulation, cannot be resuscitated and retrofitted to apply in virtual worlds. It does mean that our current understandings and analogies will often run out in these environments. We will have to muddle through for a time until it becomes clear what should count as "speaking" versus "acting" in these virtual worlds. As virtual worlds become increasingly important parts of people's lives, the need to create new approaches will become increasingly urgent.

In dividing up aspects of the virtual world into "speech" and "conduct" (or characterizing government motivations for regulation of the same), the most important distinction may be whether the virtual space is acting like a marketplace, a nexus for transactions that have real-world values, or whether it has been deliberately designed to avoid real-world commodification. A second and crosscutting distinction is whether the virtual world is offered as a space for the free exchange of ideas, or is created to realize the artistic or ideological vision of the platform owner. Regulating the platform owner's right to design in order to protect the participants' right to play is most justifiable when the virtual world serves as a public space for commerce, and when it is held open as a public space for the exchange of ideas. These two distinctions may not be perfectly clear in all cases; but they point the way to the boundaries of permissible state regulation on the one hand, and the free speech rights of platform owners on the other.

A Possible Solution: Statutes of Interration

How can legislatures navigate their way through the problems I have described while still preserving important public values of freedom of speech for players and game owners alike? One way is by creating what Professor Edward Castronova has called statutes of "interration," akin to statutes of incorporation.[35] Just as business enterprises can choose between sole proprietorships, partnerships, and the corporate form, depending on their goals and on the legal rights that each form provides, governments could offer a variety of different types of legal regimes for operators of virtual worlds to choose from. These legal regimes would set different ground rules for the legal relationships between game owners and players. Platform owners could choose from among these regimes and design their virtual worlds accordingly, knowing in advance what the law expects from them. Similarly, players could choose which virtual worlds to inhabit based on the form of interration that the platform owner chose and thus would know in advance the free speech rights they will enjoy.

For example, a government might offer a form of interration specifically designed for large virtual spaces that permit real-world commodification. In this interration scheme the platform owner must agree to protect the property and privacy rights of players, and it must recognize (and provide) public spaces for uninhibited free expression. (Other areas of the virtual world could be devoted to special purposes, or zoned as suitable for children.) This would secure free speech rights against private ownership without invoking the doctrine of the company town. Platform owners who adopt this form of virtual space also could not raise freedom of association claims to defeat public accommodation requirements.

Another form of interration might suit smaller virtual worlds that prohibit real-world commodification. Players would not have real-world rights in virtual items and the space would be devoted purely to the development of a story line or set of story lines. The platform owner would agree to respect the players' privacy but would have a greater ability to regulate the players' speech. This type of interration would be appropriate for worlds like *The Gulag Online*, in which the game owner wishes to maintain fairly tight control over the space. There might also be a special form of interration for noncommodified virtual worlds with strong interests in preserving their freedom of association from the requirements of public accommodations laws. (An example might be a virtual world run by a religious institution or political organization.) Finally, governments could create still other forms of interration for worlds designed primarily for educational purposes, medical diagnosis, therapy, testing social and economic rules, or military simulations.

This account of interration differs from Castronova's in several important respects. Castronova offered the idea of interration primarily to protect virtual worlds that he calls "play spaces" from real-world commodification. These are "closed worlds" that are self-governing and where (Castronova assumes) real-world law will not apply. In Castronova's scheme, interrated worlds must always maintain strict separation of their economies from the economy of the outside world in order to maintain their special legal status. If the platform owner fails to maintain the space as a "play space" separate from the real-world economy, the state will revoke the game's charter of interration. Worlds without statutes of interration are "open worlds" that would be subject to real-world law.[36]

By contrast, I argue that interration is most important for worlds that feature real-world commodification and in which virtual objects are freely traded. These worlds are likely to be the most popular and in the greatest need of free speech and privacy protections against game owners. Platform owners can choose between different interration schemes, some of which permit real-world commodification and some of which prohibit it. The latter schemes are the closest to Castronova's idea of "closed worlds." Nevertheless, unlike Castronova, I begin with the assumption that real-world law applies to all virtual worlds. The only question is how the law applies.

In theory, contracts between players and platform owners could produce different bundles of rights and duties for different virtual worlds. However, fixing basic rights and duties through interration statutes has four advantages. First, it greatly reduces the transaction costs between players and game owners. Second, it secures the rights of nonplayers who may not be able to contract easily with game owners. Third, it protects important reliance interests of players because it prevents basic understandings about the virtual world from being changed by the platform owner after the players have invested considerable time and formed valuable social networks there. Fourth, it protects important free speech interests that may be undervalued by market forces. Securing freedom of speech rights against private parties in virtual worlds has significant positive externalities for society. Markets will likely undervalue those rights because platform owners and players cannot capture their full value to society.

The experience of players like Peter Ludlow suggests why market forces alone might not lead large commercial game owners to protect the free speech rights of their players. Game owners do have incentives to keep their user base content, and censoring the players' speech might anger some of the participants. However, platform owners also have countervailing incentives to (1) censor speech critical of the way the owner is running the space; (2) censor speech the owner thinks will offend and hence scare customers away; and (3) censor speech that customers might (fairly or unfairly) associate with the game owner or blame the game owner for allowing in the space. Hence, like real-world governments, game owners will be likely to engage in too much censorship (and selective censorship) without legal guarantees of freedom of speech and association.

As with statutes of incorporation, governments can offer legal benefits and protections to platform owners to encourage them to interrate. In return for these legal benefits, game owners would have to agree to protect basic rights of players and third parties, and game owners would not be able to negate or undermine these rights either through code or through the EULA. (Although these basic rights would be mandatory for a given form of interration, other elements of interration statutes would be default rules that could be modified through contract).

Interration statutes might permit an existing virtual world to shift from one form of interration to another. In order to protect the players' reliance interests, however, interration statutes should require some degree of consultation and approval from the players before the basic social contract of the space can be altered. Otherwise, the platform owner might simply change the ToS or EULA unilaterally and insist that players who continue to play in the space consent to the changes in their rights. The point of interration is not to prevent modification of the basic norms of the virtual space for all time, but rather to formalize a consultation process that recognizes the interests of the player community. This is yet another way to make the point that the relationship between the game owner and the player community is one of joint governance.

Legal incentives will be particularly important to encourage interration by large virtual spaces that feature real-world commodification and virtual commerce. These are the spaces where large numbers of people will likely gather and where people will want to express themselves without fear of censorship or invasion of privacy by the platform operator. Castronova has suggested that the government could offer tax breaks to encourage interration.[37] I believe there is a more important legal protection that governments could offer platform owners that would simultaneously help protect free speech values; namely, freedom from liability for the actions of the individual players.

Plaintiffs who sue players for communications torts committed in a virtual world will probably sue the platform owner as well as the player. After all, the platform owner—especially in large commercially run game spaces—is more likely to have deep pockets than the player. The plaintiff will argue that the platform owner should have taken steps—either through the EULA or through the design of the code—to prevent the tort from occurring. The arguments will be similar to those made by plaintiffs who sue business owners for negligence for enabling third parties to commit torts on their premises. Plaintiffs will likely argue that the platform owner had the ability to take appropriate safeguards to prevent tortious activity by the players. Indeed, plaintiffs will insist, the argument for liability is even stronger in virtual worlds because platform owners have god-like powers in virtual spaces and can, in theory, control almost everything in these spaces through contract and code.[38]

To protect themselves from these lawsuits, game owners will probably insist that players waive all rights to sue as part of the EULA. Nevertheless, these waivers of liability may not be enforceable in all cases and they cannot bind third parties outside the game who may wish to sue for torts committed by players within the game space.

However, if the platform owner interrates and accepts certain duties and obligations (for example, protection of the players' free speech rights), the government will not hold him or her responsible for tortious communications made by players who are not otherwise affiliated with the platform owner.[39] If a platform owner decides not to interrate, he or she will be subject to whatever liability rules courts choose to apply. We may therefore expect that uninterrated worlds will be fairly small and noncommercial, with relatively few members.

The bargain I propose protects free speech interests in two different ways. First, platform owners who interrate will assume obligations to protect the speech of players even though the owners are not state actors. This undertaking will prove most important in the case of large commercial game spaces that are likely to be the most popular.

Second, protecting platform owners from liability also serves important free speech interests. Holding game owners responsible for harmful speech by players creates a real danger of unjustified *collateral censorship*.[40] Collateral censorship is a form of private censorship that occurs when the government holds one private party A liable for the speech of another private party B, and A has the power to control or censor B's speech. To avoid liability, A will likely err on the side of caution and censor too much of B's speech, with insufficient regard for the value of B's speech either to B or to society as a whole.[41]

Collateral censorship is a common problem in telecommunications regulation. Cable companies and Internet service providers regularly act as conduits for the speech of unaffiliated parties. Holding them responsible for the tortious speech of their customers would lead them to censor too much speech. Thus, in section 230 of the Telecommunications Act of 1996, Congress extended a special privilege to Internet service providers (and other providers and users of "interactive computer service[s]") whose customers post objectionable matter in cyberspace; it declared that, as a matter of law, service providers should not be considered the publishers of such material.[42]

It is likely that platform operators are "provider[s] . . . of an interactive computer service" and therefore already enjoy the section 230 privilege. However, section 230 is a poor device for protecting free speech values in virtual worlds. It offers game owners insufficient protection from liability, and it offers players insufficient protection for their speech.

First, section 230 only protects game owners from tort suits based on the game owner's publication of harmful or offensive material, and it does not apply to violations of intellectual property rights.[43] Game owners might still be held liable even if the law does not treat them as publishers; for example, plaintiffs may still argue that the game owner should have taken steps to prevent players from speaking or misbehaving. Second, section 230 offers players no protection from private censorship by game owners. In fact, section 230(c)(2) holds game owners harmless if they censor or block the speech of the players, regardless of whether the speech is constitutionally protected.[44]

Statutes of interration are a far better solution for virtual worlds. Unfortunately, section 230(e)(3) creates a further problem: It preempts state law to the contrary.[45] If section 230 does cover game owners, states might not be able to create new rights to protect players from private censorship or game owners from novel lawsuits. The federal government will have to amend the Telecommunications Act to permit states to create interration statutes. In the alternative, it could create a federal interration statute.

The law of Internet service providers is not necessarily the proper model for virtual worlds. In one sense, virtual worlds are chat rooms with a graphical user interface. But in another sense, they are something far greater. Virtual worlds are more than conduits or services for chat or e-mail. They are also sites of governance and community.

In the future, virtual worlds are likely to become important spaces for innovation and free expression. Properly drafted interration statutes can help promote these values. To this end, legislatures should prominently state the public values these statutes are designed to serve in the statutes themselves as guides to interpretation by courts, and courts in turn should interpret these statutes liberally to promote free speech values. We should view interration statutes as applications and extensions of the central values of individual creativity and democratic participation that we associate with the First Amendment. We should view them as "First Amendment extension acts" appropriate for a digital world in which many of the most important spaces for creative expression are held in private hands.

Virtual worlds will not remain separate jurisdictions left to themselves. The more people live in them, and the more time, money, and effort people invest in them, the more they will attract the law's attention. Intellectual property rights, consumer protection, and privacy will be three important reasons for legal regulation of virtual worlds in the years to come. Nevertheless, courts and legislatures must be careful not to lump all virtual worlds into the same category. Virtual spaces are not natural kinds: they can and will be used for many purposes in the future, including not only commerce, but also education, therapy, political organization, and artistic expression. Courts and legislatures should keep these differences in mind and avoid one-size-fits-all solutions. In this way, they will help preserve the rights to design and play in virtual worlds, and ensure that there are plenty of spaces available for new forms of creativity, expression, and experimentation.

NOTES

My thanks to Alan Davidson, James Grimmelmann, Eddan Katz, Nimrod Kozlovski, Gal Levita, Beth Noveck, Shlomit Wagman, and Tal Zarsky for their comments on previous drafts.

1. *See* Edward Castronova, *The Right To Play,* chapter 5, this volume.

2. The designers and owners of the game platform may be different people and, accordingly, may have different rights. For purposes of this discussion, I will assume that they work for the same entity, and so I will use the terms "game designer" and "platform owner" interchangeably.

3. F. Gregory Lastowka & Dan Hunter, *The Laws of the Virtual Worlds,* 92 CAL. L. REV. 1, 5–11 (2004) (describing the growing numbers of people who inhabit virtual worlds and the importance of these virtual communities to their lives).

4. *See* Robert Post, *Recuperating First Amendment Doctrine,* 47 STAN. L. REV. 1249, 1252–55 (1995).

5. *See* Post, *supra* note 4, at 1252–53; Mutual Film Corp. v. Industrial Comm., 236 U.S. 230, 243–45 (1915).

6. Joseph Burstyn, Inc. v. Wilson, 343 U.S. 495, 501 (1952).

7. *See* Interactive Digital Software Ass'n v. St. Louis County, 329 F.3d 954 (8th Cir. 2003) (digital video games protected by the First Amendment); Am. Amusement Mach. Ass'n v. Kendrick, 244 F.3d 572, 577–78 (7th Cir. 2001), cert. denied, 534 U.S. 994 (2001); Sanders v. Acclaim Entm't, Inc., 188 F. Supp. 2d 1264 (D. Colo. 2002). *See also* James v. Meow Media, Inc. 300 F.3d 683 (6th Cir. 2002) (attaching tort liability to the communicative aspect of the video games implicates First Amendment); Wilson v. Midway Games, 198 F. Supp. 2d 167, 181 (D. Conn. 2002) (video games "that are analytically indistinguishable from other protected media, such as motion pictures or books, which convey information or evoke emotions by imagery, are protected under the First Amendment"). Several older decisions held that video games are not protected on the grounds that they lack communicative content. *See, e.g.,* America's Best Family Showplace v. City of New York, 536 F. Supp. 170, 174 (E.D.N.Y. 1982) (video games are "pure entertainment with no informational element").

8. *See* Wilson v. Midway Games, 198 F. Supp. 2d 167, 181–82 (D. Conn. 2002) (arguing that interactivity cuts in favor of First Amendment protection of video games).

9. *See* Jack M. Balkin, *Digital Speech and Democratic Culture: A Theory of Freedom of Expression for the Information Society,* 79 N.Y.U. L. Rev. 1, 19–23 (2004).

10. *See* Jennifer L. Mnookin, *Virtual(ly) Law: The Emergence of Law in LambdaMOO,* 2 J. Computer-Mediated Comm. (1996) (describing the rise of community norms in the virtual space of LamdaMOO), *available at* http://www.ascusc.org/jcmc/vol2/issue1/lambda.html (last visited Feb. 27, 2004). The multiplayer online game *A Tale in the Desert* offers elaborate instructions about how players can make laws for Ancient Egypt. *See* A Tale in the Desert, Lawmaking Supplement, *at* http://www.atitd.com/man-lawmaking.html (last visited Feb. 29, 2004).

11. *See* Restatement (Second) of Torts § 559 (1977).

12. *See* Hackbart v. Cincinnati Bengals, Inc., 601 F.2d 516 (10th Cir. 1979), cert. denied, 444 U.S. 931 (1979).

13. *See* Restatement (Second) of Torts § 46.1 & cmt. d. (1977).

14. The Gaming Open Market, *at* http://www.gamingopenmarket.com (last visited Feb. 27, 2004).

15. *See* Internet Gaming Entertainment, About Us (providing services for purchase and sale of virtual currency and commodities) *at* http://www.ige.com/aboutus.asp (last visited Feb. 29, 2004).

16. *The Alphaville Herald* is now known as *The Second Life Herald,* at http://www.alphavilleherald.com (last accessed Aug. 19, 2004).

17. Amy Harmon, A Real-Life Debate on Free Expression in a Cyberspace City, N.Y. Times, Jan. 15, 2004, at A1.

18. Id.

19. *See* Paul Schiff Berman, *Cyberspace and the State Action Debate: The Cultural Value of Applying Constitutional Norms to "Private" Regulation,* 71 U. Colo. L. Rev. 1263, 1302–06 (2000) (arguing for application of constitutional norms in debates over regulation of cyberspace); F. Gregory Lastowka & Dan Hunter, *The Laws of the Virtual Worlds,* 92 Cal. L. Rev. 1, 60–61 (2004); *cf.* Peter S. Jenkins, *The Virtual World as Company Town—Freedom of Speech in Massively Multiple On-Line Role Playing Games,* 8 J. of Internet L. 1, 17 (July 2004) (arguing for company town analogy for virtual worlds that have public access, but not for worlds that select their members).

20. 326 U.S. 501, 508–09 (1946); *see also* Amalgamated Food Employees Union Local 590 v. Logan Valley Plaza, Inc., 391 U.S. 308, 325 (1968) (extending reasoning of *Marsh v. Alabama* to protect a peaceful protest by local union against shopping mall).

21. *Marsh,* 326 U.S. at 506.

22. Id. at 507.

23. Id. at 510 (Frankfurter, J., concurring).

24. *See* Hudgens v. NLRB, 424 U.S. 507, 518–21 (1976) (officially overruling *Logan Valley Plaza*); Lloyd Corp. v. Tanner, 407 U.S. 551, 563–64 (1972) (distin-

guishing *Logan Valley Plaza* on the ground that protest was not related to mall owner's business).

25. *See, e.g.,* Robins v. Pruneyard Shopping Ctr., 592 P.2d 341, 347 (Cal. 1979), aff'd, 447 U.S. 74 (1980); New Jersey Coalition Against War in the Middle East v. J.M.B. Realty Corp., 650 A.2d 757, 775 (N.J. 1994).

26. *Lloyd Corp.,* 407 U.S. at 569.

27. *See* James Grimmelmann, *The State of Play: On the* Second Life *Tax Revolt* (Sept. 21, 2003), *at* http://research.yale.edu/lawmeme/modules.php?name=News &file=article&sid=1222.

28. *See* Raph Koster, Declaration of the Rights of Avatars (Aug. 27, 2000), *available at* http://www.legendmud.org/raph/gaming/playerrights.html (last visited Feb. 27, 2004).

29. *See* Balkin, Digital Speech and Democratic Culture, at 24–25.

30. *See* Neil Weinstock Netanel, *Cyberspace Self-Governance: A Skeptical View from Liberal Democratic Theory,* 88 CAL. L. REV. 395, 456–60 (2000); Tara E. Thompson, *Locating Discrimination: Interactive Web Sites as Public Accommodations under Title II of the Civil Rights Act,* 2002 U. CHI. LEGAL F. 409, 411. But cf. Noah v. AOL Time Warner, Inc., 261 F. Supp. 2d 532, 544–45 (E.D. Va. 2004), aff'd 2004 U.S. App. LEXIS 5495 (4th Cir.) (Mar. 24, 2004) (holding that America Online chatrooms are not public accommodations for purposes of Title II of the Civil Rights Act of 1964 because they are not physical spaces); Eugene Volokh, *Freedom of Speech in Cyberspace from the Listener's Perspective: Private Speech Restrictions, Libel, State Action, Harassment, and Sex,* 1996 U. CHI. LEGAL F. 377, 390–97 (rejecting public accommodation theory and arguing for freedom of association right of cyberdiscussion group operators to discriminate among speakers).

31. Although the court in *Noah,* 261 F. Supp. 2d at 541, *supra* note 30, interpreted the language of Title II of the 1964 Civil Rights Act to require that public accommodations must involve a physical space, legislation might define a class of public accommodations more broadly. Cf. Boy Scouts of Am. v. Dale, 530 U.S. 640, 656–57 (2000) (noting application of New Jersey public accommodations statute to include organizations like the Boy Scouts of America); Carparts Distribution Ctr., Inc. v. Automotive Wholesalers Assoc. of New England, Inc., 37 F.3d 12, 18–20 (1st Cir. 1994) (holding that a trade association which administers a health insurance program, without any connection to a physical facility, can be a "place of public accommodation" under Title III of the Americans with Disabilities Act).

32. Bd. of Dirs. of Rotary Int'l v. Rotary Club of Duarte, 481 U.S. 537, 546–47 (1987); Roberts v. United States Jaycees, 468 U.S. 609, 627 (1984).

33. 530 U.S. 640, 656 (2000).

34. *Id.*

35. See Castronova, *supra* note 1, at 12.

36. *Id.* at 12–13.

37. *Id.*

38. The Digital Millenium Copyright Act (DMCA) has special provisions requiring notice and takedown that probably would also apply to platform owners in cases where a player allegedly violates the copyright interest of a third party. *See* 17 U.S.C. § 512 (2000).

39. Intellectual property will probably prove to be a special case. Given the current political configuration, it is unlikely that the copyright industry would accept liability and notice and take down provisions rules significantly weaker than those specified by the DMCA.

40. *See* Jack M. Balkin, *Free Speech and Hostile Environments,* 99 COLUM. L. REV. 2295, 2296–2305 (1999); Michael I. Meyerson, *Authors, Editors, and Uncommon Carriers: Identifying the "Speaker" Within the New Media,* 71 NOTRE DAME L. REV. 79, 116, 118 (1995).

41. Balkin, *supra* note 40, at 2298, 2302–03. The common law of defamation grapples with the problem of collateral censorship through the distributor's privilege. Generally speaking, a person who repeats a defamatory statement is as liable for publication as the original speaker (assuming the person also acts with the requisite degree of fault). *See* Restatement (Second) of Torts § 578 (1977). However, a distributor of information, such as a newsstand or bookstore, is generally not held to this standard unless the distributor knows of the publication's defamatory content. The fear is that if distributors were held to be publishers, distributors might restrict the kinds of books and magazines they sold, greatly reducing the public's access to protected expression. *See* Restatement (Second) of Torts § 581 (1977) ("One who . . . delivers or transmits defamatory matter published by a third person is subject to liability if, but only if, he knows or has reason to know of its defamatory character.").

42. 47 U.S.C. § 230(c)(1); *see* Blumenthal v. Drudge, 992 F. Supp. 44, 49–52 (D.D.C. 1998). Section 230(c)(1) provides that "[n]o provider or user of an interactive computer service shall be treated as the publisher or speaker of any information provided by another information content provider." In fact, the 1996 Act gives Internet service providers more protection than the traditional distributor's privilege, because knowledge of defamatory content is not sufficient to subject them to liability. *See* Zeran v. America Online, 129 F.3d 327, 331–32 (4th Cir. 1997), cert. denied, 524 U.S. 937 (1998).

43. *See* 47 U.S.C. § 230(e)(2) ("Nothing in this section shall be construed to limit or expand any law pertaining to intellectual property.").

44. *See* 47 U.S.C. § 230(c)(2) ("No provider or user of an interactive computer service shall be held liable on account of—(A) any action voluntarily taken in good faith to restrict access to or availability of material that the provider or user considers to be obscene, lewd, lascivious, filthy, excessively violent, harassing, or otherwise objectionable, whether or not such material is constitutionally pro-

tected; or (B) any action taken to enable or make available to information content providers or others the technical means to restrict access to material described in paragraph (1).").

45. 47 U.S.C. § 230(e)(3) ("Nothing in this section shall be construed to prevent any State from enforcing any State law that is consistent with this section. No cause of action may be brought and no liability may be imposed under any State or local law that is inconsistent with this section.").

Property and Creativity in Virtual Worlds

7

Virtual Crime

F. Gregory Lastowka and Dan Hunter

Ever since creation's peaceful dawn was startled by the death cry of the murdered Abel and Jehovah placed his mark upon Cain and set him forth a "fugitive and a vagabond," cursed from the earth that had opened its mouth to receive his brother's blood from his hand, there has been a never-ending conflict between those who make the laws and those who break them.
—Guy H. Thompson, Missouri Crime Survey,
1926, 12 A.B.A.J., 626, 632

In a recent article, we explored the emerging social phenomenon of virtual worlds and the legal issues raised by these environments.[1] We focused upon two primary questions. First, we asked whether the virtual items and properties currently being bought and sold by residents of virtual worlds should be regarded as property in a legal sense. We concluded that no obvious reason exists prohibiting the recognition of legal interests in intangible virtual properties. Second, we explored the question of whether the current technocratic, corporate, and anarchic governance systems in virtual worlds should be problematic from the standpoint of democratic governance. We concluded that due to the unique nature of the virtual spaces and the unusual and varied conventions that govern interpersonal actions within these spaces, the governance of virtual worlds is a very complicated question and would be better left to internal and market-driven forces.

In this essay, we will look at a third issue that is largely derivative of the two issues previously explored. Private property systems inevitably present the potential for social conflict by granting private ownership rights that can be infringed by trespass and conversion. In the essay, we will explore the issue of nonconsensual appropriation and destruction of virtual properties and ask whether these behaviors might be seen as truly criminal. We will conclude that such conflicts will generally not give rise to criminal liability, but that some activities involving the exploitation of game software for financial gain may give rise to criminal liability under computer trespass statutes.

Defining "Virtual Crime"

Initially, we would like to emphasize our wariness of the general concept of a "virtual crime." One of the first and most well-known "virtual crimes" was the "rape in cyberspace" reported by journalist and author Julian Dibbell. Dibbell was a participant in the LambdaMOO MUD, a multiparticipant text-based virtual environment. The "rape" in question was essentially a real-time nonconsensual textual description of the violent sexual mutilation of an online community member to other community members. The surface appearance of the "rape" was the display, on the computer monitors of several community members, of graphic and offensive textual sentences that seemed to originate from the victim. The "rapist," Mr. Bungle, was the screen name of the typist of those descriptions. As commentators have noted, Mr. Bungle's acts were insufficient to form the basis for criminal prosecution.

Many legal scholars have referenced Dibbell's report, including Susan Brenner, who wrote an article referring to the Bungle incident as a "true" virtual crime. Brenner concluded that other varieties of virtual crimes, if they could be described as crimes at all, would need to have all the elements of real crimes, and thus were not really a meaningfully new variety of criminal activity. Orin Kerr recently gave a similar skeptical appraisal of the Bungle incident, disagreeing with Lawrence Lessig's suggestion that there could be a valuable "link" between actual rape and the LambdaMOO "rape in cyberspace." Kerr has said that such a link is "tenuous at best: It is the link between a brutal rape and a fictional story of a brutal rape. Surely the difference is more striking than any similarity."

Part of the problem with the notion of the LambdaMOO rape as a "virtual crime" lies in the word "virtual" itself. According to standard dictionaries, "virtual" in some cases refers to things which are practically the same in effect as the term modified, and in other cases it simply refers to representations of things created, simulated, or carried on by means of a computer or computer network. The latter definition gained its popularity in the 1990s when the word "virtual" became almost as much a buzzword for technophiles and marketers as "low carb" is today. "Virtual" was used to describe almost all things that involved technology—especially Internet technology. Popular media embraced "virtual reality." Internet-dependant communities were described as "virtual communities," online booksellers were called "virtual bookstores," and programs that mimicked the functions of appliances were called, for example, "virtual alarm clocks." Handheld games were called "virtual pets" and an annoying animation of a paper clip that came with Microsoft Office software was called a "virtual assistant." As the cyberspace scholar Marie Laure-Ryan has observed, this widening of the term "virtual" threatens to render it virtually meaningless.

The term virtual crime can be just as meaningless as the term "virtual pet" if it is defined to include all computer-generated simulations of crime. Realistic digital simulations of mass murder occur every day on the computer monitors of those playing Grand Theft Auto III and on home entertainment centers displaying DVDs of Hamlet. Such "virtual crimes" are the subject of policy debate because they trouble many legislators and cultural commentators. However, even the representations of villainy that occur in interactive games are generally understood as speech and nothing more, and thus are within the scope of constitutional free speech protections. As Kerr has said, these activities are essentially stories.

A narrower definition of virtual crimes might equate virtual crimes with cybercrimes, defining cybercrimes as crimes committed against a computer or by means of a computer. Obviously, computers (like bookstores, alarm clocks, and paper clips) can be utilized in the furtherance of criminal conduct and there are many state and federal statutes that expressly criminalize certain types of conduct involving computer networks. But these crimes are real crimes with real consequences. In this case, there is a risk presented by conflating the actual with the "virtual" because doing so makes computer crimes seem less serious than real crimes. Those who share "virtual" programs and files (and violate copyright law in the process) are spending jail time in real penitentiaries.

But there is still a proper place for the term "virtual crime." A Japanese man recently hacked into another person's virtual world account, sold her virtual house to another player for real cash, and pocketed the proceeds. This type of activity might be described as a virtual crime because it refers to a crime which "exist[s] or result[s] in essence or effect, though not in actual fact, form, or name." This is the older sense of the modifier "virtual," and would include those crimes that somehow evoke and approach the effect and essence of real crime, but are not considered crimes. To us, this seems to be the exact nature of "virtually criminal" activities such as the "rapes in cyberspace" that occur within the context of virtual worlds and are decried by participants. Such "crimes" may cause real psychological, social, and financial harms to their victims and they may grossly transgress reasonable and sensible civic expectations of behavior, but they are not activities that tend to fall within the scope of existing criminal prohibitions due, in part, to the unique nature of virtual spaces.

As Lawrence Lessig noted several years ago, many people are spending more time in virtual worlds and it is slowly becoming impossible to ignore these places of cyberspace. It is also slowly becoming impossible to ignore the fact that virtual crimes are occurring. If we expect virtual worlds to be increasingly important and to resist external attempts at legal regulation, we can expect virtual crimes to be an increasing cause of concern for the communities engaging in the design and experience of virtual worlds.

The Bone Crusher Dilemma

To introduce the concept of virtual property crimes, we can return to an incident once again described by Julian Dibbell. During the year 2003, Dibbell took a career turn to become a professional trader of virtual goods within the world of Britannia, the virtual world environment of the game *Ultima Online*. With the help of his tiny avatar, Dibbell traded virtual currency and chattels that he had acquired within the virtual world of *Ultima Online* for U.S. dollars via PayPal. The scope of his operations and ambitions were modest in comparison to other virtual goods traders. However, he did make thousands of real dollars in profit in the course of his last few months.

Like other virtual worlds, *Ultima Online* lacks a specific quantifiable "win/lose" outcome, making it arguably a place more than a game. In other words, the precise goals of *Ultima Online* are not completely clear and one never "loses" the game unless the player stops paying a monthly subscription fee. Most players, however, do have clear goals in virtual worlds, and the predominant goal is to seek the virtual empowerment of their avatars. Players overcome challenges and obstacles set out by the game designers, and in the course of that play they obtain virtual power and wealth for their avatars. Within virtual worlds like Britannia, one can depend on the general rule that if an avatar has "lived" in a virtual world for a longer time, it will be more powerful and wealthy (in the environment) than the avatar of a new player. Longer investments in the labor of avatar existence lead, almost inevitably, to greater powers for the avatar.

The acquired power, in the form of virtual property, can be transferred to other avatars in the form of gifts or mutually beneficial economic exchanges. As Julian Dibbell has demonstrated, the economy of Britannia and other virtual worlds intersects significantly with our own, and is currently running around U.S. $3.5 million per annum. And as economist and virtual-world theorist Ted Castronova has explained, one can readily calculate a real-world hourly wage for player activities in virtual worlds as well as exchange rates for various virtual currencies. So, given the overlap of the real economy and the virtual economy of Britannia and our economy, one might well ask the question: Should virtual property crimes be recognized as real property crimes?

It is a common occurrence in virtual worlds that some avatars will surreptitiously make off with the valuable possessions of other avatars. Such "stolen" possessions may then be offered for sale to other avatars in exchange for U.S. dollars. The sale of virtual assets generally violates the standard license agreements of most games, but we might additionally ask whether, if the items were procured by theft, the sale constitutes a sale of stolen property in violation of the criminal law. Indeed, this was precisely the moral conundrum that Julian Dibbell found himself in when his avatar was offered an opportunity to "fence" a stolen virtual weapon (a "Bone Crusher mace") for real money.

At first glance, the fencing of the Bone Crusher for U.S. dollars would seem to fall within the literal text of criminal statutes in many states. The Model Penal Code states that "a person is guilty of theft if he purposely receives, retains, or disposes of movable property of another knowing that it has been stolen, or believing that it has probably been stolen, unless the property is received, retained, or disposed with purpose to restore it to the owner."[2] There is no general exemption to the statutory provisions for thefts that take place in virtual worlds.

Of course, while the language of the Model Penal Code may seem clear, one faces an interpretive difficulty in applying such statutory language to a realm constituted solely of images. René Magritte noted this problem at the heart of language by writing next to a representation of a pipe: "Ceci

N'est Pas Une Pipe." ("This is not a pipe.") Similarly, the Bone Crusher mace is not a mace but just the representation of a medieval weapon on a personal computer. One might conclude, due to the medium, that the theft of the Bone Crusher was simply a representation of theft, not a true theft intended to fall within the ambit of the Model Penal Code. Indeed, one might reasonably predict that since *Ultima Online* is commonly understood to be a computer game, the gut reaction of state and federal prosecutors to the theft would be to view it as analogous to the gruesome murder of a little pizza-shaped avatar at the hands of Inky, Blinky, Winky, or Clyde.

We think this gut reaction is a good thing for virtual worlds. Conflating Pac Man with *Ultima Online,* as many skeptics seem inclined to do, would leave the social problems of virtual worlds in the hands of the communities that understand those problems. External legal regulation of virtual worlds would be kept at bay, but not out of the sort of respect that John Perry Barlow once demanded. Instead, a healthy disrespect for the activities of virtual communities would shield them from outside interference. The short-term result, however, would still be the same.

We have doubts about the long term, however. The economic spillover effects of virtual crimes may lead some victims to petition real-world courts for more extensive involvement, as has already occurred in Asia. Virtual chattels like Bone Crushers are currently being created, traded, and socially valued in ways that are generally compatible with traditional theories of property. The money that Julian Dibbell made from fencing the stolen representation was perfectly real. So if real cash is paid for representations, and if (as we have previously argued), there seems to be no strong case for denying virtual objects the status of property, it is predictable that someday a victim of a serious virtual crime will make the case that the words "property," "owner," and "stolen" in the Model Penal Code encompass "chattels" like Bone Crusher maces.

The intangibility of the representation in such a case may not be a significant stumbling block to the application of criminal law. The Ninth Circuit recently concluded that the deceitful conversion of an Internet domain name is actionable in California.[3] Domain names, like Bone Crushers, are often viewed as being property interests by their owners, but are essentially nothing more than representations. The idea that a domain name is a property interest may seem like a social fiction. But property law itself is a social fiction. If a domain name can indeed be "stolen," then perhaps it follows logically that a Bone Crusher mace—a similar artifact at the intersection of software, databases, and networks—should be equally capable of being "stolen." If the occurrence looks like theft of property, is socially perceived as theft of property, and has the economic impact of theft of property, then Judge Kozinski's commonsense summary of the issue of domain name theft would seem to apply to the theft of Bone Crusher maces: "The common law does not stand idle while people [unlawfully dispose of] the property of others."

The Laws of Game Rules

But we are skeptical that Julian Dibbell could be prosecuted for fencing stolen property. In our view, his freedom from a punitive fine or jail term has little to do with the intangibility of the Bone Crusher representation. Instead, we believe his primary defense to a charge of theft would be that *Ultima Online* is styled as a game where Bone Crusher maces are designed to be stolen. In other words, within the *Ultima Online* setting, Bone Crusher maces have a property status similar to the status of basketballs on a basketball court in the physical world.

Like basketballs, Bone Crushers have clear value in the context of the game. Other players of the game appropriate this value when basketballs are "stolen." We unambiguously refer to this activity as "stealing"—the same word we use to describe criminal conversion or theft. The loss of a basketball game can have serious emotional and financial consequences for a basketball player. However, no player would dream of responding to a basketball's "theft" by petitioning the legal system for a remedy. Instead, the available self-help remedy must be perfected consistent with the rules of the game, which prohibit state intervention in disputes over ball owner-ship. The norms of game play supersede the standard rules of society, and the "magic circle" of game play will only be broken when a player violates the game rules.[4] A violation of game rules will result in a stoppage of play and a penalty of some sort, such as, the return of the basketball to the prior game owner.

While this game/nongame distinction is perfectly clear, it has social implications that can be fairly radical and perhaps normatively problem-atic. For instance, intentionally killing someone by throwing a rock at his head would almost certainly result in an indictment for criminal murder. For most of us, there is an intuition that a person should spend a substan-tial amount of time in jail for that type of activity. By comparison, however, what is our reaction to a pitcher who kills a batter by throwing a "beanball" or a player who seriously injures another participant in a game of hockey? One of the best known cases of beaning involved Ray Chapman of the Cleveland Indians, who died on August 16, 1920, when he was hit on the head with a fastball thrown by Carl Mays. The circumstances indicate that Mays intentionally hurled a potentially lethal projectile at Chapman's skull. However, despite an abundance of witnesses, Mays was never indicted for manslaughter.

Analogously, civil torts committed during the course of games are not only determined simply by the laws of negligence, but also take into account game rules. As the Tenth Circuit noted in *Hackbart v. Cincinnati Bengals, Inc.,*[5] "subjecting another to unreasonable risk of harm, the essence of negligence, is inherent in the game of football." Thus, the Tenth Circuit has recognized that the game world of professional football is fundamentally at odds with the social imperatives of tort law—yet law, not football, gives way in this conflict. Where the game rules prohibit certain actions, however, the law of tort will resume its rightful place, as the Tenth Circuit made clear: "[I]t is highly questionable whether a professional football player consents or submits to injuries caused by conduct not within the rules."

Even the U.S. Supreme Court has seen fit to pursue the proper interpretation of game rules in deciding how to apply congressionally enacted statutes. In *PGA Tour, Inc. v. Martin,*[6] the Supreme Court looked to the rules of golf to determine if Casey Martin should be permitted to use a golf cart to drive between golf holes pursuant to the Americans with Disabilities Act (ADA). The Court stated that the "walking rule that is contained in [PGA's] hard cards, based on an optional condition buried in an appendix to the Rules of Golf, is not an essential attribute of the game itself." Hence, Justice Stevens stated, because the walking rule was not an essential rule of golf, the ADA required the accommodation of the golf cart for Casey Martin. This implies, of course, that if the walking rule were essential to golf, no accommodation would have been required.

Justice Scalia seemed rather incensed at this intrusion of congressional statutes upon the sphere of private game rules. He asked: "Why cannot the PGA TOUR, if it wishes, promote a new game, with distinctive rules (much as the American League promotes a game of baseball in which the pitcher's turn at the plate can be taken by a 'designated hitter')? If members of the public do not like the new rules. . . . they can withdraw their patronage. But the rules are the rules. They are (as in all games) entirely arbitrary." The majority's opinion in the Martin case, as well as Scalia's dissent, both demonstrate the give and take that occurs when game rules are subject to legal regulation. In essence, the law often recognizes and respects the separate social orderings created by game rules, and gives that ordering substantial leeway.

If it is true that potential criminal prosecutions may be somehow defused by the rules of baseball and that negligence bows to football, perhaps virtual crime prosecutions will be equally unlikely due to the ground rules of computer games. After all, the societal stakes of computer games are much lower—players do not place their physical safety at risk by playing *Ultima Online*. The harms suffered by victims within virtual worlds are generally only an emotional and social discomfort and, to some extent, a putative financial harm where players have the right to trade virtual properties.

If the rules of virtual worlds indeed can play an important part in determining whether Julian Dibbell's fencing of the Bone Crusher was a virtual crime, it is clearly important to ascertain the rules that govern the game of *Ultima Online*. As we explain below, however, the rules of most virtual worlds are difficult to analogize to the rules of more traditional games.

The Lawlessness of Computer Games

Computer games are inherently different than real space games, in that they are creatures of software. Software creates the physics of computer games, gives meaning to game components, and enables player behaviors. One might argue, therefore, that the software code of a game constitutes the "rules" (if any) of the game. By contrast, physical space games such as football, baseball, and basketball, are all governed by external, quasi-legal rule systems that guide both actions and outcomes. These external rule systems constrain the actions of players and game items.

In the physical game of football, one cannot cross the line of scrimmage before the ball is snapped, not because it is not possible but because doing so will result, according to the rules, in a stoppage of play and a punitive sanction. Likewise, in baseball, a batter cannot run the bases after hitting a foul ball, not because this is physically impossible but because it would be futile and nonsensical pursuant to the rules of baseball. These player-internalized rules can be analogized to legal rules and norms. One does not walk into a stranger's home because laws and norms prospectively limit otherwise possible physical actions by the known threat of resulting formal and social sanctions.

When software rules constrain player actions, on the other hand, the player has no ability to undertake impermissible actions. So while a game program's interface must be learned (A=left, S=right), a game like Space Invaders cannot be explained by a series of prohibitions and entitlements similar to the rules governing football, baseball, or solitaire. Certainly, players adapt their behavior to avoid losses, but no possible potential actions are prohibited by any "rules" of Space Invaders. Likewise, impartial referees are not needed when two people play Combat on a vintage Atari 2600 console because the game code fulfills that function. Therefore, "cheating" at Space Invaders or Combat is impossible without modifying the game's code, which serves as its rule set. The prohibition against code breaking is the primary "rule" of computer games—players are not permitted to "win" games by severing the game designer's Gordian knots. This reliance on software as rules is perhaps the most significant difference between computer games and physical games.

Virtual worlds, to some extent, are just a massively social implementation of traditional genres of computer games. They depend primarily on software rules because, like Space Invaders, they are fundamentally code. The software code of Britannia is what makes the theft of Bone Crusher maces possible and therefore putatively "legal," as all actions are legal when playing traditionally lawless computer games. But unlike traditional computer games, virtual worlds do not rely exclusively on software for their rule systems. Instead, unlike most other computer games, virtual worlds are accompanied by explicit textual rule sets that are carefully drafted by lawyers and game designers and designed (at least in part) to curtail antisocial behaviors. These nonsoftware rules of virtual worlds are often expressed in standard end-user license agreements. Players may be additionally required to assent to Terms of Service, Rules of Play, and other varieties of contractual agreements.

For instance, in *Ultima Online,* the written code endorses the game's software code by explicitly granting players what appears to be permission to steal from other players. While code-enabled harassment is expressly forbidden by the *Ultima Online* rules, there is a particular carve-out that clearly removes the theft of another player's virtual property from the scope of harassment. As the current policy reads:

[A]nything considered a valid play style in *Ultima Online* is not considered harassment. In other words, player killing and thievery . . . is not considered harassment. By valid, we mean that there are gamer mechanics created around these play styles . . . such as . . . the thieving skill, bounty systems, murder counts, the existence of guards, etc. Ultima Online is a role-playing game that encourages various play styles, and players should seek ways of protecting themselves against these play styles through game mechanics.

So, according to both the software code of the game and the contractual agreement to which one must assent in order to play *Ultima Online,* thievery is simply a "play style." One's redress for being victimized by a thief is to resort to game mechanics.[7] If stealing Bone Crusher maces is indeed a permissible activity pursuant to both the software and the contractual provisions in *Ultima Online,* it would seem that the theft of a Bone Crusher mace could not possibly constitute an unlawful conversion. Likewise, even though there is no common-law doctrine that exempts in-game property thefts from the scope of criminal law, it seems highly unlikely that virtual property "crimes" which are entirely consistent with software and contractual game rules would be criminally prosecuted.

We should add that the software licenses provide an additional reason for removing interavatar theft from the scope of property crimes. Most virtual-world EULAs insist that the intangible artifacts in the game are the property of the game company and are never "owned" by players. Bone Crushers, therefore, never leave the exclusive possession of Electronic Arts, because they never leave Britannia. Because the game owners are not deprived at any time of their property, arguably game properties can never be "stolen" pursuant to the language of the Model Penal Code.

We do not wish to be overly sanguine about this conclusion, which seems to neatly eviscerate the notion of player rights in virtual worlds. There is some theoretical potential for the legal recognition of player entitlements to virtual property and to the legal prohibition of virtual property crimes. In the *PGA Tour* case discussed above, for instance, the PGA was essentially a game owner and it had expressly promulgated the rules of a competition that forbid Casey Martin to use a golf cart. Yet the Supreme Court did not defer to the PGA's rules of golf when they conflicted with the needs of a disabled player. Similarly, courts and legislators may conceivably refuse to defer to the private orderings created by contract and software in the case of virtual worlds. But we cannot, at this point, predict under what circumstances legislatures and courts will be willing to depart from the current default rule of nearly absolute wizardocracy. As we explain in the next section, we predict that in the short term the issue of virtual property crime will more likely have real legal teeth if game owners, rather than the game players, are the ones to press courts to recognize the existence of virtual property.

"Real" Virtual Crimes

By concentrating the legal control of and rules regarding virtual property in their own hands, game owners and designers may essentially disarm many of the difficult legal issues stemming from interavatar property crimes. However, placing the issue in the hands of the game owners does not defuse the issue entirely, but simply shifts the focus of the legal analysis from a myriad of avatar players to a handful of corporate persons who create, own, and administer virtual worlds.

Game owners are not eager to recognize the legal existence of virtual property because the issue is generally associated with player ownership of their own swords and light sabers. Historically, game owners have been hostile toward player-run markets for virtual property and have viewed the "sale" of virtual property by players as a form of cheating. Analogies have been drawn to meritocracies in sports, where transferring rights to achievement by payment is seen as reprehensible behavior. When athletes throw games, they risk disgrace and even criminal charges.

But *Ultima Online* is not a typical game. Virtual world designers generally design with the intent that players will trade virtual properties and currencies.[8] Indeed, a brisk social trade in virtual properties is generally a goal of designers, who see it as the sign of a healthy virtual economy and an enjoyable game. What game owners find distressing is not the practice of exchange but the intrusion of external economic forces on what they would rather see as an independently ordered sphere of game play. In other words, game developers strive to create the illusion of property ownership and a vibrant economy, but wish to keep player ownership, as a legal matter, strictly illusionary.

It is not unusual for game companies today to ban the accounts of individuals who engage in the business of virtual goods trading. There are legitimate reasons for game companies to take this stance. Many virtual-world participants believe that trading virtual goods for real money is unethical and breaks the spirit of the game. Designers warn that organized player hoarding and trading can destabilize virtual economies in ways that ruin game play. The perception that such unauthorized player sales are free riding on game company investments probably also plays into the general owner antipathy toward the concept of virtual property in a big way.

However, game owners may find that the concept of virtual property is a two-edged sword. Virtual-world owners have long faced difficulties in policing the security of their systems against exploiters. Combining sophisticated code exploits with virtual-property markets can be big business. In South Korea, a twenty-two-year-old student and an accomplice manipulated a virtual-world server and made off with 1.5 billion won, or approximately U.S. $1.2 million. The federal Computer Fraud and Abuse Act (CFAA)[9] would seem to apply to such activities. A criminal violation of Section 1030 requires three main elements to be made out: First, the defendant must have intentionally accessed a computer. Second, the access must have been unauthorized or have exceeded the scope of the defendant's authorization. In the case of most security breaches, these two facts can be established. The third requirement of the CFAA, however, is that the damage resulting from the unauthorized access must be over $5,000. Could the theft of virtual properties constitute real damage under the CFAA?

A recent case attempted to shed some light on this issue. On July 30, 2003 in Las Vegas, U.S. District Court Chief Judge Philip M. Pro heard a CFAA case of the *United States v. J. B. Weasel.* Mr. Weasel stood accused of directing an avatar called "Terron" to hack into another player's account in the virtual world of GettaLife, strip him of his virtual assets (especially his prized "Staff of Viagra"), and leave his avatar naked and defenseless in the game. The case was fictional ("get a life" is a common epithet cast at those who frequent virtual worlds), but the lawyers, the law, and the judge were all real. The moot court was conducted at the 2003 "Black Hat Conference" of network and computer security specialists. The most interesting outcome was a jury finding regarding the real value of virtual assets. Ted Castronova was an expert witness for the prosecution and argued that the virtual assets were indeed worth over $5,000. As Castronova recounts:

Defense counsel Jennifer Granick mounted a strong counter-argument, namely that we might, as a society, decide that it is just too difficult to classify game-related damages as real, just as we shy away from taking cases of lost sexual favors to court, even though there clearly are damages. This powerful argument suggests that losses in something we agree to call a "game" should also be free from legal oversight, even though, in fact, the distinction between game and life is arbitrary. In the end, jury and audience disagreed with this cultural stratagem, preferring instead Prosecutor Richard Salgado's argument that human activity in the allegedly virtual space is not virtual at all. It is real activity and has real values and thus, in principle, it deserves the full attention of policy and law.[10]

If such a finding obtains in a real courtroom, it would have the potential of effectively criminalizing the unauthorized creation and "theft" of virtual properties from game owners. A quintessential example would be a "gold dupe" where a player would, by exploiting flaws in the game code, generate duplicate currency. If one has enough game accounts and machines exploiting this sort of dupe, it is possible to create so much gold that it devalues the in-world currency. Of course, for the exploiter, a dupe can generate a substantial number of real-world dollars before the real/virtual currency exchange rate falls off the cliff.

Dupes and exploits obviously don't make sense as "theft" offenses, even though the individual currency "pieces" might be considered the property of the game owners. The crucial point is that a duper or exploiter is, in some sense, creating new value, not destroying existing value. Yet the devaluation of virtual currencies through massive exploits can wreak havoc on the experience of ordinary players and in some cases frustration and dissatisfaction with broken game economics may lead players to terminate game subscriptions. Thus, game owners can potentially point to real economic harms created by the "theft" (via creation) and sale of virtual currencies. These harms may, in turn, give rise to criminal prosecutions for property crimes via computer trespass statutes.

Conclusion

As we have demonstrated, the problem of virtual crime, like all legal issues that arise in the settings of virtual worlds, is exceedingly complicated. Only time will tell if one day an ambitious prosecutor will decide to indict the next Mr. Bungle and thereby assert that virtual worlds are meaningfully different from their video games ancestors. If such a prosecution should indeed occur, we will share the concern of virtual-world designer Richard Bartle, the coauthor of MUD1: "My only concern here is that laws may be drawn up prematurely, without proper consultation with those who 'get' virtual worlds, and we could be stuck with something unsuitable or unworkable as a consequence."[11]

As the Honorable Loretta A. Preska has noted, "Judges and legislators faced with adapting existing legal standards to the novel environment of cyberspace struggle with terms and concepts that the average American five-year-old tosses about with breezy familiarity."[12] Judge Preska continues in a footnote: "I recall in this respect a particularly confusing item of testimony elicited at the evidentiary hearing: Ms. Kovacs, plaintiffs' expert witness with respect to the Internet, testified that on one occasion while she was in a MUD (a MultiUser Dungeon), a malefactor sicced his 'virtual dog' on her because she had trespassed on his domain. Fortunately, the other inhabitants of the MUD came to her rescue, vehemently protesting the unfriendliness of the virtual canine attack. Relieved as I was that the story had a happy ending, I must admit that it afforded me a window into an entirely unknown world."

Judge Preska's comments are admirably honest, and show that Bartle has a point. Some degree of confusion and category mistake will almost inevitably result from judicial attempts to interpret traditional criminal laws in order to police player behaviors in virtual worlds. Ironically, if we wish to preserve the benefits of virtual worlds as free and independent social experiments, we should probably keep the criminal law at a safe distance.

NOTES

1. F. Gregory Lastowka & Dan Hunter, *The Laws of the Virtual Worlds*, 92 Cal. L. Rev. 1 (2004).

2. Model Penal Code § 223.6.

3. *See* Kremen v. Cohen, 337 F.3d 1024, 1030 (9th Cir. 2003) ("Like a share of corporate stock or a plot of land, a domain name is a well-defined interest.").

4. *See* Johan Huizinga, *Homo Ludens* 13 (1955); Roger Caillois, *Man, Play and Games* 7 (Meyer Barash trans. 1961).

5. Hackbart v. Cincinnati Bengals, Inc., 601 F.2d 516 (10th Cir. 1979).

6. PGA Tour, Inc. v. Martin, 532 U.S. 661 (2001).

7. Brad King & John Borland, *Dungeons and Dreamers* 160–62 (2003).

8. Richard Bartle, *Designing Virtual Worlds* 297–312 (2004) (providing "Tips for a Successful Virtual Economy").

9. Computer Fraud and Abuse Act of 1986, 18 USCA § 1030 (1996).

10. Edward Castronova, Report on Black Hat Moot Court, available at http://business.fullerton.edu/castronova/archive.htm (last visited July 6, 2004).

11. Bartle, *Designing Virtual Worlds,* at 621.

12. ALA v. Pataki, 969 F.Supp. 160 (SDNY 1997).

8

Owned!

Intellectual Property in the Age of eBayers, Gold Farmers, and Other Enemies of the Virtual State

Or, How I Learned to Stop Worrying and Love the End-User License Agreement

Julian Dibbell

Possession, they say, is nine-tenths of the law, and not being a lawyer myself—or even a legal scholar—I'll have to take their word for it. But having spent considerable time in the company of lawyers and legal schol-ars lately, I do know this: the remaining tenth is storytelling. As a journal-ist, therefore, I feel at least somewhat qualified to stand before this august body of lawyers and legal scholars and do my professional thing, which is to tell a story. By no coincidence, the story I want to tell right now revolves around a legal case, a case with far-reaching implications for the concepts of property in virtual worlds and of governance in online settings gener-ally. But mostly it's the story of my own evolving understanding of what those implications might be. And if that story happens to move your own understanding forward just a bit, well, as any lawyer will attest, stories can do that.

Ours begins in the year 2001, with a group of enterprising young Southern Californians who at the time were doing business under the name of Black Snow Interactive. And a curious line of business it was: they spent their days acquiring and selling, on eBay and elsewhere, the scarce virtual goods that are the obsessively coveted focus of multiplayer online role-playing games like *Ultima Online* and *Dark Age of Camelot*. For the most part they trafficked in "gold coins" and other fictional currencies, and made piles of profit doing it. But the opening scene of the story finds our heroes suddenly stymied, their operations in the lucrative *Dark Age of Camelot* space abruptly halted when the owner of that game—a company called Mythic Entertainment—suspended their accounts and, alleging intellectual property infringements, prevailed upon eBay to suspend their auctions for items acquired within the fantasy realms of DAoC.

Now, the members of Black Snow Interactive were hardly the only people engaged in this sort of trade, and they certainly weren't the first to have their goods thus confiscated. And if they'd been more like the rest of their fellow traders, they would most likely have just laid low for a while and returned to the game under some other identity—or moved on to another game altogether. But for some reason Black Snow chose to stand and fight. They filed a federal suit against Mythic for unfair business practices, and then they very publicly announced that they had done so.

"What it comes down to," declared Black Snow partner Lee Caldwell, "is, does a MMORPG player have rights to his time, or does Mythic own that player's time? It is unfair of Mythic to stop those who wish to sell their items, currency or even their own accounts, which were created with their own time. Mythic, in my opinion, and hopefully the court's, does not have the copyright ownership to regulate what a player does with his or her own time or to determine how much that time is worth on the free market."

Self-serving as the press release may have been, it did raise an interesting point: Who exactly owns the products of game-world economies—the company that creates the game, or the player whose time and efforts bring the economy into existence? Or to put it another way, did Black Snow's hard-won possession of its virtual goods indeed get them nine-tenths of the way toward legal ownership, or was this peculiar form of property simply (to cite another pertinent adage) theft?

There were other issues at stake. So many, in fact, that by the time word got around about Black Snow's suit, there were very few people with a more than passing interest in the economics of online games who had not thought and/or argued long and hard about it. And I was no exception. Having written passingly about the case for *Wired* magazine, I was invited to give a talk about it at Stanford Law School in the fall of 2002. There I spoke about the broader issues the case raised, which to my mind were two.

First, and most interesting, was the question of intellectual property in the digital sphere. And given that my invitation to speak at Stanford had come from Lawrence Lessig and his crowd, you can easily guess the direction my thoughts on the subject ran in. To me, Mythic's claim of copyright infringement was not only a weak one but a classic instance of the overapplication of intellectual property claims in digital contexts. After all, to transfer a virtual sword or gold piece from one player to another is not to duplicate the item but to move it, as it were, from one file folder to another—a procedure involving trivial copying at most and none whatsoever for any economic purposes. Thus, I argued, Mythic's restrictions on the sale of virtual items represented yet another digital-age curtailment of the so-called first-sale doctrine, which for a century has guaranteed the right of second-hand booksellers and weekend yard salesmen, among others, to sell copies of works to which they hold no copyright. Mythic no doubt owned the copyright to its fictional swords and coins, but its claim to own each copy of those fictions, implicit in its maneuverings against Black Snow, plainly ran afoul of a hallowed if increasingly embattled point of law.

Of course, the point was rendered somewhat moot by the fact that the end-user license agreement for *Dark Age of Camelot* subscribers had obliged Black Snow to waive any right to resell their items at all. And here lay the second and, to my mind, maddeningly less interesting of the case's central questions. For if it was bad enough that the agreement was the usual raw deal one sees in software and network-access licenses—a nonnegotiable contract of adhesion granting much to the issuer and little to the user—this one had the additional effect of superseding altogether the piquant intellectual-property issues the case might otherwise provoke. All a judge had to do was rule the relevant terms of the contract valid, and all discussion of Mythic's intellectual-property claims would melt into irrelevance. The end-user license agreement in this case, then, was not only the instrument of iniquity that EULAs tend to be but was, as well, a sort of wet blanket thrown upon the sparks of intellectual controversy flying from the case. It was not only bad but boring.

Thus concluded my analysis of the issues at stake. And there it might have remained had my analysis not been somewhat at odds with certain key facts of the case, heretofore left conveniently unmentioned.

It will not have escaped your notice that up to now I have said nothing about the final ruling in *Black Snow v. Mythic*. This is mainly because, as it turns out, there was no final ruling; not to speak of, anyway. A few months after the initial filing, word got out that the Federal Trade Commision had just issued a $10,000 judgment against Lee Caldwell and another of Black

Snow's principals—something to do with their involvement in a previous business, an enterprise apparently consisting of the sale, online, of computer systems they neither owned nor intended to deliver. Not long after that, the boys of Black Snow stopped paying their attorney, stopped returning his calls, and more or less disappeared, taking their lawsuit with them.

This had all transpired months before I gave my talk, and while the nature of their earlier operations hardly spoke well for the character of the plaintiffs, it didn't seem to me to diminish the essence of their claim or the gravity of the issues it raised. Neither, for that matter, did a certain almost equally undignified aspect of Black Snow's present business model, the precise workings of which bear some explaining.

I said before that Black Snow were in the business of acquiring and selling virtual goods, but I didn't say how they were acquiring them. This, it seems, involved various methods, none of which was particularly savory, but one of which was of a crassness so naked as to approach genius. To grasp what they were up to, it helps to keep in mind the economist Edward Castronova's calculation that players of *EverQuest* (the most popular of the multiplayer online role-playing games) can acquire goods within the game at an average rate of about three dollars' worth per hour. Keep in mind as well that there are places in the world where the average laborer makes less than that, and you get the picture: Black Snow had rented an office in Tijuana, equipped it with a T1 Internet connection and eight PC workstations, and hired three shifts of unskilled Mexican workers to power-play *Dark Age of Camelot* and *Ultima Online* around the clock, selling off the loot thus accumulated and paying the workers a small percentage of the proceeds.

The players whose rights Black Snow was so nobly standing up for, in other words, were in fact low-wage mouse-clickers slaving away in a virtual sweatshop. This did, of course, lend a certain irony to Black Snow's crusade—but as I said, it seemed to me an irony that the merits of their case could survive.

And yet, as I continued to think about the case after my talk, I began to have my doubts. The first turn in my thinking occurred as I embarked on a year-long attempt to duplicate Black Snow's financial success (though not their methods), buying and selling goods in *Ultima Online* and blogging my efforts as I went along. "Play Money: Diary of a Dubious Proposition" (www.juliandibbell.com/playmoney) is the name I gave my blog, and you can read the whole, sad story there if you like. For the present purposes, though, it's enough to report that the project quickly brought me in contact with players whose methods made the Black Snow sweatshop look quaint. One sent me a photo whose implications made my mind spin, a picture of a fully automated "gold farm": twenty-four computers crammed into a closet in his house, each one of them running an *Ultima Online* client, each client piped to a program that repeated the same loot-gathering operations over and over, without so much as a bathroom break. If Black Snow had hit on one of modern capitalism's great efficiency-enhancing maneuvers—off-shoring—my friend the gold farmer was working another—automation—for all it was worth.

What it was worth, in his case, was enough real money to wipe out his student loans, buy his wife a new washer-dryer, and make a nice down payment on a Prius. I didn't begrudge him any of it, but I did have some qualms about another picture he showed me. It was a chart of the price, on eBay, of *Ultima Online*'s unit of currency, the gold piece, and it was headed steadily, precipitously downward. The gold farmer told me that this was the result of overproduction by other farmers, less scrupulous than he, and a quick scan of selling patterns on eBay told me he was probably right. And here was a problem that hit home. After all, I was trying to make money myself now, selling those coins, and the faster the price dropped, the harder it would be for me to do that.

Moreover, this clear and present threat to my livelihood put me in a better position to understand how the activities of the Black Snows and the gold farmers affected the average player. It's common to hear players grumbling that those who buy their way to success in the game spoil the success of those who play their way to the top, but I never had much sympathy with that argument. Live and let live, I figured—if some players had more money to spend than time to play, while others had more time than money, what was the harm in letting each group follow its own best path to the game's upper levels? Now, though, I could see that the consequences of the "export market" (as the economist Castronova has characterized the exchange of virtual goods for dollars) weren't so easily contained. The cash market for gold drove the gold farmers, and the gold farmers drove hyperinflation within the game, until eventually there was no way for anyone, time-rich or time-poor, to keep up with the rising cost of living except by resorting to the same very effective but not very playful methods that had made the gold farmers rich.

Thus ran the argument anyway, and while I've since come to question some of its premises, what remains clear is this: The argument had almost nothing to do with intellectual property. It was an argument, rather, about a peculiar sort of economic justice, about the best way to regulate the daily life of a peculiar sort of society, about the governance, in short, of a semifictional world. And seen from within that world, the contemporary intellectual property debate, in all its vastness, was just a sideshow. What mattered here wasn't whether Black Snow had or had not violated Mythic's copyrights. What mattered, rather—and mattered indeed—was whether Black Snow had or had not done harm to the community to which they belonged by virtue of their subscriptions to *Dark Age of Camelot.*

Now, it may seem incongruous to bring up such lofty notions as governance, community, and economic justice in the context of a commercial video game, but on this point, too, my thinking was moving toward a place quite different from the one it started in. The shift here came a few months after I had laid eyes on that gold farm, when I decided to pay my first visit to online gaming's equivalent of a *Star Trek* convention: the semiannual *EverQuest* Fan Faire. The Faire was pretty much what I expected, in most ways. Wizards and dwarves roamed the hallways in hooded robes and bad makeup; small groups of doughy men and pale women huddled around cocktails trading quest stories and character stats. There was one recurring scene I hadn't expected, however: conference room after conference room was filled with players hurling questions, advice, and demands at the designers of the game, who seemed to be taking careful notes. It looked for all the world like a series of town meetings.

And as I took it all in, I remembered in a new light a talk I had heard by Dave Rickey, a leading MMORPG designer, just a few months earlier. Rickey was ostensibly talking about how customer support works in a game this complex, but by the end of his talk it was clear his point was that it doesn't. Customer support, in the traditional sense of companies walking users through a product that the company understands much better than the user, has to give way to something more like democratic politics. "You have to remember that, in aggregate, the players always know your game better than you do," said Rickey—and given that fact, he argued, the most efficient way to manage customer satisfaction is to let them tell you, to a certain extent, how to run your game.

Back at the EQ Fan Faire, I was seeing the game companies from a new angle. Caught between the demands of a not entirely captive customer base and the inefficiencies of trying to single-handedly manipulate a large, complex society, they were doing what governments of large, complex societies have a strong tendency to do: outsource decision making to the people. Needless to say, relations between the game companies and their paying "citizens" are still a far cry from the best practices defined in, say, the Federalist Papers. All the same, I realized, they come close enough to blur the line between designing a game and framing a constitution. Common principles of game design ("keeping it fun," "maintaining game balance") start to sound suspiciously like certain founding axioms of classic liberal political theory ("pursuit of happiness," "the greatest good for the greatest number"). People like Dave Rickey and Raph Koster start to sound a little like John Locke and Jeremy Bentham.

And lo and behold, the end-user license agreement—that egregious tool of corporate tyranny over the defenseless, voiceless customer (or so I had painted it)—starts to look more like the place where a complicated give and take between designers and players is finally ratified, transformed from a murky power struggle into the legally binding rules of the game. The EULA starts to look less like a contract of adhesion, in other words, and more like a social contract.

Don't get me wrong: EULAs are evil. Or at least EULAs as generally executed tend to be. But that's because the EULA as generally executed tends to be effectively nonnegotiable. Whereas the EULA for a game like *EverQuest*—as I could no longer deny after seeing its designers come face to face with the fierce enthusiasms of its players—was effectively renegotiated on a daily basis.

And in recognizing that, I was obliged to acknowledge that I had come around one hundred and eighty degrees in my thinking about *Black Snow v. Mythic*. No longer did intellectual property seem to me the most productive frame to put around the case. No longer did a U.S. district courtroom seem to me the best place to resolve the case's contradictions. No longer, especially, did the end-user license agreement seem to me an obstacle standing between the case's central questions and their proper answers.

Quite the contrary. For the most central question of all, finally, was whether or not activities like eBaying and gold farming did unconscionable harm to a community like *Dark Age of Camelot's*—and it was precisely the EULA that kept that question in the hands of the community's body politic. Weighing the case purely as a matter of intellectual property law, a judge could certainly have determined the legality of eBaying once and for all, but because the actual reasons Mythic and many of its customers wanted the practice stopped had nothing ultimately to do with intellectual property, any such ruling would have addressed those reasons no more adequately than a coin toss. Ruling the EULA to be a valid contract, on the other hand, would have sent the question back where it belonged—into the much more finely tuned evaluative process that is the ceaseless, grinding struggle between players and designers over the shape of the game.

Again, don't get me wrong: EULAs aren't perfect. There are questions they can't answer, such as, for instance, whether Mythic wasn't overstepping when it invoked intellectual property law to compel eBay's help in enforcing the rules of its game. That's one for the casebooks, to be sure. And of course no EULA can guarantee that the negotiations that produce it are genuinely fair and balanced, any more than a democratic constitution can guarantee a democratic state. As it is, I hasten to repeat, the feedback loop between MMORPG players and MMORPG designers is at best a crude approximation of democratic government—and for the sake of whatever fun inheres in these games is probably better left that way.

All that said, can there possibly be a legal mechanism better suited to the peculiar demands of virtual-world governance than the end-user license agreement? Look at it this way: The ontological ambiguities of the virtual world are such that there is probably no realm in all of human culture—aside from the bedroom, perhaps—that is so consistently difficult for the law to make sense of. Considering the novelty of this realm, we might reasonably hope for future case law and legislation to do a better job of it, but I suspect it will be a long time before enough of those ambiguities are ironed out to make a difference. And besides, why subject virtual worlds to the uniformity of a legal code when so much of their appeal lies precisely in their diversity? Ideally, they are parallel universes—alternatives not just to reality but to one another. And ultimately the only way to secure that ideal in the legal context is through that part of the law that's friendliest to variety—the law of contracts.

Contract law gives us the EULA, and the EULA gives us alternatives. Properly enforced, the EULA makes each virtual world its own parallel legal universe, immunized as much as it can be from the inability of existing law to reckon with its strangenesses and possibilities. The EULA gives us the restrictive legal regime that is *Dark Age of Camelot*, with its proscriptions against eBaying and its standard clauses demanding copyright to everything you say or do within its bounds. But the EULA just as easily gives us the radically open alternate reality of an online world like *Second Life*, where selling virtual items and virtual real estate is encouraged and all intellectual property rights remain in the hands of the players. For that matter, the EULA can put us in interesting parallel realities even outside the realm of fantasy and games: The famous General Public License, after all, legal cornerstone of Linux and other open-source software, is effectively a EULA, as are the various licenses designed by Creative Commons to carve out a space for other alternatives to copyright.

Yes, possession is nine-tenths of the law, they say, and some say too that this is best interpreted to mean that the law is overwhelmingly concerned with questions of property. And even if that isn't true of the law, it was certainly true of me when I first came upon the case of *Black Snow v. Mythic.* Fascinated by the power and scope of the intellectual property question, I failed to notice the beauty, if it's not too ridiculous to call it that, of the EULA question, which is that it's not about possession at all. In some fundamental way, it's about the same thing virtual worlds are about: creation, invention, the conjuring of abstract universes, the telling of stories. It's about that other tenth.

9

Virtual Power Politics

James Grimmelmann

Every decision made by the designers of a virtual world is a political decision. Every debate over the rules and every change to the software is political. When players talk about the rules, they are practicing politics.

Exploits

Consider the following classic story from Lucasfilm's *Habitat*, launched in 1985. A "vendroid" on one side of the world would sell a doll for seventy-five Tokens (the *Habitat* unit of currency). A pawn shop at the other end would buy dolls for a hundred Tokens each. A similar price disparity held for more expensive crystal balls: One machine would sell them for 18,000 Tokens, while another would buy them for 30,000 Tokens. When a group of players discovered this possibility for arbitrage, they took advantage of it wholeheartedly:

> One night they took all their money, walked to the Doll Vendroid, bought as many Dolls as they could, then took them across town and pawned them. By shuttling back and forth between the Doll Vendroid and the Pawn Shop for *hours*, they amassed sufficient funds to buy a Crystal Ball, whereupon they continued the process with Crystal Balls and a couple orders of magnitude higher cash flow. The final result was at least three Avatars with hundreds of thousands of Tokens each. We only discovered this the next morning when our daily database status report said that the money supply had quintupled overnight.[1]

In a game in which each player's daily income was supposed to be a hundred Tokens, the result of this arbitrage was to leave four-fifths of the entire wealth of the game in the hands of a handful of players.

In games, as in the real world, this sort of inflation in the money supply can be economically catastrophic. Prices for other game items skyrocket; other players' wealth effectively evaporates. Players who have previously made steady incomes by selling items to pawn machines see their real incomes collapse; items available from vending machines at fixed prices and in unlimited quantity flood into the game, as well. Not only do players who have invested in these items see their real value drop precipitously, but the game servers themselves may become overburdened by the sudden increase in virtual items they must track.

Today, a similar design mistake would be called an "exploit." The boundaries of what constitutes an exploit are necessarily fuzzy, for reasons I will discuss below, but the general sense is that an exploit is any activity in a game that produces rewards wildly disproportionate to the effort involved, within the context of the game's overall opportunities for reward for effort. One also sometimes sees exploits referred to as "gold duping" or "gold farming." Although both these terms technically describe more particular forms of exploits, they are used more generally. Exploits have the feeling of alchemy: arcane secrets that produce virtual gold out of thin air.

Exploits are a game designer's nightmare, but they are also nearly inescapable. Some exploits arise from outright coding mistakes, others from the unexpected interaction of game features. Every major game seems to have had exploit problems on a regular basis; game designers have learned to keep a close watch on their economies for the telltale signs that someone has discovered an exploit. When designers notice one, they first alter the game software to prevent its future use and then try to undo the damage. The following responses are typical:

- Since the *Habitat* vendroid exploit produced so much wealth, it was easy to figure out who the exploiters were. The designers contacted the newly rich players and convinced them to engage in a series of potlatches, spending their money on "treasure hunt games" for the amusement of other players.
- *Ultima Online* reduced its money supply after an inflationary exploit by introducing a special red hair dye and auctioning it off. The dye had no in-game function other than as a status symbol.

- *Dark Age of Camelot,* like many other games, has a blanket policy of warning, suspending, or ultimately expelling people who are caught using exploits. Indeed, players are instructed to report possible exploits if they discover any.
- *EverQuest* uses the threat of lawsuits and the threat of ejection from the game to try to prevent the real-world sale of in-game assets, including its currency. If other players are willing and able to pay "real" money for virtual money, then 'sploiters can convert their virtual gains into hard money. By banning "eBaying," *EverQuest* seeks to reduce the financial incentive to look for exploits.
- It is rumored that *Shadowbane,* in response to a particularly bad exploit, simply closed down the server which had been exploited. *Shadowbane*'s designers were unable to determine who on the server had taken advantage of the exploit, so they forced everyone to move to a new server, leaving behind all their gold and all their real property. The net effect was a contraction of the money supply through a massive exaction, on the theory that the vast majority of the exacted wealth would come from the 'sploiters.

The range of responses is noteworthy. *Habitat* and *Ultima Online* implicitly accepted the gains of exploiting and allowed the clever to retain their wealth; they focused instead on repairing their games' macroeconomies. The *Dark Age of Camelot* and *EverQuest* policies above are much harsher; they treat exploiting as a form of crime and the gains as contraband subject to confiscation.[2] *Shadowbane*'s reply was certainly antiexploit, but the consequences fell just as hard on people who had done nothing "wrong."

It is impossible to label these responses "right" or "wrong" in an absolute sense. We need to refer to the social consensus of a game's player base to think about a change to the game. But once we do so, then every change will have both supporters and opponents; it will privilege some players while hurting others. Whether the game *should* make the change is an issue of policy; whether it *does* make the change is a matter of politics. Every choice about a game's software is political.

One cannot dodge this point merely by referring to the end-user license agreement (EULA) of the players with the game company. The EULA is typically so one-sided, as far as the actual game goes, that it makes *any* action by the game company right. Players have no right to object if the game company closes an exploit, but they also have no right to demand that the company close one. Whether or not the game company will take action will depend on its relationship with the players and its sense of which response will be best for the game's long-term popularity. But that, in turn, will depend on the players' feelings about the issue, the kind of subjective and popularity-based inquiry that reference to the EULA was supposed to avoid.

Similarly, one cannot derive the "ought" from the "is" of the game software itself. One would like to say that the rules of the game are embodied in the software. But the problem of exploits is precisely that the software lets a 'sploiter get away with something surprising. There is nothing "wrong" with the exploit, as far as the software is concerned. 'Sploiters cannot breathe easy, however, because if the software is modified to close the exploit and confiscate the duped gold, those rules of the game embodied in the software have not been violated either. To figure out whether a given change to a game constitutes the legitimate confiscation of counterfeit virtual goods or the illegitimate taking of virtual property requires referring to something outside the software.

That "something" is the collective expectation of the players about the game they are playing.

Players and Designers

I would like to emphasize a few basic features of players' diverse motivations.

First, their motivations *are* diverse.[3] Players play games for many reasons, including the pleasure of facing a challenge and overcoming it, the pleasure of competing with others and of acquiring superior social status, the pleasure of socializing with friends, and the pleasure of collaborating with others in the pursuit of a common goal. They often play for a complicated combination of these motivations. Given that even people motivated by the same challenges will have different abilities and that people motivated by socializing will have different networks of friends, it seems safe to say that no two players play a game for exactly the same reason or with exactly the same goals.

Second, a sense of challenge is a common motivation. Psychologically, rewards tied to effort are more satisfying that ones that happen automatically. Players frequently want games in which not everything is immediately available; they want games which require interactivity. This challenge could be absolute—for example, a player must attain a certain level of skill to gain access to a particular part of the world—or it could be relative—for example, an in-game tournament that can have only one winner. Either way, players want their world to have meaningful constraints built in.

Playing a game together means squaring these two features with each other. Players with differing motivations and abilities must agree on a common set of rules that provide a satisfying set of constraints. The rules are the framework within which the game takes place; they are a compromise among the players.

Virtual worlds use software to create this common framework: the software shows players a representation of the game world and mediates between the players in determining what "happens" in that world. One might say that the rules of the game are enforced by the software, to the best of its abilities. The software constitutes the "reality" of the virtual world, by establishing a common set of metaphors for the players to share. A certain set of bits on the server and a corresponding set of pixels on the screen becomes a virtual apple; another, different set become a virtual house. These common metaphors, together with the logic by which the software responds to player requests to manipulate them, define the game as what it is. Change them too much and the game becomes a "different" one.

One of the most important ways in which the software of a virtual world fills out the content of the game being played there is by establishing a scarcity structure for the resources of the game. *Habitat* made Tokens, Dolls, and Crystal Balls into scarce resources by handing out Tokens only at the rate of a hundred a day and allowing other items to enter the world only by being purchased. *Ultima Online* made red hair dye into a scarce resource by auctioning it off.

These resources have multiple functions within the game. Some are valued by players as goals in themselves, the rewards for completing particular tasks. Some are valued by players instrumentally, as a means to accomplishing other goals. Some are valued by players as indicators of social status, either as signs of prowess or as signs of conspicuous waste. And finally, precisely because these resources are valued by players for so many other purposes, they have value as currency: They can be exchanged for other game resources, for favors, or for "real" wealth.

Game software, of course, does not spring into being from a vacuum. Someone must program it, run it, and maintain it. For most major virtual world games, that someone is a corporation whose business model involves selling access to the game on a subscription basis.

One way of looking at game designers in this model is as gods, because they have godlike powers over the game world as a world. They call a game world into being; they can also destroy it or remake it in any way they wish: the tradition of calling them "gods" or "wizards" or "superusers" reflects this virtual omnipotence. The gods can ban a player outright, block her from speaking, confiscate her possessions, or turn her into a toad. Further, under the terms of the EULA she probably clicked through when joining the world, they can banish or "toad" her for no reason, with no warning, and without offering her any compensation. Her only legally guaranteed recourse is to quit the game, leaving behind whatever accomplishments she has built up there.

Unsurprisingly, this imbalance in power casts a long shadow across virtual worlds, and frequently arouses concern among observers. Players regularly claim arbitrary mistreatment, especially where their losses due to designer action have real economic value. Indeed, courts in some countries have started to open their doors to lawsuits by players against designers for confiscating valuable virtual items.

Designer capriciousness is a real concern, especially in virtual worlds that are more than "just games." Nevertheless, I think that a focus on the conflicts between players and designers is a distraction from an even more important set of conflicts: those between players and other players. Complaints about the unaccountability of designers are sometimes legitimate, but they are often also a rhetorical posture adopted by players who lose political contests with other players. But I am getting ahead of myself.

The problem with the "unaccountable designers" view of games is that it fails to take account of the designers' motivations. The hedonic goals motivating players do not apply to designers in the same way; because designers are not "bound" by the rules of the game in the same sense, they aren't really ever "playing" the game. Baseball umpires aren't bound by the rules of baseball, but we don't fear that umpires will systematically oppress players. Yes, there is the occasional incident of abuse of power, the undeserved ejection, but on the whole, umpires aren't competitors with an unfair advantage. They may have an advantage but they will never be competitors.

As entrepreneurs, game designers are trying to make money, which they do by selling access to the game world and selling virtual resources. All their money comes from players; they make money only as long as players are willing to continue paying. Confiscating a virtual item doesn't enrich the game designer and may infuriate a paying customer. If anything, it seems as though the natural instinct of the game designer would be to pander, to hand out every in-game asset and accomplishment to anyone who asks. That way, no one would ever quit from the frustration of failure.

But this instinct runs up against players' desire for challenge and scarcity. The *EverQuest* players who play for hundreds of hours would quit in boredom if every monster could be killed with a tap on the nose. The *Ultima Online* players who lined up to bid on the red hair dye would never have done so had it been available in barrels on every street corner. Players wouldn't mind an edge here and there, but an edge available to everyone isn't an edge at all. Designers are stingy with players because *other players* demand overall stinginess.

In the end, designers are like the Genie in Disney's *Aladdin:* "PHENOMENAL COSMIC POWER . . . itty bitty living space." Their decision making in setting game rules is driven by a kind of monetary utilitarianism: they make decisions largely in keeping with their sense of long-term profitability. Whatever the overwhelming majority of players want, within reason the overwhelming majority of players get.

Game designers really are the governments of virtual worlds. Like real governments, they make the "laws" under which citizens must live. And like real governments, they are accountable, after a fashion, to their constituents. The mechanism by which that accountability is established is different—and arguably inferior—it is true, but this is not to say that no such mechanism exists. Players use designers as agents, employing them to make and enforce the collective decisions that need to be made to make a virtual world function well. Designers focus the diffuse will of the players into something actionable: software.

Conflict

As Clay Shirky has observed, any social group will witness systemic and repeated conflicts among its members; the process of resolving these conflicts is the process by which the group defines itself.[4] The advantage of applying this statement to groups whose interactions are defined by software—a category that includes virtual-world games—is that in these groups, much of the self-definition is explicit, and encoded into the software. A game is defined by its players' understandings of the rules; when those rules are to be enforced by software, the evolution of the software is a history of the evolution of those understandings.

Some measure of evolution is more or less inevitable. Players never agree completely on the rules of a virtual world; the average player doesn't even *know* most of the rules. I sincerely doubt that any *EverQuest* player knows the hit points and respawn rate of every monster in the game. Even the designers don't actually know all the rules as the software actually enforces them: every bug fix is an admission that the rules coded into the game's software didn't match the rules in the minds of the designers. Disagreement, ambiguity, and mistake are everywhere.

Most of these ambiguities are content to remain latent: a *Habitat* player probably doesn't care whether the selling price of a crystal ball at a particular vendroid is 18,000 or 19,000 Tokens. But other ambiguities are flushed out into the open. The *Habitat* vendroid exploit made it a matter of great public concern that the selling price of that crystal ball was 18,000 Tokens rather than 36,000.

A few players become rich because of an exploit; the rest of the player base wants the exploit closed off, and quickly, before their own wealth is wiped out by inflation. Exploits are not the only cause of crises over the rules in virtual worlds, but they are an especially vivid example both of the difference that rules changes can make, and of the intense pressure for and against those changes.

What makes exploits so much fun to think about is that there is no line dividing "exploit" from "feature." An "exploit" is a moneymaking opportunity condemned by most players. A moneymaking opportunity embraced by most players is a "feature." Calling something an "exploit" is a way of saying that you want the software changed to prohibit it and that you think those who are taking advantage of it are cheating. If the designers agree with you—or rather, if they think that enough players would agree with you—they will make the change. Why should you keep playing a game whose designers don't fix exploits?

What makes exploits so explosive, however, is that *not* everyone agrees on them. The so-called 'sploiters probably see their behavior as perfectly acceptable, no matter what you happen to think. Taking advantage of a good opportunity is skillful play: It indicates careful attention to the game world and good judgment among competing ways to spend your game time. You, they would say, are perfectly welcome to take advantage of the feature you insist on calling an "exploit." You shouldn't complain that someone else found it before you did. Why shouldn't better players be allowed to enjoy the fruits of their skill?

Indeed, turn the tables. Imagine that you are a long-distance merchant in *EverQuest*. You buy valuable items at a discount in remote backwaters, then carry them through dangerous monster-infested wastelands to reach the trading cities where your goods will fetch a higher price. Every journey is a risky one; you take the chance of losing your entire trading stock in an ambush. Your profit margin is large, but isn't it fair compensation for your hard work?

But now, the *EverQuest* admins intervene, saying that one plant in your bundle of goods was mispriced due to a software bug and that the 200 percent profit you were turning on it was an exploit. They fix the prices, confiscate your entire store of platinum pieces, and ban you from the game for a week. Isn't this an example of unjust designer intervention? Why should you keep playing a game whose designers fix things that aren't exploits?

There is no escaping the conflicts. Every change benefits someone and hurts someone else. The designers may claim that the overall effects are "good for the game," but their perspective reflects a kind of simpleminded majoritarianism: They will do whatever causes the fewest players to quit the game.

What is happening here is that the game's formal rules—those its software enforces—from time to time come substantially unmoored from the game's normative rules—those its players think of as the "rules," as their "social contract."[5] (Actually, the two are never entirely congruent; it is just that the differences are only noticed and fought over on exceptional occasions.) When this happens, the formal software rules need to be brought into correspondence with the players' sense of what the rules ought to be.

But it is impossible to fix the software without some clear understanding of what that "sense of what the rules ought to be" actually says. When players' senses *disagree,* there is an opportunity for a kind of metagaming. Typically, players' senses of the "right" rules favor themselves: That's human nature. Thus, whoever emerges victorious in the contest to determine "what the rules ought to say" has in fact managed to obtain an advantage within the game itself.

"Victory" in this contest, where virtual-world games are concerned, means persuading the designers, for they are the ones with the power to alter the software. The contest therefore takes the form of competing groups of players lobbying the designers, each pressing arguments why it would be better if the software were changed in the way *they* recommend. It is this triangular dynamic—two groups of players powerless to alter the world on their own competing for the favor of an omnipotent designer who nonetheless depends on the players collectively for support—that gives politics in virtual worlds their fascinating character.

Ultimately, players' power over designers depends on their ability to go nuclear: to stop playing and stop paying. It's a powerful threat, but costly for a player who has built up substantial in-game wealth or status, and each player can only quit once. Thus, the first rhetorical trope of in-game politics is the threat to quit, and the second is the accusation that the threatener is all hat and no cattle. Raph Koster has commented on the phenomenon of running a "game that people love to hate."[6] It makes perfect sense that the players most attached to the game, the most invested in it, and with the strongest opinions about how it should be run should also be the ones most often threatening to leave but never actually quitting. That threat is their biggest source of influence over the game, but they are too bound to the game to leave except under truly dire circumstances.

The next interesting pattern of virtual-world politics is that any software policy proposal is meaningless unless conveyed to the designers. The designers, it is true, have an interest in keeping an ear to the ground to know what the players are thinking, but the player who cares at all about the shape of game play really has no choice but to try and reach the designers. I think this fact underlies another familiar trope of virtual-world politics: extensive fan feedback at conventions, on public message boards, and within games.

One of the most salient forms of virtual-world politics is doubly-virtual civil disobedience: virtual once for being in a virtual world, and virtual a second time over because true disobedience is impossible in a software-controlled space. Instead, players *act out* demonstrations, even though they have no ability to withhold virtual taxes, take over virtual buildings, or topple virtual sovereigns. *Ultima Online* had a nude protest over the inflationary spike that ultimately produced the red hair dye; *Second Life* saw a "tax revolt" over the game's tax on virtual property. These were propaganda events, designed, much like real-world protests, to send a signal that many players care about an issue.

Finally, and most importantly, there is the normal grassroots work of any form of politics: persuading other people to agree with you. Your job is to convince them that your idea about how the software should be lines up with their motivations for playing, will produce an enjoyable game overall, and is most substantively just. Perhaps you will convince them, perhaps not. But you will be engaged in politics, as well as in playing the game. When it comes to virtual worlds, "politics" and "play" are one and the same.

Conclusion

Once you know to look for virtual politics, they're everywhere. Almost every design decision—even a seemingly uncontested decision—has winners and losers. It's always worthwhile asking which players benefit from a given decision, why the designers listened to them, and why the losers weren't able, or didn't bother, to put up a more effective resistance. The possible cleavages are infinite; so too are the possible coalitions.

If my argument has seemed familiar in places, that is because it is not exactly novel. My analysis of the effect and meaning of software is just a reiteration of familiar (if contested) claims about the effect and meaning of law. Perhaps it is easier to see the clash of interests and the social construction of meaning where virtual-world games are concerned. They are virtual, after all; they depend on an explicit agreement among the players. The possibility of software bugs makes more obvious the need for after-the-fact interpretation of ambiguities in that agreement. And the fact that they are games foregrounds both the sense of competition and the complete arbitrariness of the rules governing that competition.

It would be a mistake, however, to think that I am arguing that virtual worlds are somehow different from real ones. Any difference is illusory: These worlds may be virtual, but their politics are wholly real.

NOTES

1. Chip Farmer and F. Randall Morningstar, The Lessons of Lucasfilm's *Habitat*, in *Cyberspace: First Steps* (Michael Benedikt ed. 1991), http://www.fudco.com/chip/lessons.html.

2. *See generally* Dan Hunter and Greg Lastowka, Virtual Crimes (Draft 3) (Nov. 6, 2003) available at http://www.nyls.edu/docs/lastowka.pdf. Hunter and Lastowka explicitly adopt a model under which the only substantive in-game crime is "griefing," or playing "with the express intent [to] bring sadistic pleasure to the perpetrator through the suffering and emotional distress of others." What kind of play will generate "emotional distress" obviously cannot be determined without

close attention to the expectations of other players and will be highly context-dependent.

3. *See generally* Richard Bartle, Hearts, Clubs, Diamonds, Spades: Players Who Suit MUDs, http://www.mud.co.uk/richard/hcds.htm.

4. *See* Clay Shirky, A Group Is Its Own Worst Enemy, http://www.shirky.com/writings/group_enemy.html; Clay Shirky, Nomic World, http://www.shirky.com/writings/nomic.html.

5. *See generally* Julian Dibbell, Owned! Chapter 8, this volume. Dibbell argues that restrictive EULA terms can be understood as a form of social contract, a delegation of power by players to designers to enable the designers to deal harshly with eBayers and other miscreants. My argument is, in part, a generalization of Dibbell's. *See also* Raph Koster, Declaring the Rights of Players, *at* http://www.raphkoster.com/gaming/playerrights.html.

6. Raph Koster, Current and Future Developments in Online Games, http://www.raphkoster.com/gaming/futuredev.html.

10

Escaping the Gilded Cage
User-Created Content and Building the Metaverse

Cory Ondrejka

In 1992, Neal Stephenson's science fiction novel *Snow Crash* introduced readers to the concept of the Metaverse. While other science fiction had described immersive online games[1] and virtual spaces,[2] Stephenson was the first to describe an online environment that was a real place to its users, one where they interacted using the real world as a metaphor and socialized, conducted business, and were entertained:

> Hiro is approaching the Street. It is the Broadway, the Champs Élysées of the Metaverse. . . . [I]t does not really exist. But right now, millions of people are walking up and down it. . . . [O]f these billion potential computer owners, maybe a quarter of them actually bother to own computers, and a quarter of these have machines that are powerful enough. . . . [T]hat makes for about sixty million people who can be on the Street at any given time.[3]

In Stephenson's vision, the world's wealthiest and most connected people spend their time in the Metaverse. Coming on the heels of the pioneering virtual reality and interface work of Autodesk's John Walker and VPL Research's Jaron Lanier,[4] the vision of such a real place, with its social and economic opportunities, was enchanting and seemed almost within reach. Entrepreneurs and technologists immediately set out to build the Metaverse.

Unfortunately, creating the Metaverse proved to be an extremely difficult technical problem. While multiple graphical chat environments came and went during the 1990s, none of them achieved anything close to the complexity and realism portrayed in *Snow Crash.*[5] This period instead saw another type of online space establish itself as dominant: the "massively multiplayer online roleplaying game" (MMORPG). Others have done an excellent job of covering the history of MMORPGs,[6] so this essay will not cover that ground. As of late 2005 there are over three million MMORPG subscriptions in the United States alone, although some players subscribe to several online games.[7] The successes of MMORPGs combined with the failed attempts to build the Metaverse have left the concept of a broadly appealing Metaverse out of favor and out of reach.

The time has come to rehabilitate the idea of the Metaverse. Technological advances in three-dimensional graphics, network connectivity, and bandwidth have just begun to enable online spaces that embody the Metaverse concepts of user creation and broad use. Conventional MMORPGs are demonstrating the desire for online worlds that are economically linked to the real world, and also that social interaction is the dominant reason for users to spend time in-world.[8] However, MMORPGs are also demonstrating that the market for themed worlds is limited and is showing signs of leveling off.[9] Many MMORPG products have been launched under the auspices of bringing online role playing to the mass market, but none have succeeded.[10] The Metaverse has the potential to open dramatically larger markets by giving its users the vibrant complexity and dynamics of real-world cities rather than simple, repetitive game play.

This essay will argue that creating a defensibly real, online world is now possible if its users are given the power to collaboratively create the content within it, if those users receive broad rights to their creations, and if they are able to convert those creations into real-world capital and wealth. This would be the Metaverse of Stephenson's imagination.

The Need to Create

The scale of the Metaverse is difficult to comprehend. As graphics capability has increased, the cost of creating video games has increased as well. Nowhere is this more apparent than with MMORPGs, as Gordon Walton recently pointed out:

> The primary business challenge we face with art is that the costs for first-class art continue to rise faster than our market is expanding, and the

MMOGs [massively multiplayer online games] require tremendously more art assets than the vast majority of standalone games.[11]

MMORPGs are big. Really big. They have to provide hundreds of hours of game play to hundreds of thousands of players. While the challenge of entertaining players for this amount of time is helped by unscripted player-to-player interactions, much of the experience has to be designed and built by the game developers. This has led to large teams and lengthy development cycles, often involving thirty or more developers working for at least two years.

However, no matter how large a game world might become, it shrinks when compared to the Metaverse as described by Stephenson. Currently, the most ambitious MMORPGs target tens of thousands of simultaneous players in a shared space,[12] but a broadly appealing real online world might need to handle millions. Centralized planning fails on this scale, and some type of distributed creation is needed if there is to be any hope of creating an online world that dwarfs the complexity of the real world. The world's users provide a tremendous resource that must be leveraged to help create on a scale never before seen.

User Creativity

The Sims was the first mass-market game to heavily utilize player-created content. *The Sims* allows the player to control the lives of a number of virtual Sims who go about their day attempting to find happiness. Part of their happiness comes from the possessions their homes are filled with, so purchasing items like better chairs and stereo equipment is a focal point of the game. Will Wright and Electronic Arts understood that users would be able to supply more content to each other than the developers could create, so they released the tools to create content before the product was shipped. They now claim that over 80 percent of the content in use was created by the players.[13] Beyond customization, players have also built stories around screen shots captured in *The Sims*. Over 77,000 of these albums are posted and traded actively among players. The most popular album has been downloaded over 300,000 times![14]

This desire by players to make online worlds their own extends into games that do not support the type of customization allowed by *The Sims*. In *Ultima Online,* a fantasy themed MMORPG that was the first major

U.S. hit, users who wanted to decorate their homes came up with elaborate strategies for combining in-world objects in order to create images that look like real-world items. For example, there are several different techniques for making pianos[15] that involve dozens of different objects, ranging from wooden crates and chessboards to fish steaks and fancy shirts.

User creation does not end at the borders of the game. Machinima is the creation of movies within synthetic realities[16] and very often the synthetic reality of choice is an existing game engine. It is a relatively new phenomenon,[17] but it is spreading and achieving some mainstream success, including the establishment of a professional organization, the Academy of Machinima Arts and Sciences. *Quake* and *Unreal,* both extremely popular first-person shooter games where the player has full control over the camera and movement within the environment, are widely used by machinima creators. Film types include simple linear narratives, parody, and abstract exploration of the genre. These films demonstrate the quality and variety that a determined creator can produce when given the right tools.

Other forms of user-created content that extend beyond the game are mods. Mods rely on the fact that many first-person shooters, and some other games, allow users to modify some combination of artwork and game-play. The more flexible the engine, and again *Quake* and *Unreal* are standouts, the more variety in the mods, turning the original first-person shooters into everything from driving games to architectural walkthroughs. Websites devoted to mods[18] provide reviews and audiences for mods, prominently featuring the most popular mods. The mod community acts as a training ground for artists and developers who want to work on games. Particularly solid work is widely distributed and can provide the creators an entrée into the game development industry.

In Defense of User Creation

Some game developers, artists, writers, and musicians have a fear of user-created content. They say it takes a professional to provide superior content that will engage users and cause them to return. Raph Koster addressed this concern at the 2002 Game Developer's Conference:

> There's an intense amount of learning, craft and skill that goes there, and I hate to say this to all the film directors, writers, poets, painters and every-

one else out there in the world: Get over yourselves; the rest of the world is coming.[19]

While it is clear that not everyone can create great content, it is certain that some can. There are many examples that illustrate the point. *Counter-Strike* is a mod for the first-person shooter (FPS) *Half-Life*. In 1999 two avid FPS players,[20] working outside the game development world, created a game with the perfect blend of online teamwork, realism, and exciting gameplay to resonate with players. *Counter-Strike* spread virally through mod sites and quickly became the most downloaded mod. It was such a superb product that Valve Software, the creator of *Half-Life*, decided to package and distribute *Counter-Strike*. Four years later, *Counter-Strike* is by far the most played online FPS, with tens of thousands of users typically playing at any time.

It is also important to look at the desire of people in general to express themselves through creation and customization. Examples abound from the popularity of karaoke, cell phone faceplates and ring tones, to the 1.4 million active weblogs.[21] People want to be perceived as creative by customizing their surroundings. People want to have their moments on the stage. In many cases, it seems that users are just waiting for access to the right tools.

Productivity in Second Life

Second Life, an online world built by its users that launched in June 2003, is taking the first steps on the path to the Metaverse. Unlike other worlds that have attempted to allow user-created content, *Second Life* users create using built-in tools. These tools enable creation collaboratively in real-time instead of using separate programs. This allows users to create iteratively and interactively, while sharing the act of creation with other users. This encourages teams to work together on larger scale projects and creates the strong interpersonal bonds that are critical to online world success. Production occurs in-world, so there is no separate submission or preapproval process to inhibit creation.

Due to the in-world tools and lack of a submission process, *Second Life*'s users have been able to create an amazing amount of content. At the end of January 2006, users had created more than one hundred million objects, over thirty million examples of script code, and over ten million pieces of clothing and avatars.[22] Well over 99 percent of the objects in *Second Life* are user created, and users have responded positively to the idea of creating the world that they live in. Users also run classes and events to ensure that new residents understand how to create and customize within *Second Life*. Twenty percent of *Second Life* users are in-world more than fifteen hours per week; many of those hours are spent interacting and educating newcomers.[23] As knowledge spreads through the community, derived works become more important because users improve and innovate based on what has already been created.

In *Second Life*, creations are bought and sold within the virtual environment, so users provide a market for each other. They can be creators, consumers, or both. Over 6,000 different people used *Second Life* in January 2006.[24] Those people engaged in four million player-to-player transactions and spent over L$1.3 billion.[25] L$, or "Linden Dollars," are *Second Life*'s in-world currency. At the end of January 2006, the total value of the *Second Life* economy was more than L$2 billion.[26] The average transaction price was L$333 and there were 240,000 distinct objects bought and sold in-world, nearly twenty times the number of virtual-game goods for sale on eBay from all other online games combined.[27]

There is also a high degree of participation in creating the world and the economy. Sixty-six percent of *Second Life* users have created objects from scratch using the built-in modeling system in the last thirty days, and more than 15 percent have even written script code from scratch.[28] Over ninety percent have bought one or more objects from other users.[29] The average user spends more than one hour per week just on their avatar's appearance.

The collaborative nature of *Second Life* has also led to a strong and diverse social network, with users linked by both group memberships, chatting, and internal instant message (IM) buddy lists. In *Second Life*, chat provides a local method of communicating, such as saying "hello" to an avatar standing near you, while IM provides a private method of communicating over any distance. In *Second Life*, IM requires both participating users to have met and exchanged "calling cards" prior to engaging in IM. Again using January 2006 data, there were 75 million lines of Instant Message traffic.[30] Thirty-eight percent of users belong to at least one group and there are 350 groups with more than one hundred members.[31] While it has been argued that conflict is required to build strong social bonds, this is obviously not the case in *Second Life*.

True Creation

The desire to create and customize is a powerful force, and the distinction between mods and the *Ultima Online* piano illustrates a critically important point. Mods allow the creators to actually change the behavior of the game. The piano, on the other hand, is not a piano and cannot be played. It may look like a piano, but it is only a stack of crates and fish steaks. This is an excellent example of the difference between crafting and creation.

Crafting versus Creation

Crafting is not creating. While nearly synonymous in normal English usage, it is vitally important to understand what is meant by crafting in MMORPGs. Crafting is the process of advancing your character, or "leveling," through the repetitive generation of game objects.[32] Leveling relies on a complex system of skills and progressions that allows the player to unlock new abilities, visit new portions of the world, and generally become more powerful. The objects generated through crafting are chosen from the thousands provided by the developers,[33] and may be used by the crafting player, sold to other human players, or sold to nonplayer characters (NPCs) added to the game solely to act as buyers. These automated buyers are important because user leveling produces large quantities of items that are not useful or desired, so the NPCs are required to drain the unwanted items from the system.

In the real world, objects are created out of component parts of lesser value. A watch, for example, may be built from a few ounces of metal and a piece of glass. Despite the fact that the raw materials have negligible value, the watch may be extremely valuable due to the time and effort added in order to create a functional watch. This critical type of added value is present everywhere in the real world but is conspicuously absent from virtual worlds—the *Ultima Online* piano can't be played.

As many crafting systems involve the gathering of "raw materials"[34] and newer MMORPGs are adding more complicated schemes,[35] it might appear that crafting adds value in the same way as real-world creation. This is not the case. Developers use crafting based on "raw materials" to slow the rate of production, to limit the crafting of the best items, and to extend the life of content by obscuring which items are the best. Production is slowed because users must take the time to acquire the correct combination of raw materials. Crafting of the best items is limited through an artificial scarcity of raw materials. By presenting the users with a larger design space to search through, these items take more time to discover and to spread through the community. However, the users are still just choosing from the set of objects that the developers built into the game, and competitive pressures combined with communication between users will force rapid convergence onto the best items. Although the value of some of these items will be increased due to scarcity, this is fundamentally different from the value added in real-world creation. Users can't truly innovate because they are still just choosing from the items supplied by the developers.

Therefore, crafting will not work for the Metaverse because crafting has three critical problems. First, new content will not be created because the players are simply reusing content that was provided by the developers. Second, when users craft they are not adding value in the way that realworld creation does. Third, most of the objects that users take the time to craft while leveling have no market.

Users of the Metaverse need the ability to create. They must be able to create truly new objects, to add value and innovate during the process of creation, and the market must be allowed to determine which creations have real value. This requires an entirely different approach to creating inworld objects.

Atomistic Construction

Developers have long understood that creation requires a paradigm shift away from crafting. Atomistic construction, which relies on simple, easy to manipulate pieces that can be combined into large and complex creations, provides one solution. Referring to atomistic construction, Raph Koster stated at the 2002 Game Developer's Conference:

> So we can move to a meta-level of the crafting experience. We can try to take a step up and say, "We can do what Lego did," which is give them the building blocks[. . . .] That's a different level of authorship than what we are used to, but it's a really *exciting* area of authorship.[36]

Despite this knowledge, atomistic construction is not widely used because it is extremely difficult to implement. True flexibility only appears when the components assembled in arbitrary ways function and exhibit both predictable and emergent behavior. The balance between the two is critical.

Predictable behavior allows users to have some idea of how to explore the design space they are offered. People are better able to approach problems when some constraints are applied. Predictable behaviors such as "objects fall under the effect of gravity" or "objects collide with each other" provide these constraints.

Emergent behavior occurs when a set of rules interact in interesting and unexpected ways to allow experimenters and innovators to create truly new creations. For example, users working with the predictable rules of gravity and collision could have a contest to see whose catapult could throw an avatar the farthest or a user could attempt to build a chain of dominoes across the landscape.

While simplified online examples exist,[37] a real-time, interactive, fully three-dimensional, physically simulated implementation that allows multiple users to create collaboratively in a shared world is only just becoming technically feasible.[38] *Second Life* is the first and only persistent state world to offer its users this palette for online creativity, and it provides an exciting glimpse of the future of user creation and world building.

Atomistic construction becomes even more exciting when it exists in a collaborative environment where users can leverage their strengths. Specialization abounds in *Second Life,* with users focusing on everything from acting as project managers, salespeople, agents, and event coordinators, to creating script code to add behavior to objects or creating the two-dimensional textures that are applied to the objects. The combination of these users would allow an event coordinator to plan a wedding that required the project manager to hire builders and artists to build a new church. The coordinator could hire the caterer, dressmakers, and others to complete the objects and clothing for the wedding. Finally, skilled photographers would be in high demand to take in-world snapshots to create the wedding album. This importation of real-world skills into the online space is very different from role playing online worlds, where random values combined with the users' time in-game produce "skills" and "powers" that only exist within the limited framework of the game.

Building a motorcycle in *Second Life* demonstrates the power of atomistic construction. It is important to understand that nowhere in the *Second Life* software is there an object called a motorcycle. Instead, the physical simulation supports moving objects and motor forces, so users rapidly begin exploring different types of vehicles, including realistic motorcycles that can be driven and sold to other users. Motorcycles in *Second Life* are made up of a combination of geometric shapes and textures applied to provide color and detail. The geometry is constructed within the online world, so other users can help with the construction and provide feedback. The textures are uploaded into the system and can consist of everything from basic colors to details of engines and tires. The textures are actually positioned and aligned in-world, so again other users can assist in the process. For sounds, the user can upload audio samples to be played when the motorcycle is driven.

Second Life is running a full physics simulation at all times. Simple physical behaviors like falling and bouncing don't need to be created by the residents and are instead as simple as dropping an object. However, the computational power required to fully simulate a motorcycle down to the chemical energy in its internal combustion engine is beyond current server hardware. Therefore, in order to generate higher-level behaviors and effects, a scripting language is used. A script is a small piece of source code that is attached to objects in the virtual world that provides behaviors when it executes. For a motorcycle, the script handles the user's control inputs, triggers animations, plays sounds, and generates the forces to move the motorcycle. The result is a motorcycle that looks, sounds, and behaves something like a motorcycle in the real world. In addition, the flexibility of atomistic construction means that the user could modify a basic motorcycle to make it into a flying motorcycle that trailed ghostly, flaming skulls.

Looking ahead to the Metaverse, atomistic creation has another tremendous advantage because it scales with computing power. While the end of Moore's Law has been promised for years, for at least the next decade or two raw processing speed will continue to increase at approximately the eighteen-month doubling rate predicted thirty-five years ago.[39] Commodity server machines currently can simulate around 15,000 objects that range in scale from a centimeter to tens of meters, with many of those objects engaging in behavior and physical interaction at any time. The real world operates on a much smaller scale, from a hundred times smaller for even simple mechanical systems to a hundred thousand times smaller for chemical and biological processes. While computing a real-time simulation of complex mechanical or chemical processes is years away, every doubling of computer performance moves atomistic creation closer, opening up new creative opportunities. One can easily imagine a world where a motorcycle is actually simulating the motion of its engine, the transfer of torque through its transmission, and the complex friction and impulse calculations required as its tires spin loosely in a pile of small, irregular pebbles. Atomistic construction allows the system to smoothly expand what it simulates with increased computing speed in a way that conventional content creation through crafting cannot.

Economic Opportunities

Currently, the strength of online worlds is judged primarily by the number of subscribers they have. As online worlds grow and become more tightly meshed with the real world, a more appropriate measure of strength will be the health of their internal economies, the strength of their social networks, and the level of real-world wealth they generate. Less gamelike virtual worlds with vibrant internal economies powered by diversity and innovation become interesting destinations even for more casual users who do not have dozens of hours per week to spend in online worlds.

The tremendous variety enabled by atomistic construction combined with a free market and widespread participation has allowed *Second Life* users to explore a wide range of in-world professions. Some have become entrepreneurs, opening stores, bars, and strip clubs, and searching out creators to provide goods and services for them. Others choose more altruistic motives and live off the weekly L$ stipend. Fads follow innovation and waves of new ideas have repeatedly swept through the population, from wings to protest marches.[40] With rapid evolution and such a strong in-world economy, it was inevitable that users would want to own their creations.

The Question of Ownership

The status quo in online worlds is that their Terms of Service (ToS) include language that, to varying degrees, grants the rights to a user's creations to the service's operators. While there has been some user unhappiness related to these terms, most current online games offer such limited opportunities for creation—chat for example—that it has not become a pressing issue. However, using the ToS to block transfers of virtual goods is a major source of discontent and will be addressed below.

In worlds like *Second Life,* where user creation is a major component of the world and game play, a fundamental tension exists between asking the players to create the world and then having the world operators take ownership of everything they make. Users are now starting to recognize this. It was clear that the right choice was allowing users to retain as many rights as possible to their creations.

There is currently a spirited intellectual debate around the question of virtual goods and property.[41] This essay will not attempt to do that topic justice. While the argument that virtual goods are property might be flawed when applied to content created by the game's developers, it is clear that content built using atomistic creation is property and needs to be treated as such. Returning to the previous motorcycle example, intellectual property issues apply to it at many levels. The design of the motorcycle could be sufficiently new as to warrant protection. The script that provides its behavior could be particularly clever. A distinctive symbol could be used to let consumers know who built the motorcycle. Perhaps the user would want to write a graphic novel in the real world based around his or her avatar and motorcycle, and then option the movie rights. Clearly, there are laws that apply to all these situations. Rather than attempting to re-create intellectual property law, *Second Life*'s developers decided to allow real-world laws to reach into the virtual world. In November 2003, *Second Life*'s terms of service were changed to allow users to retain real-world intellectual property rights to their virtual creations.[42] The results of this decision will be closely watched in the years to come.

The real-world intrusions into virtual worlds raise important questions. Can play occur in worlds that allow real-world trade in items and currency?[43] Does commodification weaken designers' First Amendment protections in creating games?[44] As with virtual property, a complete review of these questions is beyond the scope of this essay,[45] but a few comments are warranted before moving on to why free markets and innovation are required to build the Metaverse.

The assertion that commodification prevents play is refuted by the real world, where play clearly exists alongside extensive commodification. Understanding this requires an important change in perspective, pulling back from tight focus on any particular game within the world to the level of the world itself. While the virtual world as a whole may be commodified, various activities within it will choose whether or not they want to be and will apply combinations of technical and social techniques to achieve their goal.

The freedom to create is even more interesting. Yale's Jack Balkin argues that commodification could apply as a litmus test, where virtual worlds that choose to tightly integrate with the real world lose their First Amendment protections.[46] Commodification-as-litmus test seems a poor choice for two reasons. First, as this essay demonstrates, commodification is a fundamental part of large virtual worlds. Second, basing First Amendment protection on commodification would be akin to arguing that National Public Radio has greater free speech than a for-profit broadcaster. Perhaps a richer vein would be to approach the regulation of commerce between the real and virtual worlds from the standpoint of consumer protection.

Commodification, Free Markets, and Innovation

Currently MMORPG developers are in a race that they cannot possibly win as they try to stay ahead of the users who choose to commodify their games' content and currency. The users are engaged in a highly efficient, distributed search to determine the games' weaknesses in order to exploit them for wealth and fame in both the real and virtual worlds. Raph Koster has suggested that humans work on puzzles until they master them,[47] and MMORPG players have the advantage of being extremely well connected to each other. Therefore, each patch and expansion pack becomes an attempt to stay ahead.

MMORPG game play drives its players to treat in-world items as commodities, because most players immediately realize that in order to advance their characters they will have to make enormous time commitments to the game. Simultaneously, they learn that many of the other players are students with significantly more free time than players with full-time, real-world jobs. Rather than simply not playing the game, time-constrained users can make the rational economic decision to use real-world currency to advance their character rather than time. It is debatable whether or not this is fun, but it certainly has the effect of allowing users to bypass the game designers' wishes about game pacing, advancement, and progress. It also creates a market in real-world currency for game items, game currency, and characters,[48] and rewards cheating[49] despite MMORPG developers' attempts to block the buying and selling of in-world content.[50]

Real-world markets for game items and currency reduce the amount of time players take to experience developed content by making it available to anyone willing to purchase it. In addition to attempting to block these markets, developers have converged on two approaches to stretching developed content: shards and instantiated spaces. Shards allow parallel exploration of the same content while instantiated spaces reuse content and support rapid development of specific experiences and quests. Shards also reduce the number of users a specific cluster of machines needs to support. They have the disadvantage of breaking the world up into relatively small populations and economies that cannot interact in-world—in other words, into parallel universes—but information about content and exploits still flows freely between residents of different shards. Information about instantiated spaces also moves between users and the rapid development cycles generally associated with small experiences puts limits on their flexibility and variety. So while these techniques extend the life of content, the users continue to rapidly consume existing content and to demand more.

Despite these challenges, developers and publishers should not cling to prohibition. Not only does banning users and attempting to block real-world transactions effectively criminalize and marginalize a large section of the user base, but it also fights one of the great benefits that free markets and competition bring to economies: innovation. As has already been discussed, online games have a tremendous creative resource in their players and atomistic creation provides limitless creativity. By allowing those users to freely compete in open markets, developers allow innovation to provide tangible benefits both to the innovator and the world itself.

Recently, "The Sleeper," a supposedly invincible monster in *EverQuest*, was killed through heroic effort and teamwork on the part of hundreds of users.[51] The knowledge of how to kill that monster is now available to any *EverQuest* player who wants it, and the developers are now in the position of having to spend development time and money to create a new invincible monster for the game. There was a clear desire to avoid this extra work. Indeed, the first serious attempt to kill "The Sleeper" was stopped by *EverQuest* developers.

In a world where user-created content rules and free markets allow creators to compete with each other, demand for a new invincible monster would drive users to create multiple successors. Developers would not have to fear their users' ingenuity. Many of these successors would rapidly be exposed as flawed or uninteresting, but there would be some that were exciting and worthwhile. A monster could be introduced with a new play mechanic that challenged players to defeat it in previously unexplored ways. By allowing free markets within worlds with true creation, developers grant their users power to innovate and to compete with the developers themselves. Developers should welcome this competition. The developers have enough inside knowledge and the ability to alter the underlying source code to create cutting edge content without needing tariffs or their equivalents to protect their place in the market. If a world's users are producing better content than the developers, then the developers should get out of the content business!

Of course, it may be inevitable that the residents of virtual worlds supplant developers. In the real world, innovation is the driving force behind sustained economic growth, but what factors maximize innovation? While obviously a complex issues, property rights[52] and information cost[53] appear to be the primary drivers, although significant tensions exist between the two.

Not every creator wants to capitalize on her work, but the potential to monetize creativity can be a powerful motivation. In virtual worlds, business can provide a context for creation. This is especially important in generalized spaces like the Metaverse, where the lack of a clearly defined game or progression can lead to confusion. Ownership, as will be discussed in the next section, is also necessary to support economic links to the real world. Historically, intellectual property law created limited monopolies in order to provide incentive for creators to invest the required time, effort, and money.[54] These protections are just as important for virtual-world creators as they are for creators in the real world. However, these protections must be balanced against the cost of information.

Information cost is a critical component of any economic activity. The lack of information leads to distrust, increased transactional costs, and ultimately to less innovation. Reductions in information costs, which also encompass travel and communication costs, have driven the transition to less centralized forms of government, from bands to monarchies to democracy, and corresponding increases in efficiency and economic strength. Decentralization has been so effective that modern businesses are following society's lead, with even large corporations adopting democratic and market-based approaches.[55]

Large potential payoffs aren't sufficient to force innovation, so laws and regulations that limit information flows actively impede economic growth. As Nobel Laureate Douglass C. North explains:

[T]he most fundamental long run source of change is learning by individuals and entrepreneurs of organizations. . . . The greater the degree of monopoly power the lower the incentive to learn.[56]

Before the modern era of strong intellectual property, a balance was maintained between protections and information costs, but now it is shifting toward the creator.[57] Fortunately, better intellectual property regimes exist.

In the real world, Creative Commons provides a set of licenses that attempt to maintain a better balance between the rights of creators and the cost of information.[58] Creative Commons recognizes that not every creator needs or wants his or her works to be completely protected. In fact, many creators want to enable wider distribution and copying in order to increase awareness of their works.[59] Creative Commons allows those creators to take advantage of licenses built on top of existing intellectual property law that allow numerous choices about modification, attribution, and commercial uses.[60] Creative Commons becomes even more exciting within the context of virtual worlds.

Virtual worlds, as has been pointed out,[61] have enormous potential for infringement. Everything is fixed, so many behaviors not normally protected in the real world, such as conversation or dancing, immediately become protected in virtual worlds. As such, it is easy to imagine a situation where legal concerns overwhelm the ability to share information, thus damping innovation. Creative Commons provides a method for avoiding this trap.

By allowing creators to easily choose licenses that best match their needs, and by allowing other creators to easily search for Creative Commons licensed content, a virtual world that used Creative Commons would provide far lower information costs than those that did not. Much like the real world, creators would quickly take advantage of Creative Common licenses to give away older and more commodified creations in order to raise awareness of their products and to gain new customers. New creators would be able to easily find learning material and would increase the overall competitive level within the virtual world. More importantly, Creative Commons provides a means for residents to share within a legal framework that functions both within and outside the virtual world.

Creative Commons, with its emphasis on copying with some limitations, naturally aligns with virtual property. Virtual items, after all, have no marginal cost of reproduction. Code and regulations attempt to prevent duplication, but this is clearly an artificial scarcity. In fact, there are many who believe that attempts to prevent copying are simply doomed to failure.[62] Virtual worlds will, out of necessity, pioneer solutions to virtual and digital property long before the real world does. By succeeding at this, their economies will enjoy a dramatic competitive advantage over the real world's.

By making the right intellectual property decisions, virtual worlds have the potential to be far more innovative than the real world, while still providing sufficient incentive for creators. This creative power leverages commodification rather than fearing it. This is critical, because commodification of virtual goods is happening whether developers want it to or not. Neither buying nor selling is an isolated behavior, and users are voting with their feet, using eBay and specialized auction and purchase sites, especially for worlds that explicitly ban it. PlayerAuctions, a site that grew as a result of eBay's ban on *EverQuest* items, boasts over a hundred thousand members.[63] Level 50 *EverQuest* characters cost $500 or more. It is easy to see why worlds without true user creation are scared of commodification. Fortunately for the Metaverse, free markets encourage exactly the kind of innovation that it will need.

Generating Income and Capital

The commodification of virtual goods is not enough to create the free markets the Metaverse requires. Players and businesses are already providing users with the advancement they desire, often taking advantage of cheats[64] and cheaper labor markets[65] in order to meet demand, but MMORPG operators are responding with legal action[66] and account shutdowns.[67] These responses are justified by ToS prohibitions on generating income via the product, although they are not yet a comprehensive attempt to stop item and account sales. The Metaverse must not do this.

Creating the Metaverse is such a tremendous undertaking that it will need to happen in a distributed fashion, requiring the commitment of time and resources from its diverse set of early users and creators. Current MMORPGs demonstrate conclusively that virtual goods can have significant real-world value, and any world that hopes to bootstrap itself into the Metaverse must allow these real-world economic opportunities. Distributed creation combined with atomistic construction's ability to add value to every creation means that the Metaverse must allow moneymaking activities and must allow users to own their creations. However, owner-ship is critical for another only recently understood reason.

New insight comes from Hernando de Soto's work in developmental economics, *The Mystery of Capital.*[68] In brief, de Soto argues that when property does not have recognized titles and proofs of ownership, it is not fungible. Thus, the vast majority of the developing world's population, despite having valuable assets like homes, land, and businesses, cannot leverage these assets because they do not legally own them. The ramifica-tions are far-reaching. Some may not be able to obtain telephone service because their home is not at a legal address, while others are not able to insure their business because there is no business license on record. Most relevant to the Metaverse, untitled property cannot be used to secure loans or to set up a legal business.

On the way to the Metaverse, individuals and businesses will create objects of significant value, and many will be handsomely rewarded for it. However, for some of these creators the short-term gains will not be their ultimate goal. Instead, these entrepreneurs will see the opportunity to leverage their wealth to create the next opportunity. Individual investors and venture capitalists will be approached first, but if those options fail the digital entrepreneurs could go to a real-world bank and apply for a loan, using virtual property as collateral. Virtual pioneers are going to have a hard time convincing the bank to give them the loan, but consider how much more difficult the process would be if they do not actually own the property. In the real world, lack of ownership is a fatal flaw in attempts to establish successful free markets.[69] It would be a mistake to think that virtual worlds will be any different—free markets and property rights are prerequisites to innovation.

In fact, one of the few missteps in *Snow Crash* is that its main character has significant virtual wealth but not real-world wealth.[70] For the Meta-verse to be successful, virtual wealth must be convertible to real wealth.

To the Metaverse

A decade after the first glimpses of the Metaverse, technology is now on the cusp of enabling real, shared online spaces. MMORPGs continue to advance technology and educate users about virtual worlds. They demon-strate that real-world wealth can be generated in online spaces. At the same time, MMORPG developers are fighting a rearguard action against the very users who are benefiting from this wealth while struggling to create enough content for their users to consume.

The Metaverse needs to be built differently. It will be so enormous that only distributed approaches to creation have any hope of generating its content. Thus users must build the world they live in. It must expand through viral growth and produce an increasing supply of active creators who create wealth within a generalized virtual world. These residents will draw in the casual users to play games, provide an audience, and become customers. This provides both the supply and demand for the Metaverse's enormous free market of goods and services. This free market requires creators to have ownership and rights, thereby generating both wealth and capital in order to fuel growth. By then the Metaverse tip and the world, both real and online, will never be the same.

NOTES

1. Orson Scott Card, *Ender's Game* (1985).

2. William Gibson, *Neuromancer* (1984).

3. Neal Stephenson, *Snow Crash*, 23–25 (2000).

4. John Perry Barlow, *Being in Nothingness*, at http://www.eff.org/Publications/John_Perry_Barlow/HTML/being_in_nothingness.html (last visited Nov. 22, 2003).

5. Raph Koster, *Online World Timeline*, at http://www.legendmud.org/raph/gaming/mudtimeline.html (last visited Nov. 22, 2003).

6. *Id.* See also Jessica Mulligan and Bridgette Patrovsky, *Developing Online Games: An Insider's Guide* (2003).

7. Bruce Sterling Woodcock, *An Analysis of MMOG Subscription Growth—Version 8.0, at* http://www.mmogchart.org (last visited April 9, 2006).

8. Nick Yee, *Empirical Framework of User Motivations, at* http://terranova.blogs.com/terra_nova/2003/11/empirical_frame.html (last visited Nov. 28, 2003).

9. Woodcock, *supra* note 7.

10. Steven L. Kent, *Making an MMOG for the Masses, at* http://www.gamespy.com/amdmmog/week3 (last visited Dec. 4, 2003).

11. Gordon Walton, *Online Worlds Roundtable #8, Part 1, at* http://rpgvault.ign.com/articles/455/455832p2.html (last visited Nov. 23, 2003).

12. *Wish FAQ, at* http://www.mutablerealms.com. (last visited Nov. 23, 2003).

13. David Becker, *The Secret Behind the Sims, at* http://news.com.com/2008-1082-254218.html (last visited Mar. 16, 2001).

14. *The Sims, at* http://thesims.ea.com/us/index.html (last visited Dec. 2, 2003).

15. *How to Make the Pianos, at* http://uo.stratics.com/homes/betterhomes/ essay_piano.shtml (last visited Nov. 23, 2003).

16. *What Is Machinima? at* http://www.machinima.com/displayarticle2 .php?article=187 (last visited Nov. 23, 2003).

17. *Machinima, at* http://en2.wikipedia.org/wiki/Machinima (last visited Nov. 23, 2003).

18. *PlanetQuake Featured Mods, at* http://www.planetquake.com/features/motw/ (last visited Dec. 4, 2003).

19. Jessica Mulligan, *Much Water under the Bridge, Much Beer over the Dam . . . , at* http://www.skotos.net/articles/BTH_33.shtml (last visited Sept. 3, 2002).

20. *The CS Team, at* http://counter-strike.net/csteam.html (last visited Nov. 23, 2003); *The History of* Counter-Strike: *Part 1, at* http://www.csbanana.com/ csb_page.banana?page=24 (last visited Nov. 23, 2003).

21. Jeffrey Henning, *The Blogging Iceberg—Of 4.12 Million Hosted Weblogs, Most Little Seen, Quickly Abandoned, at* http://www.perseusdevelopment.com/ corporate/news_shell.php?record=51 (last visited Nov. 23, 2003).

22. *Second Life* customer database, gathered by the author on February 1, 2006.

23. *Id.*

24. *Id.*

25. *Id.*

26. *Id.*

27. *eBay Internet Games Page, at* http://www.ebay.com (last visited April 9, 2006).

28. *Second Life* database, *supra* note 22.

29. *Id.*

30. *Id.*

31. *Id.*

32. Timothy Burke, *The Mystery of* Star Wars: Galaxies, *at* http://www. swarthmore.edu/socsci/tburke1/swgmystery.html (last visited Oct. 22, 2003).

33. *Stratics Central, at* http://stratics.com (last visited Nov. 23, 2003).

34. *Blacksmithy, at* http://guide.uo.com/skill_7.html (last visited Dec. 4, 2003).

35. *Crafting Level 1, at* http://starwarsgalaxies.station.sony.com/content .jsp?page=Crafting%20Chapter%201 (last visited Dec. 4, 2003).

36. Mulligan, *supra* note 19.

37. *Sodaconstructor, at* http://www.sodaplay.com/constructor/index.htm (last visited Nov. 23, 2003).

38. Philip Rosedale and Cory Ondrejka, *Enabling Player-Created Online Worlds with Grid Computing and Streaming, at* http://www.gamasutra.com/ resource_guide/20030916/rosedale_01.shtml (last visited Sept. 18, 2003).

39. Charles C. Mann, "The End of Moore's Law?" Technology Review,

May/June 2000, pp. 43–48; Michael Kanellos, *End Draws Near for Moore's Law*, at http://www.msnbc.com/news/999894.asp?cp1=1 (last visited Dec. 1, 2003).

40. James Grimmelmann, *The State of Play: On the Second Life Tax Revolt*, at http://research.yale.edu/lawmeme/modules.php?name=News&file=article&sid=1222 (last visited Sept. 21, 2003).

41. Dan Hunter and F. Gregory Lastrowka, *Virtual Property*, at http://www.nyls.edu/docs/hunter_lastowka.pdf (last visited Oct. 21, 2003).

42. *Second Life Terms of Service and End User License Agreement for Second Life*, at http://secondlife.com/corporate/terms.php (last visited Dec. 4, 2003).

43. Edward Castronova, *The Right to Play*, at http://www.nyls.edu/docs/castronova.pdf (last visited Nov. 23, 2003). *Also see* Chapter 5, this volume.

44. Jack M. Balkin, *Virtual Liberty: Freedom to Design and Freedom to Play in Virtual Worlds*, 90 Va. L. Rev. 2043 (2004).

45. Cory Ondrejka, *Living on the Edge*, at http://papers.ssrn.com/sol3/papers.cfm?abstract_id=555661 (last visited July 7, 2004).

46. Balkin, *supra* note 44.

47. Raph Koster, *A Theory of Fun*, at http://www.legendmud.org/raph/gaming/theoryoffun.html (last visited Sept. 12, 2003).

48. *eBay Internet Games Page*, at http://www.ebay.com (last visited Nov. 23, 2003); *PayPal Shops->Search Results for "EverQuest,"* at http://www.paypal.com/cgi-bin/webscr?cmd=_shop-search-ext&pid=0&q=everquest (last visited Nov. 25, 2003); *IGE Everquest Page*, at http://www.ige.com/main.asp (last visited Nov. 25, 2003); *Player Auctions*, at http://playerauctions.com (last visited Nov. 25, 2003).

49. Julian Dibbell, *Serfing the Web: Black Snow Interactive and the World's First Virtual Sweat Shop*, at http://www.juliandibbell.com/texts/blacksnow.html (last visited Nov. 25, 2003).

50. Bruce Rolston, *Ebay Bans EverQuest Auctions*, at http://avault.com/news/displaynews.asp?story=1192001-94048 (last visited Jan. 19, 2003).

51. Andrew Phelps, *I Saw God and I Killed It*, at http://www.corante.com/gotgame/archives20031101.html#61354 (last visited Nov. 25, 2003).

52. William Bernstein, *The Birth of Plenty* (2004).

53. Douglass C. North, *Economic Performance through Time*, at http://members.shaw.ca/compilerpress1/Anno%20North%20Econ%20Perform%20thru%20Time.htm (last visited June 1, 2004).

54. Mark Lemley, *Ex Ante Versus Ex Post Justifications for Intellectual Property*, at http://papers.ssrn.com/sol3/papers.cfm?abstract_id= 494424 (last visited June 1, 2004); Neil Netanel, *Copyright and a Democratic Civil Society*, at http://www.utexas.edu/law/faculty/nnetanel/yljarticle.htm (last visited June 1, 2004).

55. Thomas W. Malone, *The Future of Work* (2004).

56. North, *supra* note 53.

57. Lawrence Lessig, *Free Culture* (2004).

58. *Creative Commons Homepage, at* http://www.creativecommons.org (last visited on Sept. 26, 2004).

59. Glenn Otis Brown, *Cory Doctorow, at* http://creativecommons.org/getcontent/features/doctorow (last visited Sept. 26, 2004).

60. *Creative Commons Homepage, supra* note 58.

61. James Grimmelmann, *The State of Play: Free as in Gaming? at* http://research.yale.edu/lawmeme/modules.php?name=News&file=article&sid=1290 (last visited Sept. 26, 2004).

62. Cory Doctorow, *Microsoft Research DRM Talk, at* http://www.craphound.com/msftdrm.txt (last visited Sept. 26, 2004).

63. *PlayerAuctions Homepage, at* http://www.playerauctions.com (last visited Nov. 26, 2003).

64. Julian Dibbell, *Serfing the Web: Black Snow Interactive and the World's First Virtual Sweat Shop, at* http://www.juliandibbell.com/texts/blacksnow.html (last visited Nov. 25, 2003).

65. Julian Dibbell, *Play Money, Meet Big Money, at* http://www.juliandibbell.com/playmoney/index.html (last visited Nov. 18, 2003).

66. Dibbell, *supra* note 64.

67. Bob Kiblinger, comment to "Who Owns My Lightsaber?" thread, *at* http://terranova.blogs.com/terra_nova/2003/10/who_owns_my_lig.html#c273443 (last visited Nov. 2, 2003).

68. Hernando de Soto, *The Mystery of Capital* (2000)

69. *Id. at* 39–68.

70. Stephenson, *supra* note 3.

11

There Is No Spoon

Yochai Benkler

Virtual worlds are like *The Matrix*. The answer to the question: "Who should own this spoon, the provider or the user?" is, *there is no spoon.* Once you understand this, the discussions of "virtual worlds" bring about an eerie déjà vu—"it feels like you're in a room," it's a "virtual community," we should have a "declaration of independence" for "new spaces for self-governance." There is code, interface, and the social relations they make possible. There is no "governance of a virtual world." There is simply the question of governance in the relations among users of a class of software platforms that have certain degrees of freedom in their design, resulting in a variety of social affordances, and therefore facilitating a variety of social and economic interactions.

The phenomena that fall under the moniker of "virtual worlds" combine three discrete components that tend to be confused in the debate over property and governance relations among the users of these software platforms. First, the interface. They offer richly instantiated renderings of the communications of users and the interactions among them. Second, these interfaces were initially developed, and have received widest adoption, as platforms for immersive human play. And third, they have begun to be used as platforms for other types of human connection, most clearly and distinctly for collaborative creativity on the one hand, and as both platforms for and objects of trade on the other hand.

To analyze the proper institutional arrangement for the various social relations mediated by the software platforms we now call "virtual worlds" we have to get rid of the fascination with the rendering. Really. *There is no spoon.* When a richly rendered collaboration platform is used by its users to coauthor a story—as when users of *Second Life* "build" a "town" with a theme—it is a platform that is part of a category with Wikis (electronic collaboration tools), parts of the blogosphere, or Slash (the software engine that powers Slashdot and many other collaborative websites). That is, it is a form of social software, mediating a social relation among individuals who have no preexisting relations, and are weakly tied through a group interaction whose stickiness comes from the possibility of shared efficacy among its users. When the rich rendering is a fancy front end for an online store, whether for mail-order real things or for "downloads" of music, patterns, or images, as in the case of *There,* then it is part of a category of human interactions with Amazon or AOL. When users are engaged in a shoot-'em-up, bang whiz mad rush, then they are engaging in a shoot-'em-up, bang whiz. The difference in rendering matters because it may change how attractive, immersive, or dull the experience is, and it may effect whether or not the activity will seriously challenge Terminator IV. They are part of the same phenomenon as Dungeons and Dragons, and maybe *Star Trek.*

So now take the question of property. Castronova beseeches us to reject the commodification of virtual worlds so as to preserve their role as play arenas. But that cannot be a criticism of *There* any more than it would be a criticism of AOL or Amazon. *There* is not a play arena, it is an e-commerce interface. The "play" it offers is like the "play" that malls offer. There may be a movie theatre, there may be rides for kids, but it is a transactional platform. Castronova's question is not wrong. But "should there be property relations and commodification of game objects, or will this spoil the game?" is not a policy question, but a design question aimed at a certain class of platform providers. That is, it is addressed properly not to judges or regulators, but to the engineers who design game platforms and to their business managers or marketers. The claim is that, if you want the platform that you are building to be a game, make it hard, not easy, to real-world-commodify your game objects and moves. This may or may not be correct as a sociological and psychological matter. I don't know. But it is not a policy question, it is a question of marketing immersive game environment and e-commerce sites, not of governing virtual worlds.

Should there be property in *Second Life* objects, which is owned by the users who created it, and may be subject to easy-to-use creative commons licenses? Again, this is a design question, not a policy question. At baseline, as visually attractive immersive entertainment, "virtual worlds" occupy, in some part, the same role that Hollywood movies and some television shows play: escapist, engaging entertainment. On that dimension they are much more attractive normatively than Hollywood movies or the soaps. Whereas video entertainment places the users in a passive role, as pure recipients of content made by others, virtual worlds allow users to make their own stories. Users are constructed in a fashion that makes them both more autonomous and more sociable. Nowhere is this clearer than in *Second Life,* where almost all objects, and all story lines—in the sense of villages and areas—are created by the users, for the users. *Second Life* offers a model for a relationship between the market-based provider of an entertainment platform and its consumer/user that is fundamentally different from the relationship of the movie studio to the movie viewer. What makes this plausible substitutability is the quality of the rendering. But a central part of this difference depends on the kind of social interaction made possible by the platform; in other words, the kind of social software that it will be.

So should property relations be part of the social relationship for which *Second Life* provides a platform? The question is not one of prediction about whether courts will find rights here. Jack Balkin is right that someone will get hurt, some time, and particularly where there is money at stake the law will come in to this space and do its damage, or maybe its repair. But games are not company towns or regulated common carriers. Users have the option of joining one, or the other, and it takes a lot more concentration and forcing to persuade courts to void contractual terms that are not about tort liability and harm to third parties, but are about exchanges or disclaimers of proprietary claims. So the question of property is a question of institutional design of the platform: Should the EULA, or the policy adopted by a volunteer-run platform, be structured to assure that individual users retain individual proprietary rights in game objects they design using the platform, subject to case-by-case, object-by-object, user-by-user, full or partial, disclaimer through a Creative Commons license, or should there be a single moment of collective disclaimer, collective mutual commitment to share all that the participants in the social interaction build? Should the platform make the products of the acts of collective creation free as the air to common use?

"Should" is a word that calls for a normative judgment. "Should" could be answered based on a normative commitment to making money. The platform providers could ask: "Will this make us richer?" That is not a question to which I will endeavor to offer a direct answer here, but there may be indirect implications for this question too—that is, if users join a platform and pay a fee because it offers them attractive relations with others and an opportunity to be highly creative, then those characteristics that will make for cohesive social relations and heightened creativity will also increase the attractiveness of the platform to subscribers. But the interesting questions are, which approach will better foster creativity on this platform, give users greater creative autonomy, and create a more effective social network?

To answer this question we have to define the relationship that the platform is aimed to facilitate. Cory Ondrejka wrote that the vision behind *Second Life* was Stephenson's Metaverse. In other words, a richly rendered general purpose platform. The Internet with avatars. Given this broad definition, the designers of *Second Life* saw a need to provide a transactional framework and engine, alongside the tools and mechanisms for nonmarket creative collaboration and communication. Fair enough for that ambition, and if that is the ambition, building in easy-to-use Creative Commons licenses is clearly preferable to not having them, from the perspective of avoiding some of the standard dampening effects that exclusive rights in information have on incremental innovation and creativity. But a Metaverse, a social platform that has all the degrees of freedom of the real world built in, is by no means an obvious best goal from the perspective of building a creative platform for people who want to cocreate. It is possible that an environment that has different, perhaps even more limited, affordances, and hence is likely to generate different modes of human interaction, would be better. The basic position is that free social sharing of a creation is a different social experience than exchanges interlaced with markets; that free creative borrowing is a different creative experience and a different cultural form than sales-oriented pervasive licensing; and that "virtual-world" designers have at their disposal toggles that would allow them to build creative collaboration platforms that are distinctly safe for noncommodified collaborative creativity based on social sharing. The choice to use them or not to use them is not dictated by economic efficiency or by technology. It is a choice that structures the environment as a cultural artifact and as a form of social software.

To see how constraining the institutional degrees of freedom open to participants in structuring their relations with others can optimize the platform for shared creativity we need to stop looking at the pretty pictures. We need to ask why a Metaverse approach is better than Wikipedia's decision that all contributions to Wikipedia are deemed to be a license of the contribution under the GNU Free Documentation License, or the decision of the free software movement and most open source projects to license their contributions in ways that limit the ability of individual contributors to exclude others from their contributions to the common effort. The dampening effects of exclusive rights on creation are well understood in the economics literature. Existing information—software, source materials for Wikipeda articles, other user's objects and scripts for *Second Life* users—is one of the two primary inputs into new creation (human creativity is the other). If you enclose it, you make it, at the margin, less available. If you pepper the environment with potential inputs that have diverse permissions and prohibitions, you increase this effect.

Whether there are beneficial effects to introducing exclusive rights, on the other hand, depends on how one understands the motivation of the participants. If, as Eben Moglen poetically put it, "it's an emergent property of connected human minds that they create things for one another's pleasure and to conquer their uneasy sense of being too alone," then the beneficial effect of introducing copyrights is minimal to nonexistent, while its dampening effects remain. Rather than an ontological claim about the nature of all human minds, this can be taken to be an empirical claim about a subset of human beings—those who are drawn to writing free software or collaborating on a massive free encyclopedia—or a subset of human behavior—most human beings have times when we, who also know how to search for money, seek something else, namely, connectedness with others. In the case of designing *Second Life*, or maybe *Second Life* prime, the question is a very straightforward empirical one. Do users pay $x per month in the expectation that they will create something that they can later license to others for a fee, or do they pay that sum in order to get access to a platform of creative tools and connections with creative others, so that they can collaborate on cocreating story lines and pretty pictures of their own? If the latter is descriptively true of the motivational profile of Second Lifers, then introducing © into the game, no matter how modulated by (cc) (Creative Commons) permissions, mostly introduces drag. The effect of free, open collaboration that would result from everyone adopting the most expansive Creative Commons licenses for all their individual contributions could be achieved more directly by the EULA stating that, as a precondition to participating in *Second Life*, every user licenses every creation based on collaborations on this platform under a GFDL or a Creative Commons ShareAlike license.

The desirability of one licensing regime or another must be considered from the perspective of the social function. The best arrangement for *There* is an institutional design problem that is similar to AOL or Amazon user-created content. The best arrangement for *Second Life*—whose basic design characteristic is that what it offers is a collaborative creation platform—is a problem similar to Wikipedia. That the content produced on the former consists of richly rendered graphic objects rather than the textual definitions produced in the latter is irrelevant. Both are platforms for large-scale collaboration among users who are engaged in the practice because they wish to participate in the collaborative creative exercise that the platform enables. As Clay Shirky captured so well, the "user" of social software is the group, not the individual. The best design is therefore the design that will best enable the group to keep its cohesion, to avoid the centrifugal forces that our irrepressible individuality places on groups. To explain to themselves why adopting © + (cc) as its policy is a good idea for *Second Life,* the systems designers have to answer to themselves in what way they are different from Wikipedia and SourceForge, not in what way they are different than *There.* The latter question is trivial. The former, far from it.

The freedom to make together may sometimes require restrictions on the degrees of institutional freedom that participants have within the relationship, as long as they continue to choose to be participants. A rule that prohibits handling a soccer ball "limits" the freedom of players. But without it soccer would not be soccer, and no one would be able to play the game. A common creative relationship in which everyone retains the freedom to exclude everyone else from their own contributions is different from common creative relationships where all have ceded their rights to exclude anyone else. The latter emphasizes the mutual dependence and reliance of the participants on each other's creativity, rather than the individual components that each contributes. Creative collaborations like free software or Wikipedia that rely on large amounts of incremental, iterative acts of creation, built from large numbers of contributions from diverse contributors, have adopted an institutional framework through which each contributor eschews the right to exclude. They thereby create a commons, out of which everyone is free to take as they please and into which everyone is precommitted to contributing everything they add. By so constructing their institutional environment, they have become highly effective and sustainable models of creative collaboration, while retaining large amounts of freedom of action for their participants that would have been more, rather than less constrained, if every new act of creativity had required them to seek the permission of others whose work they wished to extend.

There is no spoon. There are only social relations mediated by richly rendered communications platforms. The question of "who should own this spoon?" should be understood as a question about what we want the social relations using the platform to be like. That question requires that we define a range of social relations that we believe the platform will enable, and a normative belief about how those relations should go. The rest is lawyering—constructing the detailed institutional structure within which these social relations will then be played out.

iv

Privacy and Identity in Virtual Worlds

12

Who Killed Miss Norway?

Tracy Spaight

In the spring of 2002, after more than a year in preproduction, I began work on "Real People Virtual Worlds," a documentary film exploring how people interact with each other in the graphically and textually mediated settings of online worlds. Along the way, I expected to interview people who make like they're elves or slay monsters or just hang out in virtual taverns with their virtual friends. And I did. What I didn't expect is that I'd stumble into a real-life murder mystery, complete with intrigue, deception, and, ultimately, the disappearance and death of a beauty queen.

Karyn logged onto LegendMUD for the first time in the fall of 1996. A law student at the University of Oslo, she found the novelty of Legend-MUD—a text-based virtual world that promised "adventures in a place both strange and familiar"—a welcome respite from her studies. As a newcomer to the world of multiuser dungeons, Karyn was eager to learn more about the art of being someone else. "I started out being me," she confessed at a role-playing discussion in the out-of-character auditorium (where players can take off their masks, so to speak, and just be themselves). In her charmingly broken English, she added, "I have never done anything like playing games like this." The MUD's denizens welcomed the Norwegian newcomer into their community and offered her advice on how to become a role player.

Being the sort of person who makes friends easily, Karyn decided to pursue the life of a merchant within the game. She learned how to acquire items in remote or dangerous parts of the fantasy world of LegendMUD, transport them back to town, and sell them (at a nice markup) to other players who lacked the knowledge or the time (or the patience) to set off and find the items for themselves. Before long, she had formed a mercantile group called the Norse Traders—like horse traders, but with Vikings. The Norse Traders, under her leadership, emerged as a powerful, well-respected guild. All because of Karyn.

Years later, on the other side of the world, I sit in front of my computer reading about Karyn's adventures in this virtual world. I reflect on the fact that the entire community, indeed the whole universe that was and remains LegendMUD, ran on a 486 desktop computer that sat under a desk in Austin, Texas. I page through the archives of LegendMUD, reading about her life.

"Thanks to Beam, Point, Landy, Aermid, Rummy, Outsider, Manic, and the many others who have helped me so far," she wrote on her website. These were her friends in the game—people she knew (and who knew her) only through a blinking cursor on the screen. And yet the group had formed lasting friendships. I look at the photograph on her LegendMUD web page. A beautiful young woman, wearing a "Miss Norway finalist" sash, smiles back at me. The caption reads, "This photo is taken at the Miss Norway 1995 contest. The guys on the picture are some of the contestants in the Mr. Norway contest, and the girl in the back is Monica, a friend of mine, also participating in the pageant. You should now be able to determine who's who on the picture, including who's me."

It's painful to read the details of her life, knowing that it was about to come to an abrupt and tragic end. On January 29, 1998, Karyn and a friend were out test-driving a Porsche 911. Sometime around 6 P.M., they crossed over the center lane of a stretch of highway outside Trondheim and collided head-on with a Volkswagen. Karyn and her friend were killed instantly, as was the driver of the other vehicle. Or was she? Karyn's death would soon become a cause célèbre in virtual-world circles. The more I looked into the story, however, the more I began to suspect foul play.

When your friend logs out of a virtual world, his or her avatar remains in the world for a moment or two and then blinks out of existence. You expect to see the friend again tomorrow evening. Or maybe the day after that. But sometimes your friend doesn't return. Weeks pass. Then months. Most often it's because the person has grown tired of the game and has moved on. But on rare occasions, it's because the individual behind the keyboard has blinked out of existence in the real world. And in the real world, that person won't magically reappear with an experience hit or stat loss. Death in reality is permanent.

Without Karyn's leadership, the Norse Traders began to fall apart. Weeks passed. People knew that something was wrong but couldn't figure out what. Then someone realized: Karyn was missing. E-mails were sent out, but she didn't reply. Where was she? Was she in trouble? Some friends decided to investigate. What they found shocked the community to its core. Posted on Karyn's home page was a newspaper article reporting her death and a letter from her parents. Karyn was no more. Real life had become real death. She was gone.

In a virtual world, as in real life, people mourn the passing of a friend. Given the nature of Internet communities, it's not surprising that there is often a lag of weeks or even months before news of a person's real-world demise arrives in the virtual realm. When the news of Karyn's death finally reached LegendMUD, the outpouring of grief was immediate and heartfelt. The message boards in every tavern quickly overflowed with expressions of sorrow.

"I will always remember the good times we had," one of them read, "the good laughs we shared, and the chats. I didn't knew [sic] much about you, but one thing is for sure, you were a good friend to me. You had a good heart."

News of Karyn's death soon spread to other virtual lands. Even players who had never met Karyn, or even played on LegendMUD, sent messages to express their sorrow. As a player of Discworld (an unrelated virtual world) wrote: "We play 'games' like this one here on the Internet, often without realizing how our actions affect *real* people, perhaps thousands of miles away, on the other side of a telnet session. We form friendships that outgrow the boundaries of any simple 'game'; sometimes, we even fall in love. How can this be, that we experience such profound emotion from a game, with people that we have never met face to face? It is my hope that those that read of your story will reflect upon the relationships that *they* have built, playing these 'games,' and try to realize the importance of building lasting, caring friendships wherever possible, because life is fleeting."

In response to player requests, the immortals (the administrators of the MUD) decided to construct a "Garden of Remembrance" to honor Karyn's memory. After many hours of wandering around LegendMUD, I finally stumbled across it. When I (metaphorically) entered the room (actually, a database record), the following text was displayed:

The Garden of Remembrance

This ever-lit room exists in memory of the people that had brought light to the land of Legend and left us prematurely. The grass grows soft and green, the sky above seems always to be a perfect, endless blue. The memories of friendship and laughter and joy abound. A rose garden lies to the east and a quiet pond to the west. An imposing arch of trees leads out to the north.

A small tree is here, lovingly planted in memory of Karyn. A brass plaque has been placed in front of the tree.

The plaque reads: "In Memory of Karyn whose kindness and companionship will always be missed."

Raph Koster, at the time one of LegendMUD's administrators and now the lead designer of Sony's *Star Wars Galaxies,* wrote a eulogy for Karyn that has been widely reprinted over the past five years. He called it "A Story about a Tree," and originally told it at a luncheon for *Ultima Online* players (he was also the lead designer of UO) in May 1998. In his essay, Raph describes the friendships that Karyn made in the game and the difficulty players had in articulating the grief they felt over the loss of someone they had never met in real life. The Garden of Remembrance, in Raph's view, marked a defining moment in the consciousness of the online gaming community:

> In the end, that garden and that tree served not only as a memorial to a well-loved and much-missed person, but as a marker of a moment, a moment in which the players of an online game realized that they weren't "playing a game." That the social bonds that they felt within this "game" were Real. . . . Sometimes it takes a moment of grief to make people realize it, and sometimes people just come to an awareness over time, but the fundamental fact remains: when we make a friend, hurt someone's feelings, suffer a loss, or accomplish something in an online world, it's real. It's not "just a game." I am not going to let anyone tell me that the Garden of Remembrance isn't Real, or that the grief we all felt over Karyn's death was not Real. And I hope that UO players aren't going to let anyone tell them that their experiences within UO aren't Real either, that it's "just a game." It may be for some people, but we all know better, don't we? For Karyn's sake, and also for our own.

This "Garden in the Machine" helped the community come to terms with the loss of their friend in the virtual and real worlds. Five years later, however, the wounds would be reopened in a way few could have imagined.

In the spring of 2002, I mailed a demo tape of my film to Richard Bartle, cocreator of the first multiuser dungeon. The tape included footage of Raph Koster talking about the Garden of Remembrance. Karyn's story immediately set off alarm bells for Richard; he'd seen similar situations in other online communities and smelled a rat. Had anyone actually checked the story? Was there corroborative evidence? I decided to do some research.

According to Karyn's memorial page on LegendMUD, she attended the law school at the University of Oslo. I decided to start there. I contacted the university to see if they had some record of a twenty-four-year-old female law student dying in January 1998. The woman I spoke with reported that they had no record of any law student of any name dying in a car wreck in January 1998. OK, so perhaps Karyn exaggerated her educational attainments a bit. It wouldn't be the first time that someone had padded their résumé.

I next turned to Karyn's foray into the glamorous world of beauty pageants. I sent a letter to Geir Hamnes, the director of the Frøken Norge competition, asking about the identity of the woman in the photograph posted on Karyn's memorial page on LegendMUD. Geir replied that her name was Trine Solberg Lepperød, a finalist in the 1995 competition. Had I stumbled across the real Karyn? Excitedly, I fired off an e-mail to Geir, asking if Trine had died in a car crash a few years back. "No," Geir replied, "she's alive and lives in Oslo." He gave me her e-mail address.

I sent Trine an e-mail. Two days later she replied that yes, she was the woman in the photograph, but that she had never heard of LegendMUD. Trine was startled to learn about her own death. "I was scared by all these letters this 'Karyn' person got," she told me, after looking at the memorial on the website, "since the picture is of me and I am alive!" Trine, who is now a product assistant in a textile business, had no idea how anyone who was not at the competition could have acquired the photo, since to her knowledge it had never been published anywhere.

This left the matter of the newspaper article that had been posted on Karyn's web page. Surely a scanned newspaper article demonstrated that someone had died on that highway? I set to work tracking it down. While searching, I learned that only 352 Norwegians died in traffic accidents in 1998. That's less than half as many that die on U.S. highways in any given week! Of all those deaths, only 89 involved people between the ages of fifteen and twenty-four. So if a young woman and her friend had died on

January 29, 1998 while test-driving a Porsche 911 on the E6, there should definitely be a record of it.

While Babelfish and other nifty web translation programs will translate from English to Norwegian, none of them seem to go in the other direction. So with a borrowed Norwegian dictionary, I started plodding through the online archives of Norway's leading newspapers—*Dagbladet, Verdens Gang,* and *Aftenposten.* After many frustrating hours of getting "søket fant o dokumenter," I tried a key word search for "bilulykke" and "frontkollidert" and there it was: "Woman Dead in Car Accident near Skogn," January 29, 1998—the same headline and date of the newspaper article that had been posted on Karyn's web page. Translated, the text read:

> A woman was killed in a car accident on the E6 near Skogn in Northern Trondelag Thursday afternoon. According to witnesses, the woman's car crossed over into the opposing lane and collided head-on with a truck. She was alone in the car and died instantly, according to the officer on duty at the Levanger police station. The driver of the truck was not injured in the accident. The road was icy in the area where the accident took place.

Only one fatality? What about her friend and the driver of the other vehicle? Something was fishy here. I called the Levanger police department (fortunately, the receptionist spoke English) and asked him to look up the accident report. Although the receptionist was unable to divulge the woman's name, citing privacy concerns, he did tell me that she was "a lot older" than twenty-four, did not die in a Porsche, and was not named Karyn. He also said that Karyn was not a Norwegian name. A quick search of Norway's bureau of statistics showed that only three women in all of Norway go by the name Karyn. Yet LegendMUD's Karyn claimed that her name was Karyn in and out of the game.

It strained the bounds of probability to suppose that there had been two accidents on the same date at the same time on the same road, both involving a head-on collision with fatalities. Was the newspaper article actually scanned, as some Legendites remembered, or was it simply a transcription? If there was a scanned image, then perhaps Karyn had changed the wording of the *Aftenposten* article in Photoshop, and then posted it on her GeoCities web page?

I contacted GeoCities and asked about its privacy policy. Would Geo-Cities consent to allow a third party (such as a person's parents) to access an owner's web page and post a letter on it? After some checking, a company spokesperson replied that no, they would not, since they have no way of knowing if a third party is actually related to the owner of a given GeoCities web page, and in any case to grant access would violate the privacy policy.

The conclusion seems inescapable: "Karyn" fabricated her death just as she'd fabricated her life. So who killed Miss Norway 1995? Karyn did. Or rather the person behind the Karyn mask.

Who was Karyn? Someone logged into LegendMUD night after night from September 1996 to January 1998. Then that person disappeared. The individual was likely Norwegian, or at least Scandinavian, since according to all involved she routinely chatted with friends in Norwegian. There are several suspects within the world of LegendMUD itself, including the Norwegian-speaking player who translated the original newspaper article. I even considered the possibility that Trine might be Karyn after all, except that her surprise and bewilderment seemed so genuine.

Unless Karyn steps forward, we'll probably never know who the real-world Karyn was. I say "she" guardedly, however, since it's quite possible, and indeed probable, that the person behind the Karyn persona was actually a man. It wouldn't be the first time that someone engaged in virtual cross-dressing. As MIT sociologist Sherry Turkle points out, "gender swapping on MUDs is not a small part of the game action. By some estimates, *Habitat*, a Japanese MUD, has 1.5 million users. *Habitat* is a MUD operated for profit. Among the registered users of *Habitat*, there is a ratio of four real-life men to each real-life woman. But inside the MUD the ratio is only three male characters to one female character. In other words, a significant number of players, many tens of thousands of them, are virtually cross-dressing."

For his book, *Designing Virtual Worlds*, Richard Bartle compiled a set of guidelines for spotting a "female-presenting male player." According to Bartle, players will claim that their alter ego is physically attractive; avoid players of the same gender they are pretending to be; use the same real-world name as their alter ego; invent reasons they can't go to real-world player gatherings or talk on the phone; and finally, "have their alter ego succumb to injuries or ailments that lead to absences or promised absences."

Now let's look at Karyn again, with Bartle's list in hand. She claimed to be a Norwegian beauty queen. Check. Most of her companions in the game were men. Check. Her name was Karyn, both in and out of the game. Check. She lived in Norway, which prevented her from attending player gatherings. Check. She never talked to other players on the phone. Check. She died in a car crash while test-driving a Porsche. Check. Karyn fits the profile for a female-presenting male player rather well. The person behind the Karyn mask probably logged on to explore aspects of his identity, got in over his head, and then bowed out of the community when a newspaper story about a car crash suggested a dramatic and compelling exit strategy.

Last spring, when I talked with Raph Koster about the Garden of Remembrance, he made an analogy between virtual communities (as exemplified by the friendships people formed with Karyn) and the children's book *The Velveteen Rabbit.*

"The rabbit desperately wants to be real with a capital R," Raph reminded me. "But the love of the child who owned the rabbit is what makes it real. I think it's unfair to say that virtual communities aren't real with a capital R. I'm not going to let anyone tell me that that wasn't real. No one's going to say that the friendship wasn't real because I know the grief was definitely real."

Raph was referring to the community itself becoming real or realizing that it was real, through the experience of losing Karyn. But what if Karyn, the catalyst of community formation, was herself not real with a capital R?

In a simulated world, the line between real life and fantasy is easily blurred. For many, that's clearly part of the attraction. Race, gender, age, and other markers of identity are rendered invisible behind the veil of the Internet and the anonymity it confers. You can be anything that you want to be, since all that other people "see" in a virtual world like LegendMUD is your avatar. As I learned in shooting the film, many people find it liberating to be judged solely on their ideas and actions, rather than their physical appearance or real-life limitations. But as the Karyn story illustrates, the anonymity of the Internet also allows for hurtful deceptions.

The heart of "A Story about a Tree" is Raph's assertion that "the social bonds of the people in a virtual environment make it more than just a game. They make it real." In one sense, he's right. People do form friendships and even meet their significant others through online worlds—and they will probably do so in far greater numbers in the years ahead, as online gaming becomes more immersive, more compelling, and more mainstream. But in this case, the "real" existed only in people's heads. Karyn was only real because the players who encountered her in a virtual world believed that she was real.

The point is not to poke fun at a community for being hoodwinked. After all, she could have been real in reality too; players simply don't know who's behind the blinking cursor. Like the velveteen rabbit, Karyn wanted to be real with a capital R. And magically, through the love of the community, she got her wish.

13

Who's In Charge of Who I Am?

Identity and Law Online

Susan P. Crawford

As we enter this new century, identity online seems full of opportunity. Someday "virtual-world" identities will be just as important as "real" identities—just as "e-commerce" has become indistinguishable from "commerce." Control over online avatar identities will have many real-world consequences, because these clouds of bits may include our credit records, our buddy lists, our job records, personal references and other reputational information, medical histories, certifications, and academic transcripts. As soon as something is valuable and persistent, we seek to associate rights and duties with it. What will be the law of online identity to which those rights apply? And what will those rights be?

Virtual worlds partake of the beauties of networks and the glories of hierarchies. The player-avatar feels himself to be part of a new world of interactions and relationships, a richly contextual network of bits made para-flesh. The player may feel that no one is really in charge of this world—certainly, most of the time, there is no police presence, no sirens howling in a virtual world to remind the player that he is being watched. But the reality is, of course, that omniscient game gods can (if they want) observe everything that is happening and wield switches that are the digital equivalents of weapons of mass destruction. Focusing on the central question of identity sheds light on potential conflicts between the networked and the hierarchical aspects of virtual worlds, and brings home (yet again) the central question of many of the essays in this volume: What should be the role of traditional law in virtual worlds? The question before us is:

Who can destroy a life online? And should those outside the world have any say about its destruction?

I suggest a set of preliminary responses to these questions about law, rights, and destruction in this essay. First, online identities are emergent. Identity is by definition a group project, something created by the context in which the identified operates. My avatar has certain characteristics, affiliations, and interests that arose from its adventures in a particular world—all of these, taken together as a cloud of reputation and experiences and objective facts, constitute its "identity," and could not have been predicted at my avatar's moment of birth/creation. Identity, both virtual and real, is not a matter of "rights" that we can think of in the abstract or in advance. Indeed, the very notion of "rights" assumes a preexisting set of understandings operating to protect an individual against a hierarchy, and does not fit the dynamic, contextual world of identity. For this reason, having some centralized one-size-fits-all "law of identity" (and associated rights) does not make sense: The context for identities does not arrive before us fully formed, and different groups have and will continue to have different ways for dealing with identity-removal questions. It is futile (and perhaps destructive) to presume that humans can design, in advance, rules about identity removal to which virtual worlds should adhere.

Second, just as we are getting comfortable with the idea of these contextual, group-shaped, customized online avatar identities, it is disturbing to learn that online intermediaries (the companies who create online spaces—now, games, but in the future, walled worlds that will be our internets)[1] now have "ownership" of online identities, together with hooks allowing them to remove identities they don't like. In other words, the gods of the virtual worlds are making all the rules (or laws) about identity.

But because there is no norm of transparency with respect to these laws—no way for an individual to understand or predict how his/her identity will be treated by any given intermediary—accountability is difficult. We are not used to asking the question, "Who is in charge of who I am?" But this question is becoming more important.

Third, it does not look as if traditional sources of law will assist in rationalizing this state of affairs. Indeed, traditional statutory or judge-made law likely will not fit the identity context. Judging from past experience in similar domains, traditional lawgivers will either support without question the contractually based actions of online intermediaries to remove identities (because the whole matter is just too complicated to get into, and the intermediary's terms of service have reserved for it complete discretion), or promulgate centralized rules about identity that are unenforceable as a practical matter.

So we have something important that we don't yet completely understand (online identity), that although created by groups and relationships is subject to the unaccountable, invisible actions of private intermediaries. If we individual players/avatars/users were kings, what would we do to address this problem?

The bad news is that "we" (as individuals) will not be kings in these walled worlds that will be our future internets. The people who erect the walls will have a great deal of power that they will be unwilling to devolve. The good news is that, when it comes to identity, the "gods"[2] will need to recognize the power of the groups that live within their worlds. An administrator who makes his or her walled world hospitable to groups (and defers to group "rulings" about identity) will make that world wildly successful. Groups, or guilds, may provide some help when it comes to deciding what to do about identity questions. Groups, in short, provide the answers to this series of conundrums.

1. What is identity online? The interesting and new thing to realize is that identity is something that groups do. Identity is emergent. We are not used to this way of thinking about identity; we prefer, unasked, to think of ourselves as fully formed by our own actions within our chosen environment. Or, if we think of ourselves as having various role-playing identities, we imagine ourselves to be voluntarily, purposefully role playing. But these conjectures of ours are only partial: We are, in fact, constantly bumping up against and watching and learning from everyone around us. Everyone who makes up our "group" has a hand in our identity, and we emerge over and over again changed by the interactions we have with that group (or those groups). The chamber music played by groups and individuals is constant, seamless, and endlessly productive of identity.

To be sure, subsets of virtual identity data can be used in slices—to authenticate for the "truth" of who an actor is, to signal permission to enter a particular area, and to permit associations across areas, for example. But identity is much broader than these mechanical matching practices. It is all these data points, plus more. The being perceived by others (in games/virtual worlds, the avatar) is that being's identity, and that being's identity is in turn shaped by the others who interact with him or her. Identity and reputation go hand in hand, as individuals gain reputations that are connected to particular contexts and groups.

As defined by the U.S. General Accounting Office, "identity theft or identity fraud generally involves 'stealing' another person's personal identifying information . . . and then using that information to fraudulently establish credit, run up debt, or take over existing financial accounts."[3] It is amazing that the GAO has undertaken the task of describing "identity theft." It is not surprising that the GAO has emerged with a crabbed description of identity.

Identity is not just credit card data or clickstream information or address details. In *The Presentation of Self in Everyday Life,* Erving Goffman (1969) suggested the notion of identity as a series of performances, where we use "impression management" to portray ourselves appropriately in different environments. Some part of identity is controlled by the individual, but most of it is created by the world in which that individual operates. We can think of identity as a streaming picture of a life within a particular context. Each of us has multiple identities.[4] The role of groups in shaping "real-life" identities is implicit, as is the multiplicity of "real-life" identity. What is interesting and new about virtual worlds is that they make this group shaping explicit, and the multiplicity of identity actionable.

Indeed, as Richard Bartle puts it, "[t]he celebration of identity is the fundamental, critical, absolutely core point of virtual worlds."[5] The combination of interactions with fellow players and code-driven constraints produces a "stream of challenges" that shapes the identities of virtual-world inhabitants in an explicit way over a compressed period of time.[6] It may be that people now go to virtual worlds at least in part because of this compressed, playful, group-based identity-creation experience.

Once we recognize that identity is a networked group project, the tension produced by the physics of virtual worlds is obvious. The "gods" of the online world, the people writing the code that makes the world run, can have a conclusive effect on identity: They can remove all trace of anyone and anything. (Indeed, the "gods" may see themselves as shaping identity; their shaping is done through code rather than hints, actions, and conversations.) What happens when emergent, group-shaped identity is threatened with hierarchical erasure?

2. What may happen to these online identities? Right now, e-mail addresses are the most widespread form of digital identity in cyberspace. E-mail handles do not seem very rich or meaningful, and having recently been through a substantial change of address I can attest that losing this

particular element of online identity leads to very few consequences other than less spam.

But future (nongame) online worlds may be far more serious, as we usually understand that term, than games—they may have consequences for our wallets and our way of life. They may involve transactions that are more and more inseparable from our "real" lives. If an avatar is walking through an online world as "you," making friends, doing work, and transacting in all kinds of ways, loss of that digital identity will be far more meaningful. Indeed, it does seem that something like an early version of *Snow Crash* is already happening.[7] Cyberspace users may be getting used to the idea of identity online being different from identity offline: Identity that is "unbundled" and exists only in an online space may be a concept whose time has now come.

This movement toward meaningful online identity is happening at the same time that more online "gods" are being promoted into position. Online privately governed internets will soon become more prevalent than they are in 2004, as concerns about security, viruses, spam, and the unknown increase, as valuable content is made accessible only to those who have been given permission to see it, and as hardware and software systems made available to the masses increasingly taken on "trusted" aspects.[8] Online games are precursors of these future, more serious, private competing internets.

As we know, key characteristics of both games and walled worlds are their limited access, clear boundaries, rules, roles/players, and feedback mechanisms that create reputational information. As Caroline Bradley and Michael Froomkin (Chapter 15) make clear, these characteristics of games make them ideal laboratories for experimentation with rule sets, particularly in an era of increasing harmonization in the real world.[9] David Johnson suggests that new kinds of organizations may arise in the online context, as we begin to take the screen seriously and understand its ability to allow new kinds of roles, new kinds of writings, and new kinds of visible interactions to shape our imagination. My view is that games can provide early-warning alerts about identity issues that may arise in the "serious" virtual worlds of the future.

Choosing (and holding on to) an online identity in an online world is likely to become even more meaningful in the future than it is now. At the moment, who I play in *EverQuest* is certainly meaningful if I obsessively work at improving the life and abilities of my character. But in the future, in this next generation, who I play in *EverQuest* may morph into the question of who I play generally online, and whether who I play has just bought a house or a car, and whether who I play has a new job contributing to a peer-production group effort of some kind, and whether who I play has a sterling reputation. Who is in charge of this identity becomes something I care about. When people pay attention to something, and want to associate rights and duties with it, they talk about the law.

3. Should we have an international (or national) "law of identity"? Because identity is an emergent group project—in a permanently beta, contingent form—it is difficult to imagine how anyone could write an effective "law of identity" or a "bill of rights" of the identified. "Those who act badly under the Terms of Service of walled worlds have a right to notice and arbitration before an international online identity tribunal before their identity may be affected or destroyed" seems like a nonsensical legislative enactment in this contextual arena. What if the virtual world is a private listserv, or a thinly populated chat room, or the network of a multinational corporation? Would it even be possible to enforce such a centralized rule? How would the putative enforcer know what "identity disputes" to address or what punishment to mete out? Many of these same issues have arisen in the data privacy context, and it is fair to say that enforcement of privacy rules has proven to be extremely difficult. What does "notice of affected identity" mean in a world of swirling, undifferentiated bits? And won't the groups who transact in a particular walled world want some say in what happens to the identities of their members? A single "law of identity" is likely to be even more difficult to articulate (much less enact into law or enforce) than privacy rules have been. On the other hand, individuals who are dependent on the continued actions of their avatars for their livelihoods will seek assurances that these identities will not be frivolously altered or destroyed by walled-world administrators.[10]

I want to suggest to you that the answer to this puzzle may lie in the activities and decisions of voluntarily formed groups of one-hundred-fifty-or-so members—the size of group that we as individuals can deal with daily and understand, and the size of successful "guilds" in current virtual worlds.[11] It is true that group jurisdiction over identity management in walled worlds is unexplored territory. But such groups can be trusted by individual users, and their rules can map to (be congruent with) the desires of their members in a way that a centralized source of rules never will. So a group's assertion of some say over what happens to identities and reputations is very likely to occur whether or not legal rules exist supporting this assertion.[12] Groups, after all, will have assisted in creating these identities.

4. What are the relevant existing rules about identity in virtual worlds? Just as we are getting comfortable with the idea of these contextual, group-shaped, customized online avatar identities, it is disturbing to learn that online intermediaries (the companies who create online spaces—now, games, but in the future, private internets) now have "ownership" of online identities. These providers may not be very accountable or transparent. And their rules may be effectively unreviewable by any terrestrial court or legislature. This means that online intermediaries will be handing out "law," whether we like it or not. Online intermediaries are a different source of law than those we are used to (like courts and legislatures). This difference presents both opportunities and risks. We will start with the risks.

a. *Risks.* As several online services (such as MSN, EA, and AOL) ramp up to provide a platform for all online interaction, bringing hardware and software and single sign-on benefits into one seamless secure virtual-world whole, how they treat identity becomes more relevant.

One representative example of how online services treat online personas is found at the MSN Gaming Zone. MSN says:

1. Microsoft reserves the right to immediately terminate or suspend a user's Zone.com account for violations of our Code of Conduct.
2. Microsoft also reserves our right to amend or change the Code of Conduct at any time without notice. You agree to periodically review this document to ensure you are doing your part.[13]

This means that, in MSN's discretion, they can decide whether to terminate a user for any action they view as violative of their (mutable) Code of Conduct.

AOL says much the same thing:

America Online reserves the right, in its sole discretion, to terminate your access to all or part of this site, with or without notice.[14]

And Electronic Arts retains similar discretion:

If you, or anyone using your Account, violate our online conduct or Content standards, EA.com may take action against your Account. We may issue

you a warning about the violation, or we may choose to immediately terminate your account. You acknowledge that EA.com is not required to provide
you with notice before terminating your Account, but it may choose to do
so.[15]

It seems clear that the current state of play is that an identity chosen in
a particular online world (such as the worlds of MSN, AOL, or EA, or any
subworld within those contexts) can be wiped out by the intermediary
who runs the online garden. Such an event would not be subject to First
Amendment scrutiny.[16] A private online intermediary has no particular
legal requirement to be neutral as to viewpoints or actions of users.

Courts will defer to extraordinarily broad (and ever-changing) terms of
service for these online worlds.[17] So the law of identity online is private,
contractual law. The use of force online—the removal of identity—has
been handed over to private parties.

Because an intermediary's control will trump any legal requirement
found in the "real world" to be neutral, the possibility for abuse exists.
One can imagine particular online worlds kicking members out whose
actions (graphical or text-based) don't fit the values of clerks working in
the compliance department of the online intermediary. Particularly if you
have invested a great deal in your life in a particular online world, and
have gathered a rich reputation through your persistent involvement in
relationships with others online, you may be quite upset to lose that
investment because of pique on the part of the intermediary. And you will
have no meaningful recourse.

Who owns identity? Who owns reputation? From the intermediary's
perspective, software creates rules that control what social context can be
moved elsewhere. Your identity is "really" a database entry, and the intermediary can argue that your identity is their intellectual property, not
yours. You may attach great importance to it, but this identity (and its reputation) will not as a practical matter survive outside the world in which it
was formed. Virtual-world designers have incentives to raise switching
costs and capture all the value of this reputation.[18] But users may defect
from environments that attempt to constrain the persistence of their reputations and identities. The difficult task for developers and intermediaries
is how much freedom to give their users. This takes us from the realm of
risks to the realm of opportunities.

b. *Opportunities.* It is true that online intermediaries very readily defer
to national laws regarding content, and are likely to do the same when it

comes to identity.[19] It is also true that there will be attempts from some sectors to encourage providers of online worlds to kick off users. For example, in the United States ISPs have been asked to terminate subscribers who were uploading music files.[20] But given a service provider's fervent desire to hang on to as many subscribers as possible, it is unlikely that service providers will be receptive to requests to terminate their customers. It is far more likely that they will be very cautious in responding to requests to terminate, even when pressed by governments or well-funded industry sectors, for fear of the precedent that might be created by acceding to such requests.

Similarly, it is unlikely that service providers will internally be trolling their online worlds, looking for subscribers to zap. The monitoring costs of looking for "bad" behavior are substantial.[21] And every subscriber is a no-cost revenue stream as long as the service doesn't spend any time looking at what those subscribers are doing. Service providers, by and large, want to remain dumb and are not by nature devilish. They want to get as many people as possible interested in their online worlds. So, as long as we ensure that users have choices at all—in other words, as long as membership in MSN's virtual world is not required for your online life to continue[22]—users will have some (limited) ability to control their identity. With any luck, online individuals will retain the ability to leave the roles they have taken up online. (I am not saying this will be an easy thing to do; indeed, your investment in your online identity may be such that leaving it will be extremely painful.)[23]

But we shouldn't have to go bowling alone.[24] Short of exit, we may have other options online that allow us to route around the extreme actions of intermediaries. Group online interactions, just beginning now, provide interesting ways to construct an embedded online self. The "social software" discussion going on right now is dealing with questions of online identity.[25] Games already allow groups to do very interesting things.[26] Gaming conflict brings comrades together in the tribal relationships that humans crave.[27] As real work becomes a more common online activity (in addition to buying airplane tickets and keeping a diary), identity created in connection with groups will be more and more meaningful. Why, though, should intermediaries care about the groups whose interactions they facilitate (as more than aggregates of individual subscribers)?

5. Why groups are important. Here's why. We know (and MSN and EA know too) that the total value of a communications network grows with

the square of the number of the devices that it interconnects. This is Metcalfe's Law, named for Bob Metcalfe, the inventor of the Ethernet. Metcalfe's Law has been critical in understanding why applications that run on top of the Internet spread as quickly as they do. The more people who use a particular piece of software, or a particular standard, the more useful that software or standard is to each participant.

But we also know that "[n]etworks that support the construction of communicating groups create value that scales exponentially with network size" much more quickly than Metcalfe's law.[28] This is David Reed's law. In other words, if ordinary networks scale at an N^2 rate, where N is the number of subscribers who want to reach all the other subscribers and do peer-to-peer transactions, networks that facilitate group communications (like team rooms, chat rooms, discussion groups, and the like) will scale at a rate of 2N, because potential groups can form easily and people can find others who share their interests.

Where Metcalfe's Law is dominant, because a network is seeking to add many new users, one-to-one transactions are the most important communications that take place on that network. But where Reed's Law is dominant, collaboration and jointly constructed value become the most important content distributed by the network, and the formation of groups the key longed-for activity. David Reed calls these changes "scale-driven value shifts." A frequently cited example of a 2N kind of network is eBay, whose affordances allow individuals to easily form marketplaces.

Human nature will always tend toward groupness. We are by nature social animals. We form bonds immediately and look for people with whom we can share our time.[29] We know that scale matters. We care deeply about twelve to fifteen people, and we are probably not capable of caring so deeply about more than that number. Psychologists call this "channel capacity." But we also know that humans have "social channel capacity" (caring, but not so deeply) for about one hundred fifty people.[30] It turns out that functional fighting units in the real world are often about groups numbering one hundred fifty people in size. Virtual worlds work the same way: Guild sizes show a "knee" (trail off) beyond about one hundred fifty members.[31]

Reed's Law will be important to virtual-world administrators. Networks that want to scale at a 2N rate will want to facilitate easy group formation (particularly of groups that are about one hundred fifty strong). Users may even exit if group interactions are not facilitated as part of the virtual world. As Raph Koster puts it, "You could probably kill off another

game by persuading all its guild leaders to switch to your game simultaneously. Offer 'em free accounts. Conversely, don't expose who your hubs are
to competitors. . . . You want them to stick with your game. It makes good
business sense to offer incentives to hubs."[32]

The single most important action a world designer can take to improve
a virtual world is to increase the bandwidth of social interaction. This
means, in turn, that identity created in the context of group work should
be particularly respected by online intermediaries. That's the kind of identity an online intermediary will want to encourage in order to keep its network strong.

Indeed, network administrators who do not facilitate (and defer to) the
workings of groups will have to expend more energy moderating their
worlds than those who do defer to group jurisdiction over identity. To the
extent that any network administrator wants to retain the ability to turn
off troubling identities, aggregate information (how is the group behaving?) is easier to watch over than individual information.

6. If individuals were kings, what would they do to address this disconnect between group creation of identity and intermediary control over
online existence?

a. *Ensure that choices of online intermediaries are real.* It is very clear that
no one is going to stop an online intermediary from cutting off a user.
These intermediaries set their own laws and serve as judge and jury.
Courts routinely defer to such decisions, citing the very broad language of
intermediaries' terms of service. The ratchet here may be one-way: governments and interest groups will want a lever over private online intermediaries that they can use to ensure that a disliked user "disappears." It is
essential, therefore, to keep choices of online intermediaries available. This
is the role of antitrust law. But individuals also have a role in ensuring that
choices remain. They can make this happen by voting with their feet,
demanding reasonable terms of service and moving on (with their guilds)
when they are not satisfied.

b. *Demand visible online laws and disclosures relating to identity dealings
by online intermediaries.* The key insight here is that games and online
worlds give us the opportunity to understand the law by seeing it. It may
be that we have never really understood the regimes to which we are subject because we have not seen them for ourselves. We see the buildings and
the texts, but in order to understand these things as institutions and laws
we need interpreters—we need lawyers. In the online world we have a

chance to understand the law directly, as it is applied, without making an analogy or writing a paragraph. This visual presentation of the law will allow us to make the direct connection to comprehension without an intermediate step.

There will be many interesting questions with which we will grapple:

Should we (can we) make the interaction of real-world identity law with online intermediary law visible? Should we show when someone has been "disappeared" by an intermediary for failure to adhere to a particular nation's rules?

Will an intermediary ever show anyone voluntarily what it is up to when it comes to questions of identity? What legal enforcement mechanisms are needed? or can this entire development be left to market pressures and the perceived need for an "identity seal"?

What would be made visible? The fact that someone's identity has been taken away, and the reasons why? Or speech-related actions of the intermediary that have an impact on identity (but are less than "disappearing" someone?)

What about reputation? Is it right that a user must leave her reputation behind when she leaves a particular online world? Is "reputation portability" possible? Or is reputation so context-dependent that the online world should be permitted to own it? And what does the online world "own," exactly? A group-created construct?

Is this entire problem avoided by staying out of "walled gardens" and maintaining our own domains? Will this be possible as online worlds become more and more attractive, and as hardware and software increasingly intertwine? Will we have to live in the online equivalent of Ted Kaczynski's Montana cabin?

In order to understand the rules that affect our identities online, we should be able to see them. If we see them (and, indeed, are part of these decisions), we should be able to act on them by leaving intermediaries who are acting abusively (or at the direction of a third party with which the individual doesn't agree). We should demand and use patterns of identity decisions to help us decide which intermediary to trust. Requiring publication of such patterns does not mean requiring publication of private individual data. We need to be able to understand the trends that our intermediary is displaying (with our help), and compare them to others' activities. Establishment of a seal program would be a key step toward making identity removal visible. Another key step might be to have the removals of users' identities made possible only if the online community agreed—a sort of online death penalty procedure. Because identities are contextual and mutually created, it makes sense to have the community involved in deciding whether they will persist or not.

c. *Join groups—and then route around any attempt to squelch identity.* One key way to retain identity is to link yourself to others. This may seem paradoxical. But if the identity of a member of a functional group is attacked, the group can move elsewhere—intact. By forming groups within these online worlds, individuals can create identity that cannot be taken away because it resides within the minds and memories of others. And intermediaries will be interested in facilitating these groups because of the 2N impact on the overall health of their networks. As Raph Koster has noted to an audience of game developers, "Your guild structure had better support 150 comfortably. . . . You need interdependence, so that groups do notably better than soloers."

d. *Take seriously the idea of group banishment.* I have not, perhaps, made enough of the severe losses that might accompany a loss of identity caused by an intermediary. Given the elaborate and ever-increasing investments that people will be willing to make in walled worlds, the loss of someone's reputation (her win-loss records) may have a real impact on her ability to make a living. One approach to this disconnect may be to establish within new walled worlds the idea that the community is responsible for government. This means that only the community can act together to trigger rustication of a member. No one can take such an action unilaterally. "In the end, it boils down to the fact that the best government is the one that you can trust, which will be the one you know personally: the people close to you in your virtual community, who are held accountable precisely because of community ties. Your best government is going to be each other, because the man behind the curtain isn't going to know you any more than you know him."[33] Banishment can be the tool that enforces the community's rules.[34]

Conclusion

We are still at the early stages of the first two steps in dealing with any technology: fear and opportunism. Enlightenment is not far away. I want to suggest that we skip quickly through the fear, linger on the opportunism (for the good it will do for jobs in Silicon Valley), and move on to human betterment. This social benefit may come (as so many good things do) from playfulness. Games have a great deal to teach us about how we establish and maintain identity.

The fundamental problem that has yet to be addressed is that while reputations and identities are group projects, the legal ownership of collectively created intangible identities currently appears to reside (by default) in online intermediaries. We need to forge a direct link between the way we live and work online (especially within virtual worlds) and the way we structure control over online resources. If the new mode of work online is collaborative peer production of resources,[35] who will own a shared online space of identities? This ownership itself should be collective.

NOTES

Thanks to Richard Bartle, Raph Koster, and Ren Reynolds who very generously and kindly came up to me after my presentation at "State of Play" and told me how much I had not yet learned. Thanks particularly to Dr. Bartle, who told me to read his book (DESIGNING VIRTUAL WORLDS, 2003). I heartily recommend this book to anyone who is interested in virtual worlds. It is a touchstone. *See* p. 298, n. 56: "To anyone who bought this book with the aim of studying virtual worlds from the perspective of some other discipline: Hi!"

1. See David R. Johnson, Susan P. Crawford, and John G. Palfrey, Jr., *The Accountable Net: Peer Production of Internet Governance,* 9 VA. J.L. & TECH. 9 (2004) (accountability for future online interactions will be found in individuals' decisions to connect to (or exclude) particular individuals; the Internet we know in 2004 will be replaced by many smaller internets) (available at http://www.vjolt .net/vol9/issue3/v9i3_a09-Palfrey.pdf).

2. "Deities create virtual worlds; designers are those deities." Richard A. Bartle, DESIGNING VIRTUAL WORLDS, 247 (Cambridge: MIT Press, 2003).

3. U.S. General Accounting Office, Identity Theft: Greater Awareness and Use of Existing Data Are Needed, H.R. Rep. No. GAO-02-766, at 23 (2002).

4. *See, e.g.,* Roger A. Clarke, "Human Identification in Information Systems: Management Challenges and Public Policy Issues." 7 INFORMATION TECHNOLOGY & PEOPLE 4, 6–37 (1994), *at* http://www.anu.edu.au/people/Roger.Clarke/DV/ HumanID.html:

[I]dentity is used to mean "the condition of being a specified person" or "the condition of being oneself . . . and not another." It clusters with the terms "personality," "individuality" and "individualism," and, less fashionably, "soul." It implies the existence for each person of private space or personal *lebensraum*, in which one's attitudes and actions can define one's self. . . . The dictionary definitions miss a vital aspect. The origin of the term implies equality or "one-ness," but identities are no longer rationed to one per physiological specimen. A person may adopt different identities at various times during a life-span, and some individuals maintain several at once. Nor are such multiple roles illegal, or even used primarily for illegal purposes. Typical instances include women working in the professions, artists and novelists, and people working in positions which involve security exposure (such as prison warders and psychiatric superintendents).

5. Bartle, Designing Virtual Worlds, *at* 159.

6. *Id. at* 161.

7. Neil Stephenson, Snow Crash (New York: Bantam, 2000) (Hiro Protagonist spends his time in the "metaverse," an open world wide web–like virtual-reality world, and foils a plot to control minds through use of a virtual drug called Snow Crash (which destroys avatars by showing them a special bitmap pattern in the form of snow on a scroll in the Metaverse)).

8. The public, worldwide Internet is increasingly perceived as a polluted space, and individuals, enterprises, and ISPs all have good reasons to protect themselves against spam, viruses, and spyware. The results of the aggregated filtering/connecting efforts of these actors can be viewed as a kind of collective online governance. The spaces across which sets of such rules will operate can be viewed as walled gardens (the traditional term) or, more optimistically, as privately governed internets that will compete against one another for customers and attention by filtering out dangerous bits and connecting to desirable material. Pessimistically, such privately governed internets could be monopolistic, government-mandated spaces that greatly control access to content and require identity certification before entry is allowed. In late 2003, a rumor swept Internet mailing lists to the effect that someone from the Recording Industry Association of America (RIAA) had suggested that users should be identified with digital certificates before being allowed online. While the RIAA denied saying this, it is true that such a "drivers license" would be a benefit for the content industry. *See, e.g.,* Jonathan Weinberg, *Hardware-Based ID, Rights Management, & Trusted Systems,* 52 Stanford L. Rev. 1251 (2000) (discussing Intel's Pentium III architecture, and Intel's Processor Serial Number and its function as a globally unique ID for Internet-connected computers); Ross Anderson, *Trusted Computing Frequently Asked Questions, at* http://www.cl.cam.ac.uk/~rja14/tcpa-faq.html:

> Identification could be required as a precondition for access to cyberspace using law, technology, or a combination thereof. Using law, the government

potentially could regulate access to cyberspace whether access is obtained through government-subsidized or private ISPs. In the case of private ISPs, the government could require the ISPs not only to require identification as a pre-condition to access, but also to keep logs of cyberspace users linking their cyber-aliases to their real world identities.

A more optimistic view of the future of the Internet would include many private internets that are affirmatively chosen by end-users rather than mandated, and that feature security/spam/spyware protections. *See* Johnson, Crawford, and Palfrey, note 1 *supra.*

9. Caroline Bradley and A. Michael Froomkin, *Virtual Worlds, Real Rules,* Chapter 15, this volume.

10. In the gaming world (which is a precursor of future, more "serious" walled worlds of transactions and work), such altering and destroying has unquestionably taken place.

> Full purges can be great fun if you are bored . . . wipe a tenth of the persona file, randomly. This way everyone worries it may be them. . . . Personally, I used to like going onto a game as a wizard and threatening someone. . . . [Admins] are there for the people above them to abuse, but as a sideline, they are there to abuse the people below them. . . . To be successful at being a "big" arch-wizard you need to be extremely arrogant . . . wipe them and all of their friends out in one fell swoop. Make a point of doing it loudly. . . . The odd act of kindness, like say, making a novice with a cute name a wizard, can really annoy people who have been playing for months.

Quoted by Raph Koster in his 2003 slide presentation, see note 31 *infra,* and written by Michael Lawrie, aka Lorry, for MYST back in 1991. More serious alterations have occurred as well. *See, e.g.,* The Age.com.au, September 16, 2002 (20,000 players of Warcraft III kicked off for cheating; banishment extended for two weeks, and win-loss records were permanently deleted).

11. Robin Dunbar, "Co-Evolution of Neocortex Size, Group Size, and Language in Humans," *Behavioral and Brain Sciences* 16 (4): 681–735 (1993) *available at* http://www.bbsonline.org/documents/a/00/00/05/65/bbs00000565-00/bbs.dunbar.html ("[T]here is a species-specific upper limit to group size which is set by purely cognitive constraints: animals cannot maintain the cohesion and integrity of groups larger than a size set by the information-processing capacity of their neocortex . . . 150 may be a functional limit on interacting groups [of humans].");
see also Robin Dunbar, GROOMING, GOSSIP AND THE EVOLUTION OF LANGUAGE (Harvard Univ. Press, 1997). Robin Dunbar's conclusions are that social channel capacity is correlated to the size of the neocortex, and arrives at a figure for humans of 147.8; asserts that the average number of members in hunter-gatherer tribes is 148.4; and points out that functional fighting units are often scaled to be around 150 soldiers in size.

12. Paul Schiff Berman, *Globalization of Jurisdiction,* 151 U. PA. L. REV. 311 (2002), is instructive on this point. Why should we privilege state assertions of jurisdiction over nonstate assertions? Groups online will have (and should have) some jurisdiction over identity questions, as a matter of self-enforcing norm development.

13. http://www.zone.com/zzzz/help/zonehelpcodeofconduct.asp.

14. http://www.aol.com/copyright.adp.

15. http://www.eagames.com/official/thesimsonline/home/index.jsp, link to Terms of Service.

16. *See, e.g.,* Noah v. AOL Time Warner, Inc. (261 F. Supp.2d 532 (E.D.Va. 2003) (where plaintiff claimed that AOL had violated his First Amendment rights by briefly terminating his account, allegedly in response to his pro-Islamic statements, court finds that AOL is not a state actor and so the First Amendment cannot support plaintiff's claim); *see also* Hudgens v. NLRB, 424 U.S. 507, 513, 96 S.Ct. 1029, 47 L.Ed.2d 196 (1976) (First Amendment does not protect against actions taken by private entities, rather it is "a guarantee only against abridgment by government, federal or state.");Green v. America Online, 318 F.3d 465, 472 (3d Cir.2003) (noting that AOL is a "private, for profit company" and rejecting the argument that AOL should be treated as a state actor); Cyber Promotions Inc. v. American Online, Inc., 948 F.Supp. 436, 441–44 (E.D.Pa.1996) (rejecting the argument that AOL is a state actor). It is also clear that the intermediary retains the discretion not to eliminate any particular identity. *See, e.g., Noah v. AOL Time Warner, supra,* 261 F.Supp. 2d at 545: "The plain language of the Member Agreement makes clear that AOL is not obligated to take any action against those who violate its Community Guidelines. Thus, the Member Agreement provides that AOL 'has the right to enforce them in its sole discretion,' and that 'if you . . . violate the AOL Community Guidelines, AOL may take action against your account.'" Paul Schiff Berman, *Cyberspace and the State Action Debate: The Cultural Value of Applying Constitutional Norms to "Private" Regulation,* 71 U. COLO. L. REV. 1263, 1302–5 (2000) (state action is unlikely to apply to ISPs, given that we don't really "live" in cyberspace).

17. So far, my research has not revealed cases in which members thrown out of virtual worlds have successfully challenged these contracts.

18. As Raph Koster puts it, "Make sure that players have a reasonable expectation of future interaction. This means persistence of identity and limited mobility." Slide presentation, note 31 *infra,* at slide 114.

19. *See, e.g.,* Pedro Gomes, "The Case of Yahoo! in China," InfoSatellite.com, July 24, 2002 (noting that Yahoo! agreed to refrain from "producing, posting or disseminating pernicious information that may jeopardize state security and disrupt social stability.")

20. *See, e.g.,* Recording Industry Association of America (RIAA) v. Verizon

Internet Services, U.S. Court of Appeals for the District of Columbia, Nos. 03-7015 and 03-7053, 2003 WL 22970995 (Dec. 2003).

21. When the Children's Online Privacy Protection Act became effective in April 2000, mandating monitored chat rooms for children online, many services reacted by simply dropping chat for kids. Providers of online worlds are low-margin businesses, and are likely to become more so as revenues for providing online access continue to drop.

22. *See* Eli Noam, The Internet: Still Wide Open and Competitive? at TPRC, Sept. 2003. http://intel.si.umich.edu/tprc/papers/2003/200/noam_TPRC2003.pdf (finding "pronounced horizontal and vertical trends of concentration in the Internet sector"); CCIA report, Cyberinsecurity, Oct. 2003, http://www.ccianet .org/papers/cyberinsecurity.pdf.

23. *See, e.g.,* F. Gregory Lastowka and Dan Hunter, *The Laws of the Virtual Worlds* 92 CAL. L. REV. 1 (2004) ("Is the option of virtual exit real if you have to give up family, friends, property, and your very form?").

24. Robert D. Putnam, BOWLING ALONE: THE COLLAPSE AND REVIVAL OF AMERICAN COMMUNITY (New York: Simon & Schuster, 2000).

25. *See, e.g.,* Many2Many, a group blog on social software. http://www.corante .com/many/.

26. As the Multiplayer Online Games Directory puts it, "What would an RPG be without guilds???" Guilds often have many staff positions, can tax their members, can provide health coverage, and generally provide an identity for the user.

27. *See, e.g.,* Arthur Jacobson, *Origins of the Game Theory of Law and the Limits of Harmony in Plato's Law,* 20 CARDOZO L. REV. 1335 (1999) (contrasting idea of law as an instrument for achieving harmony, and playful law needed for games in which conflict exists).

28. David P. Reed, That Sneaky Exponential—Beyond Metcalfe's Law to the Power of Community Building, http://www.reed.com/Papers/GFN/reedslaw.html.

29. Gary Marcus, *The Birth of the Mind* (New York: Basic Books, 2003) (very few genes are responsible for brain development; genes code flexible circuits that continue to adapt in response to the environment); Steven Johnson, MIND WIDE OPEN (New York: Scribner, 2004) (basic neuroscience introduction).

30. *See* the work of Robert Dunbar, British anthropologist, cited in note 11, *supra.*

31. Richard Bartle's book, at p. 225, n. 118, pointed me to Raph Koster, *Small Worlds, Competitive and Cooperative Structures in Online Worlds,* San Jose, *Proceedings of Computer Game Developers' Conference,* 2003, http://www.legend-mud.org/raph/gaming/smallworlds_files/frame.htm; this is a very well-done 125-slide presentation about network theory, groups, and gaming, and includes an extensive bibliography.

32. *Id.* at slide 105.

33. Raph Koster, The Man behind the Curtain, essay at http://www
.legendmud.org/raph/gaming/.

34. *See, e.g.,* Paul Schiff Berman, *The Globalization of Jurisdiction,* note 12,
supra (overview of jurisdiction literature; asking why nonstate actors should be
privileged in the consideration of jurisdictional questions). *See, e.g.,* David R.
Johnson & David Post, *Law and Borders—The Rise of Law in Cyberspace,* 48 STAN.
L. REV. 1367 (1996) (advocating the self-regulation of cyberspace as a jurisdiction
independent of territorial sovereigns); Dick Morris, *Direct Democracy and the
Internet,* 34 LOY. L.A. L. REV. 1033 (2001) (advocating direct democracy via Internet mechanisms). "For most people feeling out the limits of the network it only
takes one short gline (global ban) to elicit an apology for their behaviour. It's
amazing what effect denying access to social networks can have, especially on
hardcore online games players." Tom "cro" Gordon, message to MUD-Dev list,
April 5, 2004.

35. Yochai Benkler defines peer production as a new mode of collaboration in
which individuals contribute to the construction of some valuable work product
in exchange for recognition or reputational gain rather than as part of an
employment relationship or in the course of a market-based transaction. Yochai
Benkler, *Coase's Penguin, or Linux and the Nature of the Firm,* 112 YALE L. J. 369,
375 (2002).

Privacy and Data Collection in Virtual Worlds

Tal Zarsky

Introduction—Joseph K. in a Virtual World

Virtual worlds pose new and specific privacy concerns that are at times greater than those arising in other online interactions. To see why, consider the examples in the following story:

It was early in the morning when Joseph K. heard a knock on his door. Joseph, who spends forty hours a week in an online virtual world while using the avatar "Castleman," rushes to the door where he confronts the neighborhood mailman, who with a sly smile hands him his mail. "Here you go, Castleman," he says. Joseph slams the door angrily, as he was hoping to avoid sharing information regarding his online endeavors with his offline neighbors. He then turns to his mail, which includes some surprises: An advertisement for an anti-insomnia drug which Joseph assumes has been sent to him as a result of his gaming activities (Castleman is active during the night), and a warning from the U.S. State Department— stating that he must cease his dealings and communications with several avatars that were traced back to actual citizens of enemy nations. The drug company and the State Department indeed received personal information regarding Joseph directly from the game controllers—while the mailman has heard of the link between Joseph K. and the "Castleman" from other neighbors on his route, who reached this conclusion after noticing that their online friend Castleman tends to disappear at the same dates Joseph K. goes on vacation.

The next day, there is a knock on Joseph K.'s door—but on his virtual rather than physical one. When responding, Castleman is approached by a "wandering merchant" who is in fact an automated program—or "bot" constructed by the game operators. The bot offers him several special "deals" for online and offline game-related merchandise. It is clear to Castleman that these offers have been constructed on the basis of his previous online actions and transactions. In addition, Castleman notices that other such "merchants" have approached his online virtual friends, yet does not know the content of their conversations or the actual offers such "bots" might have made his fellow avatars.

This story of Joseph K. exemplifies many of the characteristic privacy concerns arising in virtual worlds, while illuminating two basic categories: (1) privacy concerns that result from moving personal information between the "virtual world" and the "physical world" (such as those in the first part of the story); and (2) privacy concerns that pertain to the collection, analysis, and use of "personal" information exclusively within the virtual realm (such as those illustrated in the second part of the story).

The story also suggests the vast extent of personal information that can be collected in virtual worlds. This information includes complete records of what users said and did within these realms (including the body movements and facial expressions of the virtual persona), the persons they interacted with, and the times at which they did so. This information also includes data about the players' consumer preferences—information that may prove particularly valuable to the growing commercial markets inside virtual worlds. These records can be connected to the specific users' consistent online identity, and can sometimes be linked to their "offline" identity as well, by tracing the source of their network connection and their method of payment for the game services.

Finally, the story of Joseph K. demonstrates that privacy and the magnitude of the various forms of privacy concerns depend on the level of access to the flow of personal information available in virtual worlds. Game controllers—the people who own and maintain virtual worlds—and their business affiliates are privy to the entire scope of data described above; using this data, they can construct an overall profile of the actions of an online persona. Game controllers and their affiliates also have multiple opportunities to link this virtual identity to the real, "offline" individual. By contrast, the government, unaffiliated commercial entities, and other players have access only to a narrower realm of information about the player's avatar, and have weaker links to the offline persona.

In this chapter, I draw out an overall framework for addressing privacy in virtual worlds, while returning to the issues these examples illuminate. In doing so, I confront the "usual suspects" of privacy law: the *government, other users* interacting in "game space," and the entities *controlling the game* (as well as their business affiliates).

Sources of Privacy Concerns: Government

The government's collection and use of personal information in virtual worlds, and its attempts to connect virtual and physical identities create significant privacy concerns. Government agents may gather information by maintaining a presence in a virtual world—for example, by posing as players. The government could analyze this information, and, if it generates suspicion, try to deduce the identity of the offline persona that stands behind the online avatar from the data it gathered.

Avatars/persons subjected to this form of government surveillance can rarely argue that their privacy has been breached according to today's law, because all the information the government collects and uses has been viewed and gathered in an open, public forum where there is little expectation of privacy. However, virtual worlds offer a new twist. Unlike the real world, where manpower constraints limit the government's ability to engage in ongoing undercover activities and surveillance, virtual worlds might provide almost limitless opportunities for the employment of "bots"—automated programs that can interact in virtual settings—while "eavesdropping" or soliciting information that the government finds helpful. Should these practices of automated intelligence gathering become commonplace, legislators and courts might want to reconsider the legality of these forms of data collection in virtual worlds. They might choose to require governmental automated "agents" to identify themselves, or require government officials to give reasons for suspicion before launching these bots.

Governments can also discover the real-world identities of avatars by requiring game controllers to surrender this information directly. This echos the ongoing debate concerning the rights and duties of Internet service providers (ISPs) to provide the government with identifying information about their subscribers. End-user license agreements (EULAs) between players and game controllers already detail when the game controllers are entitled to provide the government with identifying information. However, these provisions may not (and perhaps should not) always be enforceable; courts must balance users' privacy interests against the government's interests in crime control and national security. That balance, in turn, will depend on whether virtual worlds have become a fertile ground for the exchange of information and funds by crime rings and terrorist cells.

Sources of Privacy Concerns: Other Users

Actions by other game users also raise special privacy concerns. Other players in virtual worlds may learn of the real-world identity of a virtual persona from data they gather while playing. They might publicize or threaten to publicize this information in order to harm or gain advantage over a player.

Disputes concerning the disclosure of private facts about others have been part of privacy law for many decades. However, virtual worlds create privacy problems in two directions—there is a danger of revealing embarrassing facts about what real-world players do as avatars and a danger of revealing the avatars' real-world identities and activities. Consider *Player A*—an average citizen who does not want his offline friends and neighbors to learn of his escapades in virtual worlds, where he portrays a particularly grotesque avatar. Player A hides his physical identity when he plays in virtual worlds, and he might be greatly concerned if other players publicize in the real world the connection between him and his avatar. But players are not merely worried about their virtual identity being revealed to their real-world acquaintances. They are also worried about information about their offline life compromising their virtual-world identity. Players in virtual worlds invest a great deal of time and money in creating and maintaining their online reputations. Because their virtual persona might be very different from their real-world selves, players might consider information regarding their offline lives, jobs, gender, or age as quite harmful to their virtual reputations. To illustrate this point, consider *Player B*—another average citizen who is interested in hiding where she lives and information regarding her job from her virtual friends, because she fears that she might appear too boring or too different from the virtual identity she has constructed. Her virtual-world mystique or influence might well be undermined if it is widely known that she is a meek, boring individual with pedestrian tastes who labors in an unglamorous dead-end job.

Online virtual personas have become increasingly important to people, and allow them to evolve in a new environment. Therefore, courts will have to confront this new variation of the tort of public disclosure of private facts, and decide whether the reputation and privacy of this new form of online identity should be protected from unwanted disclosures about a person's offline identity (as in the case of Player B). This privacy right might have to be established on a case-by-case basis, based on the subjective importance of the relevant virtual identity to the plaintiff, and objective factors such as the time and funds the plaintiff has invested in its development.

Sources of Privacy Concerns: Game Controllers

Other privacy concerns arise from the manipulation of personal data by game controllers (as well as their affiliates and other third parties who might receive such data from the game controllers on the secondary market). Game controllers have access to information concerning both the players' online and the offline identity and might use this information to meet corporate objectives while contacting players in the offline world. Even though the information derived from play in virtual worlds might appear innocuous (such as the number of hours played), it might lead to powerful inferences (for example, that a player suffers from insomnia) and to advertisements or other commercial actions that players might consider offensive (for instance, the recommendation of a drug to cure insomnia). These concerns resemble the familiar fears that ISPs and website operators will sell or misuse their customers' personal data. However, once again virtual worlds raise special privacy problems. First, game operators by themselves are privy to a great deal of personal information that could be easily and efficiently aggregated and analyzed. By contrast, in the general online setting, users divide their attention (and thus the data trail they leave behind them) among several e-commerce vendors, content providers, and other online applications. Second, players in virtual worlds might be unaware of the extent of surveillance and its consequences (given the "playful" setting), and may have comparatively limited options to escape from it, especially if other competing game controllers have similar abilities to collect and analyze personal data, and similar policies regarding its subsequent use.

Because privacy concerns are enhanced in virtual environments, courts and legislatures should adopt more protective legal standards for interpreting terms of service agreements and EULAs governing virtual environments than for interpreting similar documents concerning Internet service providers and other Internet applications. In addition, regulators should consider overriding the privacy standards game operators adopt in their EULAs. Market forces may protect the end users' privacy preferences to a significant degree, but the law needs to step in where markets cannot effectively do this.

Finally, virtual worlds may create a special form of privacy concerns stemming from the collection and use of personal information exclusively within virtual worlds themselves. The game controller can collect information about a specific player and, even without linking it back to the physical user, use it to the player's detriment. This results from the fact that game controllers have the ability to collect vast amounts of interesting data about every user, such as data regarding the times of the day the user plays; the parts of the virtual world the user visits and the goods he or she buys, exchanges, and consumes; the other avatars he or she chooses to interact with, and the times and duration of these interactions. Let us refer to all this as *Player Data*. Even without connecting Player Data to users' offline identities, game controllers can still threaten privacy interests. These threats to privacy will result from the expansion of commercial activities within virtual worlds, as game controllers strive to capitalize on their ongoing and extensive access to a large audience they "know" quite well. In this context game controllers will take advantage of their ability to tailor specific advertising messages to each individual player in accordance with their personal data, preferences, and attributes derived from the Player Data game controllers obtain. In doing so, game controllers can use Player Data to unfairly discriminate among players while offering different players different products or services. In addition, game controllers might also use Player Data to manipulate players by providing them with advertisements and marketing materials that play to their personal insecurities.

In the "general" online context, consumers have demanded that website operators and Internet service providers limit their use of personally identifiable information that links Internet activity to an end user. However, website operators and Internet service providers generally reserve their right to engage in extensive analysis and use of "nonidentifiable personal data." But in virtual worlds, the category of "nonidentifiable personal data" includes Player Data. Therefore, regulations designed to protect privacy in ordinary Internet contexts may not be sufficient for virtual worlds, and courts and regulators must closely consider the privacy concerns arising from the analysis of "mere" Player Data, even if game controllers insist that it is not directly personally identifiable. Players, in turn, need to understand the possible threats to privacy that stem from the use and collation of Player Data, and signal their discontent to game controllers (and regulators). Furthermore, if regulators construct a code of proper privacy practices for virtual worlds, they must pay close attention to Player Data and set stricter standards to its analysis than those set for nonidentifiable personal information in the general online context.

Conclusion

As technology and patterns of use change, additional privacy concerns will emerge in virtual worlds. But the examples I address above should be sufficient to demonstrate that there are special privacy issues in this context. As more online activity moves into these environments, players, privacy advocates, and regulators alike need to remain open-minded and vigilant.

V

Virtual Worlds and Real-World Power

15

Virtual Worlds, Real Rules
Using Virtual Worlds to Test Legal Rules

Caroline Bradley and A. Michael Froomkin

In virtual worlds such as *Ultima Online* and *EverQuest*,[1] the Internet may accidentally provide an environment that lends itself well to the testing of legal rules. We argue that the ability to test legal rules in these virtual worlds could help solve a long-running and worsening problem in the design of legal rules—the barriers to experimentation caused by an increasing tendency to the harmonization of law. Legal harmonization occurs for many reasons, including regional integration,[2] a wide acceptance among policy makers that good rules promote economic success,[3] and lobbying by business interests.[4] Obviously, it makes sense to try to harmonize on good rules rather than bad ones as the costs of bad harmonized rules increase with the number of countries that adopt them.

Legal harmonization is often accomplished by transplanting what are perceived to be good rules from one place to another. However, legal rules do not exist in a vacuum but in complex institutional and cultural contexts which affect how the rules operate.[5] Some commentators argue that effective legal transplantation is difficult or even impossible as a result.[6] For example, rules of contract law may work differently in different social contexts with different enforcement mechanisms.[7] It would therefore be useful to be able to identify how and why rules work, and to explore how to carry out successful transplantations.

Increased legal harmonization reinforces the need for a new way to test legal rules: As legal diversity decreases, there are fewer alternate rules to draw from, and thus potentially useful de facto experimentation with alternative rules becomes rarer and more difficult. As legal harmonization gathers momentum, the argument for experimentation in virtual worlds grows ever stronger, if only because of the lack of alternatives.

Given that the adoption of less-than-optimal rules involves costs, it is desirable to test rules before adoption to examine their likely effects. Real-world empirical studies of the effects of actual rules suffer from the risk that a study will not identify crucial factors affecting the operation of the rules in practice. In particular, studies that leave out specific institutional and cultural factors may suggest erroneous conclusions. Some studies on the effects of social programs do seek to experiment with and compare different policy interventions, but they tend to focus on disadvantaged groups.[8] Economic models can give some indications about how rules may work, but are always subject to the risk that their assumptions are inaccurate and that any inaccuracies in the assumptions undermine the reliability of the test results.

Behavioral economists have begun to examine the behavior of economic actors empirically, using relatively simple studies where "real subjects make decisions with real monetary consequences in carefully controlled laboratory settings."[9] These studies suggest, for example, that people may not always behave in the self-interested way that traditional economic theory would suggest: Instead of simply being economic maximizers, many people are concerned about fairness.[10] Subjects of these experiments tend to behave more altruistically than economic theory would suggest. Some games test other ideas, such as how trusting people are.[11] Researchers also test whether players from different cultural backgrounds play games differently.[12] Results of some experiments suggest that people in some countries are more trusting than people in other countries.[13]

These experiments focus on people's behavior rather than on the effect of legal rules, and are oriented to the testing of economic assumptions about behavior. Thus, they are important for academic lawyers who are interested in the economic effects of legal rules. In particular, academic lawyers are interested in how people value assets differently in different contexts. A person may be willing to pay much less for a thing than the amount he or she would expect to receive to give it up.[14] This cultural difference has implications for ideas of property rights and for a range of rules of business organization law.

The design of behavioral experiments may affect the results—which raises questions about how much they tell us about the real world. Game experiments often use students as the participants in the games rather than a range of people with different characteristics.[15] The student test subjects may volunteer for the experiment,[16] and may receive small payments for participating.[17] Experiments to test endowment effects may involve testing how students value the mugs the researchers give them.[18] The context, however, makes a difference.[19] Students may respond differently to ownership of a mug depending on whether they "feel their status as owners has an independent moral justification."[20] Using students as test subjects may skew the test results. If one wanted to test levels of trust, age and life experience might make a difference. As a result, the controlled settings for the experiments necessarily means that they are artificial.[21]

Virtual worlds could be a better venue for testing legal rules and persons' responses to those rules than the laboratory.[22] Any experiment that used virtual worlds could attract a large number of enthusiastic—even fanatical—players who would have a real investment in the game. Their investment in the game would be closer to an investment in real life than the types of investments the student volunteers used in academic studies tend to have in simple games. Some virtual-world participants prefer to live in the online world than in the real world. Indeed, some players become "immersed" in the games and begin to take their virtual life so seriously that they forget that it is a game.[23] Of course, any attempt to harness a virtual world as an experimental tool would require the informed consent of the experimental subjects—a somewhat ironic problem for any experiment that might be designed to test consumer comprehension of rules.

Inhabitant-players in virtual worlds are likely to have a greater sense of investment in those worlds than participants in mug games have in their mugs. In this sense the virtual worlds may seem more like meat-space and conclusions drawn from studying the virtual worlds and their inhabitants may be more valid than those drawn from the simpler behavioral experiments.[24] However, inhabitant-players in virtual worlds may have different characteristics from most participants in meat-space economic activity. For example, they may be more aggressive and risk-tolerant than the average consumer. Any such generalized tendencies for virtual worlds' inhabitant-players character traits to diverge from the traits of the general population (or that sector of it which is involved in the relevant types of meat-space economic activity) would reduce the usefulness of the virtual worlds as test-beds for legal rules.

With the notable exception of *The Sims Online* and *Second Life*, the virtual worlds most popular in North America involve fantasy, magic, and violence. It seems therefore that they may attract an unbalanced sample of the population unless, of course, the taste for fantasy, magic, and violence is in fact very widespread. This suspicion seems particularly plausible given the excesses in the most violent of the virtual worlds. For example, a leading game industry expert once described *Ultima Online*'s community as "a Hobbesian war of all against all, a chastening reminder of anarchy and lawlessness" marked by "a palpable feeling of terror in the streets . . . [that] makes you appreciate cops, or at least, makes you realize the value of living in a society that is policed."[25] This does not sound like a good model on which to base tests of the Uniform Commercial Code (UCC), although it might have some use if one were seeking to model police strategies for the most dangerous neighborhoods in the United States— which might actually be a good idea, as current policing policies seem unable to make them safe.

Ultima Online is the extreme case. Other games either do not allow players' avatars to kill each other, or limit the gankage[26] to well-demarcated kill zones. Many other games, such as *EverQuest,* do not allow characters to kill one another. In the less extreme games, the only players who may attack each other are those who have explicitly and mutually assumed the risk of injury caused by interplayer mayhem, or those who choose to play on predefined "player killer" servers.[27] It may be that people with violent tendencies gravitate to games like *Ultima Online,* where player-killing is allowed.[28] In other games, where players have a choice as to whether they venture into "kill zones" where players are allowed to kill each other, only a small fraction of the players choose this option.[29] Indeed, many players avoid the games with rampant player-killing.[30]

In fact, Hobbesan violence is a characteristic of only a small subset of the virtual-world population.[31] One game development pioneer suggests that there are four types of people attracted to online shared environments, "achievers, explorers, socialisers and killers." They are attracted respectively to "achievement within the game context," "exploration of the game," "socialising with others," and "imposition upon others."[32] Others have emphasized the social nature of online gaming.[33] These commentators suggest that what goes on when people play games is much more complicated than simply venting murderous urges.[34]

In addition, Castronova's work documents the extent to which virtual behavior mimics the real-life experience of labor, even labor at repetitive and boring tasks.[35] Furthermore, there is evidence suggesting that whatever the demographics of MMORPG players, the population of online game players more closely reflects the population at large.[36] The earliest adopters of the Internet were predominantly a certain type of white male, but now Internet users more closely reflect the U.S. population as a whole, and indeed some day may comprise nearly the entire population. It may be only a matter of time before the MMORPG population undergoes a similar transformation, although this is certainly an issue that requires careful monitoring and study.

Although they are artificial, virtual worlds are artificial in different ways than are experiments such as trust games and mug studies. Yet virtual worlds are similar to these games in that they are more controllable and modifiable than the real world. Virtual worlds are more complex than simple experimental games (making them more like the real world) and yet they are, for now, simpler than the real world (making them more manageable). Virtual worlds are also more easily manipulated than are real-world experiments: The game's designers can choose which variables to modify while leaving the others constant. Different versions of the game, or "shards," can run at the same time, thus allowing us to test how rule variations affect players' behavior.[37] One can imagine different ways of structuring the experiment: In one version the operator of the game might allocate players to different shards at random; in another, players could choose which rule set they preferred ex ante; in another, players could participate in the development of the rules by expressing their views about what proposed changes to the rules they would like to see. In this version, the game would not merely test different rules identified by the experimenters but would also harness player creativity to design better rules.

While virtual worlds have characteristics that make them look like useful test-beds for legal rules, existing games do have characteristics that may limit their usefulness. Virtual worlds seem like the real world in that they are interactive, social environments.[38] But in a number of ways the assumptions built into the games may not track reality. Games may assume scarcity,[39] whereas in the real world some things are scarce while others are not. Games may assume that it is better to cooperate than to work alone.[40]

To the extent that virtual worlds' usefulness as test-beds for legal rules is based on their similarity to the real world they also threaten to raise the legal transplants issue mentioned earlier: Just because a rule works well in Norrath does not mean that it would work in the same way in Newark, much less Nepal. But the very simplifications that make game worlds possible also allow researchers to decide what to model, what to leave out, what to hold constant, and what to vary. Thus transplanters of legal rules from a virtual world into a real-world context might find it easier to think about how the conditions in the real world differ from those in the virtual world than would be the case in a real-world to real-world transplant. Moreover, virtual worlds themselves allow researchers to experiment with the way different conditions affect the application of the rules. Furthermore, if experimenters are able to control the nationality of who plays in their shard, virtual worlds offer the additional advantage that the players can be drawn from the same society as the one for which the rule is being tested. Any unknown and unstated cultural assumptions are likely to be replicated in the model, rather than being missing from it, because the players naturally bring their assumptions with them. Thus, rather than have to trust that Newark's rule fits Nepal, one need only have reason to believe that Newark's gamers, or the United States' more generally, act online in ways that sufficiently resemble their earthbound selves.

We think we could use virtual worlds to test a wide variety of questions about how the law works, but not all of them.[41] In general, virtual worlds would seem to be more useful for testing relatively simple rules and also more complex rules in relatively simple contexts. Even with this substantial limitation, however, virtual worlds provide a fertile testing ground for a number of existing legal beliefs and potential innovations.

Virtual worlds generate a range of different transactions, and participants in these worlds inflict harm on other participants in various ways. Virtual worlds therefore inherently invoke ideas of property, contract, and tort. A player in *Ultima Online* or *EverQuest* owns weapons, may buy and sell those weapons, and may use them to hurt other players. As a result, the game needs to have rules regulating the types of property rights a player can have in weapons, the ways in which transactions in weapons may be accomplished, and the consequences of inflicting harm on another player.

Real and Chattel Property Regimes

De Soto and others who focus on development emphasize the significance of property rights on economic success. Participants in virtual worlds' own property, and some items of the property they own are more valuable than others. But perhaps the property rights thesis could be tested—or sharpened—by having parallel virtual worlds with different types of property rights. One version of a game might be designed to see how players would react to a wide range of different rights that could exist with respect to a particular item of property. Players might be able to lease their property to others for a number of days or weeks or for certain hours in the day. Lease contracts might allow subleases, or they might not. A player with many swords might get into the business of leasing swords to other players. A player might sell swords on credit and expect to have a security interest in the transferred, but not-yet-paid-for sword, allowing for investigation of different arrangements for security interests and for rules about the transfer of risks. Different versions of a game might demand compliance with formal requirements for the transfer of property, or could allow for the recognition of informal transfers. A virtual world could experiment with socialism and dispense with individual ownership of property, or provide for the redistribution of property.

Tax Policy

In the same way that virtual worlds might allow for the testing of different allocations of property rights, they might also allow for the testing of some basic general ideas of tax policy. Clearly it would be difficult, if not impossible, to test detailed technical rules in a virtual world, but different shards of a game could have different tax regimes. One shard could impose taxes at a flat rate, while another could have a progressive tax system, allowing the experimenter to compare the results. One could also measure players' attitudes toward different trade-offs between tax regimes and social expenditures. For example, one could measure the effect on player satisfaction of making healers more effective in a game with higher tax levels.

Transactional law

Characters in virtual worlds enter into simple transactions with each other. They meet to buy and sell items in the game, or agree that they will journey together to a new place in order to find a needed item. Games may be structured so that success at a particular task requires a number of different skills that one character alone is unlikely to have. Therefore, players need to negotiate how to obtain the benefit of another character's skills. Such agreements may look like agency or employment relationships, or even partnership, if the players agree to share the profits of the expedition. Thus, in virtual worlds one could not only expect to see simple transactions involving the buying and leasing of property, and perhaps loans of money, but also simple business relationships. It would be possible to run different versions of the virtual world where some had limited liability business forms and others did not, although these different arrangements would clearly be sensitive to tort rules in the game. One could explore the relationships between tort and contract rules by testing, for example, the effects of allowing tort damages for breaches of contract (which seems to match the expectations of many nonlawyers). Different versions of a game could implement different arrangements for the enforcement of contractual obligations.

Tort

Characters in virtual worlds can suffer physical harm and economic losses, although the implications of physical harm are different. Virtual worlds would not be useful test-beds for rules about the measure of damages—characters may have to pay for the services of healers, but this is unlikely to be as expensive or complicated, and certainly not as physically painful, as acquiring the services of doctors and hospitals in the real world. On the other hand, it should be possible to test the effects of having, or not having, an economic loss rule precluding damages for economic loss except where there is physical damage. Virtual worlds could also be used to supplement the results of simpler experiments investigating endowment effects, or status quo effects, which would be interesting for many areas of law that rely on the Coase theorem,[42] including environmental law.

Insurance

Players in virtual worlds might want to insure against the risks of harm or economic loss, so the games could be used to test different rules about what risks are insurable, and different arrangements made for dealing with moral hazard.

Dispute Resolution

Virtual worlds may also provide a test-bed for some features of dispute resolution mechanisms. In the real world, judges may tailor the rules they develop in order to limit the number of disputes that may come to court in the future. In virtual worlds, one could experiment with costless access to courts. In this model, players would experience the costs of dispute resolution primarily as costs in time, rather than money. Comparing the litigiousness of participants to a different shard in which litigation was expensive (or even to similarly situated real-life litigation) might provide valuable information about the sensitivity of the quantity of litigation to financial cost.

Jurisprudence

Virtual worlds might also allow for the testing of various moral intuitions at the foundation of important strands of modern political philosophy, although some obstacles would need to be overcome. A major theoretical move in John Rawls's *Theory of Justice*[43] presupposes an imaginary "veil of ignorance" that prevents rational actors in a hypothetical "original position" from knowing what their physical, cognitive, familial, racial, national, and economic endowments will be in society, and then asks what rules they would choose if ignorant of their actual role and abilities. Rawls—implicitly taking people to be risk-averse rather than risk-loving—argues from the premise that rational people behind the veil of ignorance would agree on two principles of justice. Their first principle would affirm an equality of basic rights. Their second principle, known as the difference principle, would hold that all inequalities are unjust, unless removing them would worsen the situation of the worst-off members of society. It would be trivially easy to design a virtual world in which players were unaware of their future avatar's characteristics and endowments. Faced with the prospect of participating in such a game, players could be polled, or even asked to come to an agreement, as to their preferences for how abilities and endowments should be handed out and what social policies should dominate the game. Since players would be making these choices before the game started, however, it might be difficult to get them to take it as seriously as they would take rules that affected an avatar in which they had expended substantial effort. In particular, in order for the experiment to be meaningful, players would need to believe that they could not simply quit the game and start another one if they got stuck with a lousy avatar.

We also can identify a number of different factors that would get in the way of using virtual worlds to test real-world rules. In essence, these factors are all consequences of the ways in which virtual worlds (inevitably?) differ from the real world. Virtual worlds are less complex than the real world and relationships in virtual worlds are different from relationships in meat-space. Virtual worlds do not (currently) have elected governments and they do not have nations, although they do have tribes, factions, guilds, clans, and racial (or species) groupings.

Complex Rules

Virtual worlds are less factually complex than the real world. Any area of law dealing with highly complex factual situations in real life would be difficult to translate to the virtual world. In a virtual world, players might seek a remedy for misrepresentation about the characteristics of an item for which they believe, after the transaction, that they overpaid. But business enterprises in online games do not ordinarily issue securities to other players, and even if players did offer people the opportunity to invest in their business activities in return for a share of the profits, the legal issues involved would look much more like those involving simple fraud than like complex securities regulation.

One set of implications of this lower level of complexity in virtual worlds is that they do not (so far) include lawyers.[44] While it is possible to conceive of the development of *EverQuest* lawyers in response to a development of law, until that time it would be advisable to avoid using legal rules that are so complex that players need to consult a lawyer to understand them. In fact, this idea of using the games to examine the extent to which people can use legal rules without the involvement of lawyers could be interesting,[45] but a range of complex rules—such as tax rules, and detailed rules of civil and criminal procedure—would fall outside the scope of testing through this sort of game.

Family Law

Many rules of law deal with relationships. We suspect that rules of family law and inheritance would not translate well to virtual worlds. Characters in virtual-world games may "marry" other characters but these marriages are very different from real-world marriages (players can select the gender of their avatars much more easily than people currently can), and are insulated from the stresses and strains of everyday life. Even if characters in virtual worlds have children, those children are never related to them biologically. Your real-life kids may not play the same game, and if they do they are unlikely to want to play as your virtual kids (although they might want to be your parents!).

Administrative Law and the Legislative Process

Virtual worlds do not currently have elected governments—most seem either anarchic, feudal, or mysteriously governed by "gods" who are in fact the game operators. Some have authorities who exercise police powers, and different games could include different rules limiting the freedom of action of the policing authorities. It might be possible to imagine a virtual world in which players elected representatives who would act as legislators within the world, but they would do so within a system run by designer/gods/experimenters who set the fundamental rules, and are not term-limited, so there would inevitably be a limit as to what the player/legislators could decide. Legislators in the real world are often limited by a constitution, but designer/gods/experimenters of virtual worlds are unlikely to want to allow the players to amend the worlds' constitutions. In the real world constitutional change may be arduous or bloody, but it can happen. On the other hand, the operators of virtual worlds may change their worlds in response to market pressures. If players dislike particular constitutional features in one world they may migrate to another. To the extent that we could examine constitutional and administrative law issues in virtual worlds, we would run again into the fact that the virtual worlds are less complex than the real world.

Transnational and International Law

The absence of anything resembling modern governments in the major virtual worlds means that even when separate nations exist in current virtual worlds, their relationships are unlikely to be meaningful representations of international law. Thus, a range of issues in transnational and international law arising in the real world cannot be reproduced in existing virtual worlds. Because virtual worlds have no international trade, there is no scope for international trade law other than, perhaps, tariff law. There is no need for rules of public or private international law.[46] Moreover, one could imagine a need for admiralty law only in games with substantial sea-based trade.

Zoning

Some real-world property problems may be too complicated to model in virtual worlds. In games like *The Sims Online* where players try to make Simoleans by attracting customers/renters to the properties they develop, it might be possible to experiment with different zoning regimes. Two shards of the same game could have different zoning arrangements: one unregulated and the other with zoning controls. One could then study the patterns of development under the different systems and test which outcome players preferred.[47] Clearly, however, zoning in the real world is very different from zoning in a virtual world, and the implications of having a toxic waste dump next to your apartment building in the real world are likely to feel very different from the same experience in a game.

Intellectual Property

Like zoning, intellectual property involves complex technical issues in the real world that a game could not test. However, arguments about IP law often center on arguments about whether strong IP rights are necessary to encourage entrepreneurial activity. We think it is possible that one could test such claims in virtual worlds, although it would be necessary to run the games for a long time in order to obtain useful data.

In a world where real-world experimentation with legal rules is likely to be useful, but also difficult and expensive, experimentation with legal rules in virtual worlds may be a valuable substitute. Large numbers of enthusiastic players in virtual worlds could test legal rules in an environment closer to the real world than many of the experiments that behavioral economists run to test economic behavior. The cost of running these experiments would involve the expense of developing the games, but one could free ride on the existing market for games. One would, however, want to sell the games, because giving them away would risk undermining the market for existing games. Experimenting with rules in virtual worlds also avoids the real-world economic and psychological costs of experimenting with interesting, but ultimately harmful, rules.

NOTES

We would both like to acknowledge the University of Miami School of Law's support for the writing of this essay. Comments are welcome at cbradley@law.miami.edu and froomkin@law.miami.edu.

1. Edward Castronova, *Virtual worlds: A First-Hand Account of Market and Society on the Cyberian Frontier* (CESifo Working Paper Series No. 618, 2001), *available at* http://papers.ssrn.com/sol3/papers.cfm?abstract_id=294828 (last visited Sept. 26, 2003) (describing the *EverQuest* universe and giving an overview of the economic and social impacts these games have generated in the real world).

2. *See, e.g.,* G. L. Davies, *Justice in the Twenty-First Century,* 7 INT'L. TRADE AND BUS. L ANN. 181, 185 (2002) ("Economic and cultural convergence brings legal convergence. This movement is accentuated in the countries of the European Community.")

3. *See, e.g.,* World Bank, WORLD DEVELOPMENT REPORT 2005, A BETTER INVESTMENT CLIMATE FOR EVERYONE, 1 (2004) ("Government policies and behaviors play a key role in shaping the investment climate. While governments have limited influence on factors such as geography, they have more decisive influence on the security of property rights, approaches to regulation and taxation (both at and within the border), the provision of infrastructure, the functioning of finance and labor markets, and broader governance features such as corruption. Improving government policies and behaviors that shape the investment climate drives growth and reduces poverty.") *available at* http://siteresources.worldbank.org/INTWDR2005/Resources/complete_report.pdf. *See also* HERNANDO DE SOTO, THE MYSTERY OF CAPITAL (2000).

4. For example, consider the spread of the limited liability partnership. *See, e.g.,* The Law Commission Consultation Paper No 159, The Scottish Law Commission Discussion Paper No 111, Partnership Law. A Joint Consultation Paper and 1.13 (2000), *available at* http://www.lawcom.gov.uk/library/lccp159/cp159.pdf.

5. *See, e.g.,* Daniel Berkowitz et al., *The Transplant Effect,* 51 Am. J. Comp. L. 163, 171 (2003).

6. *See, e.g.,* Pierre Legrand, *What "Legal Transplants?"* in Adapting Legal Cultures 55 (David Nelken and Johannes Feest, eds., 2001).

7. *See, e.g.,* Paul Collier and Jan Willem Gunning, *Why Has Africa Grown Slowly?* 13 J. Econ. Perspectives 3, 11 (1999) ("The problem of contract enforcement thus makes markets less competitive and reduces the potential gains from trade, while tending to perpetuate the dominant position of minorities in business.").

8. *See, e.g.,* David Greenberg et al., *The Social Experiment Market,* 13 J. Econ. Persp. 157, 159 (1999) ("The scarcity of experiments involving the middle and upper class is extraordinary").

9. Ernst Fehr and Klaus Schmidt, Theories of Fairness and Reciprocity—Evidence and Economic Applications 4 (Institute for Empirical Research in Econ., Univ. of Zurich, Working Paper No. 75, Feb. 2001), *available at* http://www.iew.unizh.ch/wp/iewwp075.pdf.

10. *See, e.g., id.*

11. Joyce Berg et al., *Trust, Reciprocity and Social History,* 10 Games and Economic Behavior 122 (1995).

12. *See, e.g.,* Hessel Oosterbeek et al., *Cultural Differences in Ultimatum Game Experiments: Evidence from a Meta-Analysis* (2003), *available at* http://www1.fee .uva.nl/scholar/mdw/sloof/Ultimatum MetaMarch03.pdf; Rachel Croson and Nancy Buchanan, *Gender and Culture: International Experimental Evidence from Trust Games,* 89 Am. Econ. Rev. 386 (1999).

13. *See, e.g.,* Marc Willinger et al., *A Comparison of Trust and Reciprocity Between France and Germany: Experimental Investigation Based on the Investment Game,* 24 J. of Econ. Psych. 447 (2003) (suggesting that Germans are more trusting than the French).

14. *See, e.g.,* Jennifer Arlen et al., *Endowment Effects Within Corporate Agency Relationships,* 31 J. Legal Stud. 1, 2 (2002) ("the maximum amount a nonowner would be willing to pay for an entitlement is often significantly less than the minimum amount she would demand to part with it if she initially owned it."); Russell Korobkin, *Empirical Legal Realism: A New Social Scientific Assessment of Law and Human Behavior: The Endowment Effect and Legal Analysis,* 97 Nw. U. L. Rev. 1227, 1228 (2003).

15. *See, e.g.,* Willinger et al., *supra* note 13, at 456–57; Berg et al., *supra* note 11, at 129.

16. *See, e.g.,* Willinger et al., *supra* note 13, at 456–57.

17. *See, e.g.,* Berg et al., *supra* note 11, at 129. Research suggests that even small payments may have an effect on participants in the experiments.

18. *See, e.g.,* Daniel Kahneman et al., *Experimental Tests of the Endowment Effect and the Coase Theorem,* 98 J. POL. ECON. 1325 (1990).

19. *See, e.g.,* Korobkin, *supra* note 14, at 1242 ("legal scholars need to take care to ensure the closeness of their contextual analogies and not to lose sight of the fact that their conclusions will often be contingent on the soundness of such analogies.").

20. Arlen et al., *supra* note 14, at 9.

21. *See, e.g.,* Arlen et al., *supra* note 14, at 33 ("experimental research is necessarily constrained within a specific, controlled environment, purposely isolated from other aspects of the real world. This isolation is both its great strength and its profound weakness. Observing a predictable behavioral pattern within a controlled experimental setting enables researchers to make causal claims with minimal fear that unobserved phenomena or reverse causality are driving their results. Yet this very controlled setting makes it difficult to generalize to real-world settings that are the focus of policy reform proposals.").

22. The idea that virtual worlds might have something to teach us about reality has not escaped other commentators. *See, e.g.,* F. Gregory Lastowka and Dan Hunter, *The Laws of the Virtual Worlds,* 92 CAL. L. REV. 1, 33 (2004) ("A third reason for exploring the laws of virtual worlds is that they represent an amazing experiment in law-making, and provide a serious challenge for real life legal systems."). Our aim in this essay is to make the case, and to discuss where it is most, and least, likely to work.

23. *See* Jane McGonigal, *"This is Not a Game": Immersive Aesthetics and Collective Play, available at* http://hypertext.rmit.edu.au/dac/papers/McGonigal.pdf.

24. "Meat-space" is what is commonly regarded as the "real world."

25. Alexander P. Macris, Imaginary Worlds, Real Communities: Understanding the Future Architecture of Cyberspace Through the Study of Massively Multiplayer Games, 15, unpublished manuscript. Feb. 1999 (quoting GREG COSTIKYAN, FUTURE OF ONLINE GAMES 57 (1999))

26. To gank is to kill another player's avatar. Gankage is the noun meaning the process of ganking.

27. Macris, *supra* note 25, at 9.

28. *See* Macris, *supra* note 25, at 22–23.

29. This is 10 percent of the players in *EverQuest. See* Macris, *supra* note 25, at 23. On the other hand, the relative unwillingness of players in *EverQuest* to risk kill zones may be an economically rational calculation based on the chance of being killed as a function of population density:

> [T]he number of violent encounters between players will go up as roughly the
> square of the increase in population. And it's not hard to accept the assumption

that being killed in PvP is a more frustrating experience than having to wait in line to kill a popular item-dropping mob. . . . [T]his theory . . . would predict that if the amount of territory available on a "Zek" server [an *EverQuest* server with a ruleset that allowed players to attack each other at any time] was increased, then so would the population. . . .

[When the *EverQuest* Scars of Velious expansion pack] came out, and the populations of the Zek servers rose significantly, then stabilized at a higher level. The theory that all of the players in EQ who wanted to play PvP, already were, was disproven, and the theory that the lower populations of "hardcore" servers were lower due to different parameters of population pressure was strengthened.

Dave Rickey, *If you can't say anything nice. . .* , Engines of Creation #6 (August 12, 2003), *at* http://www.skotos.net/articles/engines06.shtml.

30. For example, Macris quotes Tessa, described as a "high-level Everquest player" as writing:

I don't think I'm overgeneralizing to say that 90% of those who've moved to EQ from UO did so because of a cowardly refusal on the game designers' part to "protect players from aggression before the fact" (to use Koster's phrase), i.e., to deal with the PK problem straightforwardly, as EQ has done. I came to absolutely detest, loathe, hate, abominate UO for that reason.

Macris, *supra* note 25, at 17 (quoting Tessa, *Gamers General Forum, at* http://eq.stratics.com).

31. Macris finds evidence for all three of the following hypotheses: (1) human nature becomes more violent in *Ultima Online* than it is in realspace (virtual sociopathy), (2) a disproportionately large number of humans who are violent in realspace play *Ultima Online* (player-killers), or (3) the level of violence in *Ultima Online* would occur in real space but for some nonarchitectural factor (laws and norms.) Macris, *supra* note 25, at 20.

32. Richard Bartle, *Hearts, Clubs, Diamonds, Spades: Players Who Suit MUDs, at* http://www.brandeis.edu/pubs/jove/HTML/v1/bartle.html (suggesting that each ludic type approaches the game differently: Achievers see them as games like chess or tennis; explorers see them as hobbies akin to gardening and cooking; socializers see them as entertainment; and killers treat them as sports like hunting or fishing. Unfortunately, these categories don't seem sharp enough to be useful).

33. *E.g.,* Mikael Jakobsson and T. L. Taylor, *The Sopranos Meets* EverQuest: *Social Networking in Massively Multiplayer Online Games, available at* http:// hypertext.rmit.edu.au/dac/papers/Jakobsson.pdf ("social networks form a powerful component of the gameplay and the gaming experience").

34. Arguably the *virtuality* of the killing in the more violent MMORPGs such as *Ultima Online* liberates or encourages antisocial behaviors that people would not engage in in real life: "Killing an *Ultima* character does not kill the *Ultima* player, just his avatar. The result is a guilt-free opportunity to commit mayhem

which *Ultima Online* players seem to revel in at least part of the time." Macris, *supra* note 25, at 21.

35. *See* Castronova, *supra* note 1, at 14 ("developing the avatar's skills takes time; monsters must be killed, axes must be forged, quests must be completed. The result of all this effort, which can take hundreds of hours, is "avatar capital": an enhancement of the avatar's capabilities through training").

36. *E.g., Adult Women Like to Play Games,* Reuters, Aug. 27, 2003, *at* http://www.wired.com/news/games/0,2101,60204,00.html.

37. Unless the purpose of the experiment was to see which rule system players preferred, players would have to be randomly assigned to different rule systems.

38. "[S]ince the VWs are inherently social, the achievements are relative: it is not having powerful weapons that really makes a difference in prestige, but in having the most powerful weapons in the world. In a postindustrial society, it is social status, more than anything else, that drives people to work so diligently all their lives. In this respect, VWs are truly a simulacrum of Earth society." Castronova, *supra* note 1, at 17.

39. *See, e.g., id.* at 16. As well as being subject to scarcity of economic resources inhabitants of Virtual worlds may be subject to "budget constraints" which affect their avatars' abilities, so that an avatar with good healing capacities may not be an effective fighter. This fact forces specialization. *See, e.g., id.* at 12.

40. *See id.* at 18 ("It turns out that grouping is essential to advancement.").

41. Virtual worlds could also shed light on some economic issues, such as how to identify people who would be likely to be successful entrepreneurs. People who showed entrepreneurial approaches to playing online games by developing new strategies that took advantage of particular characteristics of the games might also be successful entrepreneurs in meat-space. Venture capitalists could decide to allocate capital to people who showed success in making simoleans. Note that this would only work if one could guarantee that the simoleons were self-made rather than bought on eBay.

42. The Coase theorem holds that if private parties can bargain over the distribution of resources without cost, then they will allocate the costs of externalities in a manner that efficiently allocates resources. It follows that if the bargain cannot be reached, or if there are transactions costs, efficient allocation in the face of externalities may require the intervention of a third party. *See* Ronald Coase, *The Problem of Social Cost,* 3 J. L. and Econ. 1 (1960), *available at* http://www.sfu.ca/~allen/CoaseJLE1960.pdf.

43. John Rawls, A Theory of Justice (Belknap 1999) (1971).

44. We would argue that this shows that game developers lack imagination when it comes to creating seriously aggressive monster classes.

45. The Canadian province of British Columbia recently proposed introducing a new simpler system of securities regulation. *See, e.g.,* British Columbia Securities Commission, New Concepts for Securities Regulation, A New Way

TO REGULATE 5 (2002), *available at* http://www.bcsc.bc.ca:8080/Historycomdoc.nsf /0/ffb85755a68dce2e88256b64005970f8/$FILE/New_Concepts.pdf; BRITISH COLUMBIA SECURITIES COMMISSION, SECURITIES REGULATION THAT WORKS. THE BC MODEL, COMMENTARY ON DRAFT LEGISLATION 3 (2003), *available at* http://www.bcsc.bc.ca/Publications/BC_Model/Commentary.pdf. Issuers suggested that they would be more likely to interpret simpler, "plain language" rules themselves rather than consulting a lawyer. CHRISTINA WOLF, BETTER DISCLO-SURE, LOWER COSTS: A COST-BENEWT ANALYSIS OF THE CONTINUOUS MARKET ACCESS SYSTEM 16, *available at* http://www.bcsc.bc.ca/Publications/CBA _Report.pdf (2002).

46. Migration between different shards is very different from immigration in the real world.

47. One could run the test either by seeing which system players preferred to enter initially, or by allowing players to move from one shard to the other.

The New Visual Literacy
How the Screen Affects the Law

David R. Johnson

Online games have given us a whole new set of tools with which law and legally significant relationships can be created. The tools we first try out in the context of multiplayer online games may open up fundamentally new modes of communication and collaboration. Games may show the way toward new kinds of legal texts, new institutional forms and, ultimately, new kinds of social order.

Our new computer and network capabilities won't change human nature or fundamentally alter governments. But they may well change the way we form and act in social and economic groups. They may allow for the creation of new kinds of organizations—including complex, stable institutions that ultimately may demand and deserve legal personhood. The creation of new kinds of legal persons could have a profound effect on all our lives.

Let's examine how we might get from here to there.

Online Places Have Rules of Their Own

Virtual worlds have given us a sense that online "places" (particular screens that can be reached only in particular ways, sometimes only by particular groups, sometimes only under certain conditions) can have rules of their own. We've always had real-world places that are associated with particular sets of rules: churches, courthouses, homes, stadiums, military bases, restaurants, and so on. As bandwidth improves and computer graphics become more powerful, it becomes increasingly easy to deliver the visual cues necessary to differentiate one online space from another. These spaces are often provided by nongovernmental third parties. The nature of rules applicable to online activities is impacted by this in subtle yet important ways. AOL has a law of its own regarding user conduct (its "terms of service" define incivility). eBay has a different set of rules. *EverQuest* has still another. The use by virtual worlds of three dimensions and in-world physics—coupled with their persistence and development even while we are not present—reinforce our sense of the "placeness" of online locations. We may soon take it for granted that the act of visiting a particular online space corresponds to submission to the special rules that apply to actions in that context, just as we understand that traveling to another country subjects us to its local laws. When in Rome. . . . When in *Second Life.* . . .

Graphical Objects on the Screen Can Define Roles

Avatars have given us a sense that we can define new ROLES in the context of such rules. Online spaces are not merely virtual geographies—we see people, including ourselves, "there." Even the thinnest of graphical cues may serve to represent the role the user is playing (and her current state). When the cursor changes to a hand, or pointer, or insert bar or wand, that visual cue sends a self-referential message regarding the nature of the activity in which the user is or might be engaged. It's a short step from the cursor to the use of a graphical object that represents the user more explicitly and persistently. (Consider the labeled dot around the circular virtual table in UnChat, for example.) An avatar (or, indeed, any other graphical object) can change its state (color, size, costume, etc.) to reflect the state of mind, or intentions, or promises, or reputation, or circumstance, *or rights and duties* (!) of the user. And, as discussed more fully below, it's a short step from there to the creation of graphical conventions that can represent the relationship of a person to a social group. (The screen will show us who is entitled to act as moderator or who has responsibility to complete particular tasks shown on the Pert chart we are all viewing together online.) Ultimately, we'll use graphics to show the emergent state of mind of an entire group of persons who share a context (I'll say more on this later). In short, rules and the roles they create combine to define a social context.

New Forms of Legal Writing

The development of graphical interfaces has enabled a new form of "writing"—graphical groupware—that involves decisions by users to place particular graphical elements in particular locations within a larger graphical environment. This "semantic placement" has the potential to give us a new form of asynchronous group communication. The key point is that graphical objects can "stand for" ideas or people or things—and that the placement of such objects against a background (or, in effect, in a location in a particular online place) can communicate the relationship between such persons or things (or the view of such persons or things or ideas held by the person doing the placing).

Online games use graphics to create the illusion of a "real world" of tangible objects located in relationship to one another. If we apply the metaphor of "objects" placed in a "space" to the intangible—to the world of ideas—new forms of graphical communication may open up. For example, we can create a shared online diagram. Graphical objects representing particular risks or opportunities can be placed, by members of a group, against axes that represent urgency or magnitude of impact. The result is a jointly created "radar screen" that shows the state of mind of the group regarding its collective future.

Creation of a shared diagram is fundamentally different from the creation of shared documents, or even shared pictures of virtual worlds. A "diagram" has at least two layers—a background (which can provide a context or a metric) and a foreground (which can contain graphical objects that relate to identified ideas, persons, or things) and are placed or controlled by multiple users. A dynamic online diagram has both the advantages of compact symbolism and the efficiency and richness of visual perception (the parallel processing of the eye allows us to see more, more quickly, than we can read.) Nonpictoral graphics have previously been the stuff of math. One thing we have learned from the interfaces of games (particularly from the option of allowing graphical elements to be placed for purposes of communication with a group) is that complex nonpictoral graphical constructions can facilitate collaboration. If everyone in a group separately places "their" graphical elements against a background, and a composite view is "rolled up" by averaging these placements, the resulting pattern is an emergent representation of the views of the group as a whole. Each member of the group may be surprised by the result the group has collectively created.[1]

The use of computation to alter the state of a dynamic graphic provides us with a new method for seeing emergent relationships between facts and conclusions and between individuals and groups. When law is expressed as text, it can only be about things reasonably expressible in text. If the law could also consist of structured, dynamic pictures, it could express some kinds of legal ideas more precisely or accessibly. For example, a dynamic model of a contract or statute is capable of conveying legal relationships more completely, less ambiguously, more obviously, than traditional text. Putting a statute or regulation into the form of a graphical diagram forces disambiguation of the "or's" and makes the structure of "and's" obvious. Making that diagram interactive allows a "user" of the law to play "what if" games that enhance comprehension. Turn the (graphical objects representing) facts "on" or "off" and the (graphical objects representing) conclusions recompute.

Similarly, a dynamic, emergent organizational chart that shows patterns of relationships that emerge from networked interactions and decentralized decisions can change how we see—and how we think about—our involvement in social groups. Many of our most important advances have come simply from new technologies that allow us to see phenomena that were previously invisible to us. The shared screens of online games give us the beginnings of designs for a new legal microscope, telescope, x-ray. At a minimum, it seems likely that new graphical interfaces, based on what we've learned from online games, will help to make the intangible world of law and legal relationships more accessible to all.

Enriching Online Contracts

Long since, we've gotten used to those "click to agree" buttons. Oddly, few of those debating laws designed to make e-signatures binding have raised concerns about the lack of "channeling"—the absence of the signal provided by a "real" signature, its unusual formality implicitly warning that there may be potentially serious consequences from entering into a contract. We might reasonably be concerned that the screen does not offer rich enough cues to give users a sense of when they should be careful. What is the minimum required electronic indication of assent? Does it make a difference that your avatar can now nod in agreement, or virtually shake hands? For now, our ability to challenge any credit card charge helps mitigate the dangers. But online games provide richer contexts—and may create new traps for the unwary. Maybe we'll insist that, in order to bind a user to significant obligations, avatars be made to appear to use a virtual pen to sign a virtual document. We might come full circle.

Once we take the screen seriously as a context in which legally significant relationships can be formed, there are many options in addition to indicating agreement with a contractual text. We can drag an online "object" to a semantically significant location—the "buy this" bucket, or the screen location that indicates that another party may have that particular item or concession. Or we can indicate subtle shadings of opinion on various alternatives by arraying the objects representing all alternatives along axes that represent different views (e.g., the extent to which the user favors or disfavors a particular contract term or option). We already click to vote. Why shouldn't we also drag and drop to indicate various shades of opinion, or commitment, or willingness to accept various roles, or agreement to provide compensation to others who do so? If I place my avatar into a particular unoccupied seat at a virtual table, that may constitute acceptance of a particular role or job (with corresponding rights and responsibilities in relation to the rest of the group admitted to the online space in question). Surely we will develop new visual forms of consent to contractual relationships.

From Contracts and Games to Organized, Persistent Entities

Contrary to often parroted doctrine, most legally respectable social organizations have arisen from private custom or agreement, rather than from a charter granted by the state. Even corporations (joint stock companies) basically arose long before the sovereign purported to license them. To be sure, the state must decide to respect and defer to an organizational form if it is to be viable. The difference between a corporation and an illegal conspiracy is just that the state refuses to allow the latter to persist (and won't protect its bank account). If we can form contracts online, we can form legally significant organizations online. The interesting questions are whether the new electronic medium through which we meet, contract, and collaborate may lead to new and different types of organizations—and whether governments will defer to them.

In a sense, it already has. Yochai Benkler has explained why peer production flourishes in an online environment where the cost of finding opportunities to add value to a shared informational commons is dramatically reduced.[2] But peer production is now really "just" a new mode of production, not a new organizational form. It will only really become a new persistent organizational form insofar as online groups discover how to collectively appropriate the product of their shared work. Such groups might form, in effect, an emergent producers' cooperative, in which self-selecting producers collaborate to decide both how to create valuable work product together and how to capture some of the value of their shared work product in the context of a larger marketplace.

What does this have to do with games and graphics? The fundamental challenge for any organizational structure (or market or mode of production) is figuring out how to allocate particular tasks to particular people (and how to coordinate related tasks and people). The new "visibility" of social relationships provided by gamelike interfaces may provide an answer. Graphics can be used to represent both a task (let's say, with a box) and a person (let's say, with a circle or a face). Put the circle/face in a box and you've got a work assignment. That could be done by a supervisor. But it can also (perhaps more cheaply) be done by the person undertaking to do the work. If work is divisible into small chunks, this allows a movement away from large-grained employment contracts toward finer-grained "jobs." If the workers self-select, the online place may produce emergent teams. If the teams can use graphics to allocate the "ownership" interests in their joint work product, this may result, in effect, in emergent corporate (or cooperative) organizations. Even if the teams disperse, the resulting "organization" might persist insofar as their work-product retains value vis-à-vis the external marketplace and some mechanism remains for making decisions on how to realize that value and distribute net proceeds.

The Persistence of Graphical Online Places

One striking attribute of multiplayer online games is that they persist and evolve even in the absence of a particular player. That same attribute is also a most striking feature of corporate entities of all kinds. The difference between the two may be just that we have learned how to realize one in graphics, while we typically realize the other (the corporate entity) in text. Both may evolve toward an appropriate mixture of graphics and text, on the asynchronously shared, persistent screen.

There are many possible approaches to the creation of what we might call an organizational interface. As noted, the consequences of undertaking and completing a job can be represented graphically, perhaps with backup text as necessary to explain the conventions in question. We already regularly communicate online applause—reputational feedback sufficient to motivate many contributors to open source projects (think of eBay ratings). But that doesn't exhaust the possibilities. We might exchange more than applause. We might create an online knowledge assembly line at which all who can add value may find their most productive places, from which those who contribute substantially might reasonably expect to receive financial compensation. Wiki's now allow large groups to collaborate to build valuable online texts. If access to such texts by noncontributors were charged for, the group collaborating to create the texts might be rewarded financially. The simple elements of agreement, roles, and communication of task status, all conveyed with dynamic graphics, can combine to create something much more complex than a shared text—a persistent social/economic organization.

Managing Assets Created by Online Groups

Any effort to collectively appropriate the work product of collaborative online production would require the group in question (the producers) somehow to arrange to make joint decisions about how best to exploit their property in the wider market. A traditional corporate structure would do this by delegating decision making to agents, top down. The online game environment suggests another possibility—emergent "management" of jointly owned assets, by means of direct (or proxy) voting by a persistent group of constantly shifting composition. Games can create a new kind of agent—not in the top-down principal and agent sense but in the bottom-up sense that decentralized decisions by individual contributors can be computationally cumulated into decisions that bind the group (with respect to the disposition of its collective work product) over time.

The net allows us to pool effort, not just capital. Shares in the resulting proceeds are not necessarily securities (within the legal meaning of that term), because they do not depend for their value solely on the actions of others. Should we characterize online collaborations as partnerships? That would substantially deter valuable collaborations, because it is our received doctrine that partners are liable for each other's actions. So we quickly come upon an old question in this very new context—should we provide "limited liability" for those who contribute their time and effort (not capital) to a collective online enterprise? Drawing on the long-standing debate about corporations, we might suspect that the answer turns on whether the limitation can be made visible enough—so that those dealing as outsiders with such entities will be warned and will remain free to decide whether or not to take the risk.

We are not that far away from the use of the net to allow emergent consulting firms. Teams of software engineers are assembled for projects on the fly. Contributors to slashdot bulletin boards collectively rate and select the most relevant postings. Bloggers motivated to investigate an issue in aggregate assemble relevant details, correct each others' mistakes, and evaluate claims and options. These kinds of efforts don't persist or achieve legal personhood (or own a bank account). But it is possible that increasing use of graphics will make such groups seem more real and, therefore, allow them to become more persistent.

Visualization of Legally SigniWcant Relationships

One of the key challenges facing any attempt to create online organizations of any kind is the need to make the rules that define various roles clearly enough for all to see. This may be one place in which visual contextual cues and the interactive character of the screen become very important. As noted, it is possible to translate an authoritative text into a series of interactive "fact" buttons that, when toggled, turn appropriate conclusion buttons on or off. Expressing a set of rules as a dynamic virtual (software) machine has the potential to reach more users, many of whom might only tune out if required to read a traditional legal text.

In some cases, the combination of user input and network connectedness may enable a new source of authoritative rulings: the online jury. If the question presented is what is "reasonable" in a particular online social context, maybe we should use our newfound ability to ask the relevant group that question! (The obviously relevant group consists of the users whose interests and values the online space in question is designed to serve.)

Whoever makes the decisions, we'll need to overcome one key current problem for any form of online decision making—getting even a small group to make decisions together online requires too much text. Real-world meetings are bad, but online meetings (to produce real decisions and buy-in) are even worse! Why? Current systems don't provide enough feedback regarding the state of mind of the group. Here again, the new affordances provided by online games may prove important. You can tell a lot at a glance about what the person behind an online avatar is paying attention to, how that person feels, and whether he or she and others assembled in an online meeting support a particular idea or course of action.

The most important aspect of the screen used in multiplayer online games is the fact that a group of people are looking at it and treating it as the context for their own actions and comments. In the military, they call this "situation awareness"—a shared image that dramatically increases communications efficiency. In the online context, the "situation" in question is the online context itself and the state of all participants. When a shared image is used to represent the state of mind of the group itself, a new kind of collaboration results. Each individual reacts in relationship to his or her relationship to the group. Effective online group decision making thus becomes possible.

From Online Organizations/Entities to Legal Personhood

However we use the new affordances of the screen to form legally significant relationships, it appears very likely that we will begin to enjoy a more explicit, self-referential view of our mutual undertakings. Whenever we act together in groups, offline, we often do so in ways that create a persistent identity for the group itself. When we act in groups online, we will end up creating composite entities that may be represented by visible avatars of their own and may seek rights and duties independent from those of particular individual participants. How will the (traditional, offline) law react?

If the affordances of online games (graphically conveyed roles, the new writing by means of semantic placement, and the computationally determined location and state of graphical elements) enable us to create new kinds of organizations, then we'll face the question whether and to what degree to grant these organizations legal personhood. Will an online game, active as a collective, be allowed to open a bank account? What ultimately distinguishes a game from a corporation? If the participants want to act collectively with respect to the external world, for purposes that we would not otherwise brand as illegally conspiratorial, why shouldn't we let them do so? If the rules are clear, the roles established and otherwise permissible, and the status of the entity as a limited liability sharing of time and effort are disclosed to those with whom the entity deals, why shouldn't that new kind of "web of contracts" be respected?

Some might respond that it's easy enough to "touch down in Delaware" and adopt a standard corporate form for any activity one might engage in online. But I don't think it is that simple. Most corporation statutes require traditional ownership and the appointment of named officers with particular powers. These laws do not anticipate emergent decision making by a group with constantly shifting members. Unincorporated associations of various types are recognized by the law, but perhaps without the necessary assurance of limited liability or the desired ability to bring suit to protect jointly owned property rights. I think the law will have to adapt to take into account new ways of "owning and controlling" the end product of our new electronic modes of production.

We will clearly not be dealing just with "legal fictions" or "mere games." Groups that coordinate their activities online can take action that impacts the real world. The growth of "smart mobs" is an early example of use of the net to coordinate collective action in the real world.[3] If the next "smart mob" were to cause a group to come together to raise a barn, or write a song, who would own the work product? Is that a function of the terms of the online notice? Could the group's work product be sold? What mechanism would be used to set the price? If the "mob" came together, solely online, using electronic tools to do collaborative work, would the ownership and control of their collective product stem solely (or primarily) from the rules of the online context (virtual place) within which they assembled?

Collaborative work is at least as old as our first efforts to surround prey to increase our chances in the hunt. We can now assemble online, from all over the world, to perform many different kinds of collaborative work. How could we not begin to exploit this new potential? If what is necessary to make it happen is legal recognition of the assembled collective having rights *of its own* to the fruits of its labor, we'll give such entities rights (and corresponding duties). The resulting increased stake of individual contributors in the online enterprise will make it easier to enforce whatever rules make this new form of collective productivity possible.

New Types of Organizations?

Another interesting question is whether the flexibility of the screen will allow us to create institutions that have a more diverse set of goals than do our current organizations. Current (nongovernmental) organizations that claim legal personhood tend to sort into two distinct piles—those dedicated to seeking profit and those established for what some local sovereign considers permissible "nonprofit" purposes. Online groups might blend these two types in unpredictable ways—for example, collectively creating an intellectual work product for fun and profit and the betterment of the world. Is online collaboration to create an annotated map of the world, complete with links to local pictures, a game? What if noncontributors were charged for access to the map, with the proceeds shared by those who contributed data or pictures?

The ultimate question posed to local sovereigns will be how to sort out those collaborative activities that should be discouraged from those that ought to be welcomed and legally recognized and enabled. One possible determinant of the answer to that question will be whether the activities of the group primarily impact willing participants (or parties whose well-being is sought by the group). Because online groups can form and act easily across physical boundaries, there is in this online context less than the "normal" assurance that their activities will primarily impact those who participate. It's one thing for a state to defer to local churches, charities, and clubs. It's quite another for a local state to defer to a group that might consist entirely of noncitizens, taking action that might well affect many who have not voluntarily joined the group. However we deal with these challenges, it will be important to be able to see what is happening. The use of graphical, gamelike interfaces for collaborative action may thus provide part of both the problem and the solution.

Conclusion

If the law is about the collective creation of rules that define roles that guide and enable collective action, then multiplayer online games surely involve, create, and will inform the law. More importantly, if games are collective activities engaged in through roles established by rules, then our new appreciation for how best to design and play games online will lead to new insights into how best to create new social institutions of various kinds.

Some of the new organizations we form online will be more visible than any we have created, offline, in the past. We will begin to see the social fabric, and our own place in it. How we will react to a gaze into this new mirror is anybody's guess. I'm hopeful that we will be encouraged to take actions that make us proud of what we see. And I hope that we remember to use our collective imaginations to the fullest, because what shows up in that mirror won't be limited to the organizational forms that our previous ways of writing, our previous ways of forming contracts, and our previous ways of playing roles and sharing decisions, made possible.

NOTES

1. As Surowiecki notes, in *The Wisdom of Crowds: Why the Many Are Smarter Than the Few and How Collective Wisdom Shapes Business, Economics, Societies and Nations* (New York: Doubleday, 2004), the result may be more accurate than the views of any members of the group.

2. Benkler, "Coase's Penguin, or Linux and the Nature of the Firm," 112 *Yale L.J.* 369 (2002).

3. Howard Rheingold, *Smart Mobs: The Next Social Revolution* (New York: Basic Books, 2002).

Democracy—The Video Game
Virtual Worlds and the Future of Collective Action

Beth Simone Noveck

The Wisdom of Crowds: Three Stories[1]

The CEO of United Parcel Service is not a happy man. Fundrace.org,[2] the website which allows visitors to search the campaign contribution database of the Federal Election Commission and to create maps of Red and Blue buildings, streets, and neighborhoods, makes it easy to find out that he gave a substantial sum of money to George W. Bush.

During the Moveon.org on-line conference with Michael Moore[3] following the release of *Fahrenheit 9/11*, the computer screen showed the Director in his baseball hat but it also indicated "hot spots" of activity—big colored nodes—where people were participating. Not to be outdone by another region, increasing numbers of people volunteered, generating a higher level of engagement.

"[The] Washington monument had been replaced by a giant tower of tea crates; . . . the Route 66 gas station set ablaze by an insurrectionist midget shooting off seditious fireworks." A group of outraged "Lifers" or subscribers to the *Second Life* virtual world, were protesting newly imposed (and, as a result of their protests, subsequently revoked), taxes levied on digital possessions.

What do these stories have in common? In each of them, the visual computer screen helped people to see themselves and the community to which they belonged. When we can see the group, we can act as a group.

All the fundamental activities of public life in a democracy are group activities. The group in its myriad forms is the basic unit of social organization. Activism and organizing require the mobilization of communities of interest. Lawmaking and legislating in a democracy demand the public deliberation of a group. The people affected by a decision are expected to play a role—be it through deliberation, voting, or providing input in some form—in decisions that are made. Through public and shared participation in making law and policy, we arrive at legitimate and informed solutions. Not only is it group decisions that are viewed as legitimate but collective vision sees reality more clearly and collective conversation gives rise to greater truth. While our legal and political culture is strongly liberal individualist, its institutions are centered on the commonplace idea that democracy requires the involvement of the *demos,* the group participating in shaping the life of the polity. In other arenas, including economic and business life[4] and creative and cultural life,[5] there has been a keen interest in the role of groups in making forecasts, creating value, sharing risks and rewards, and making decisions. But there is no account at all in the legal literature about the relationship between technology and collective action.

If we want to understand the impact of technology on our democracy, we must look at the way technology affects groups. We need to know what technology does to people's ability to organize, protest, deliberate, resolve disputes, and engage in the basic collective actions of democratic life. Most of the technologies we use on the World Wide Web today, what I term the "web world," are premised upon disconnected, individual users. Even popular chat tools are either one-to-one instant messaging devices or unstructured systems for talk radio ranting. While this first generation of text-based cybertechnology has created new opportunities for communities to form, the lack of face-to-face interaction has made trust building and collective action difficult. Groups are easy to form but hard to sustain. Yet in the second generation of virtual-world technology, we may be evolving interfaces better suited to new kinds of collective action.

What makes virtual worlds particularly interesting for the future of democracy is that they are conducive to groups coming together, working together, and staying together. Virtual worlds and visual technologies reintroduce place and space, they allow people to "get next to" each other in real time and to assume discernable identities. This reintroduction of space and place renders cyberspace more hospitable to social interaction. But, even more profoundly, what typifies the new virtual landscapes is the primacy they assign to *visuality and seeing,* which transform the relationship between people and information on the Internet. By allowing participants to see themselves within the context of the group and exchange information and assets, virtual worlds permit members of a group to manage the division of roles and responsibilities that allow groups to do productive work in participatory fashion. It is not simply a matter of visualizing information but using technology to visualize people and their roles. Virtual worlds, because they allow people to see the group and to divide labor and share tasks necessary to accomplish the work of the group, enable collective action that may bridge the chasm between real-world power and virtual-world play. This is significant because when groups can work together effectively, they can wield power.

My argument about virtual worlds and groups navigates between those who propound an exclusive focus on deliberation and those who offer the equally unrealistic notion that networks—like markets—will produce a flourishing of free speech, association, and democracy. Instead, I want to focus on how technology that "foregrounds" social interaction can help groups govern themselves. In this introductory exploration of the subject, the goal is not to predict which groups will flourish online[6] but rather to develop a theory of technology design that can be used to help groups succeed in an era of relentless technological change.

Group Life

Groups,[7] in the sense that I use the term here, are not the same as communities, a term that has become ubiquitous to describe the emotional attachments of people online. A group is unlike two people talking or ten people on a street corner or even unlike ten thousand people on Craig's List. A group is not only more than the sum of its individual parts; it is an agglomeration of people with an affirmative purpose. A group *aspires* to do something in the world. It is an intentional collective that creates a sense of belonging to something and manifests a shared purpose. In the group roles and responsibilities are shared, with boundaries and membership. Interaction must be sustained over some period of time, during which a group develops its own internal norms or culture. Perhaps most important, a group does its work through the participation of its members.

Admittedly, there are terrorist cells that fit this description of a group. But from the perspective of fostering a new electronic civil society, it is participation—not membership, nor subject matter and not even conversation—directed toward accomplishing something together that is most relevant to defining the group. Often, to be participatory, a group has to be small enough to enable a clear delineation of roles and responsibilities. But with new technology, opportunities emerge for larger-scale participatory working and internetworking of smaller groups into larger collectives. Groups wield power as collective actors and through participation that power is legitimized, enabling groups to make decisions and take action.

Participation, especially in the Internet era, takes many different forms and is not limited to equal time in a conversation. New technology is changing the opportunities for intentional collaboration. Members of a group participate through discussion and deliberation to inform decisions taken and also through active participation in the decision itself. But they also participate through taking on a task aimed at achieving the group's goal. The means for doing so may be explicit deliberation processes or emergent mechanisms for coordinating disparate opinions into collective action across a network,[8] enabled by peer-to-peer technology such as that used for music file swapping and sharing. Deliberation and conversation can take place in real time or asynchronously, using a variety of face-to-face and software mechanisms. Participation in the life of a group may also entail a sharing of responsibility that does not result in everyone participating co-equally in every decision taken.

Participation and the Work of Groups:
Physics, Culture, and Information

We need to focus on the three essential elements to the work of groups. They are: (1) group physics, (2) group culture, and (3) group information.

The *group physics* are what give shape and direction to the work of groups. By physics, I am referring to the rules and structures which determine how participants in a group interact. The physics are the basic structures that allow the group to form and give it boundaries. All groups operate according to some kind of governance or organizational rules. My assumption is that structure and rules are essential to give shape and direction to the work of groups and that, without rules, the communication necessary for collaboration cannot take place. Is it legally incorporated or simply a loose agglomeration? Does the group have an explicit policy about who can join and what membership requires? Are decisions taken by vote and by whom? Having a structure also gives participants a clear indication of their role and function within the group, which in turn contributes to a sense of belonging.

Group physics may enable a group to form, but to maintain a group requires that participants have a sense of shared purpose, belonging, and solidarity. In other words, there must be a *group culture.* Culture reflects the organizing principles, mission, and purpose—the ties that bind—of the group. Participants have to be aware of the identity of the group and to perceive shared values, a collective purpose, or common mission.

That identity of the group is, in turn, reinforced by the perception by each participant that he or she belongs. A successful group does not require a common cause; people can be joined by difference. But for the group to have an independent identity, participants must consider themselves to share a purpose and to rely on others not to defect. Participants have to be able to build trust. A common uniform, logo, or other symbol of belonging help to create a sense of the group.

Finally, participatory problem solving by a group depends not only on physics and culture, but also upon having access to information that is useful to the group. It is not information per se; it is *group information*[9] in the context in which it can be used and understood by a group of people. That information may come in the form of outside data or may be the information exchanged through deliberation and dialogue within the group. It is paramount that the information be manageable enough to exploit, clear enough to understand, and transparent enough to minimize manipulation. The ways of understanding the relationship between the information, the desired outcome, and the different roles of members of the group vis-à-vis that information are crucial.

The Political Sociology of the First-Generation Internet

Group Physics

For groups, the technology has been a mixed blessing. The first-generation Internet has made communication cheap and plentiful, reducing the initial costs of forming groups. But cyberspace also eliminates the familiar structures and rules of real space that contribute to sustaining groups over time. It is a familiar observation that life online is characterized by decentralized, many-to-many interactions that undermine attempts at top-down control. The celebration of distributed, hive intelligence was part of the ethos of the early Net. But Larry Lessig has powerfully demonstrated the fallacy lurking behind the idea that technology and life online are not subject to control.[10] While such "regulability" creates problems for civil liberties when done by government or corporations, control and structure by the group itself are necessary to organize group life.

While it turns out to be very easy to launch an open-source software development project where the collective mind of dozens of programmers are channeled into a common project, this is only half the story. Most of these projects are never completed. They are difficult to manage because the division of roles and responsibilities is hard. In the end, those that do get done are largely the work of a handful of people.[11]

The problem is that networks make communication vastly cheaper. More people have access to a means of expression, such as a weblog or electronic mail. This is very promising for participation, which depends upon open and easy expression. Yet cyberspace erases the structures upon which groups rely in real space to manage their conversation. The social clues, cues, and etiquette are gone. People interact with handles rather than names. The organization imposed by physical constraints or the threat of violence is absent. The lack of structure for coordinating plentiful communication and information makes it harder to define the boundaries of the group and to organize work within the group over time.

In other words, it is easier to form a group, independent of the bounds of geography, about bridge or poodles. But the fact that I can start such a group does not make it any easier to sustain it, especially where there is so much communication and so many channels competing for people's loyalty and attention. It is easy to speak but difficult to be heard. Even where a group commits to forming, there exist few of the familiar constraints that help it cohere.

So while it may be simpler to talk to people, it is generally hard to find them. Though communication is cheap, it is harder to be heard. Even when people "get next to each other," without structure they do not know where to stand. While networks may aggregate huge numbers of anonymous actors to rate books on Amazon or rate postings on Slashdot, the lack of structure makes it harder to create participatory groups that engage in affirmative (rather than reactive) action.[12] There is nothing inherent about cyberspace that makes communication easier to structure.

One partial solution to this problem is the ability to program rules and structures into the code itself to facilitate communication and deliberation.[13] The Harvard Berkman Center's H2O Rotisserie discussion software,[14] for example, requires all participants in a given group to respond to a particular question before the answers are displayed to the members. This feature encourages everyone to participate and limits the "cascading" problem of one person swaying the debate by being the first to respond. While some Wikis, such as the Wiki Encyclopedia,[15] the user-written and edited encyclopedia, are open, other WIKIs are limited by password to a predefined group or show a history of the group's editing as a way to manage posting. This transparency creates an incentive to appropriate participation. By translating methods of interpersonal communication used for offline deliberation to the web, technology can help manage conversation, to an extent, by building the physics into the code of the software.[16]

Group Culture

Another problem for groups in text-based cyberspace is that, while there are addresses, there is no place and without place there can be no sidewalks.[17] While the lack of space liberates people from the constraints of geography, it also eliminates opportunities for civic encounters and events. This profoundly changes the way group culture forms. The decoupling of cyberspace from physical place impedes the opportunities that foster belonging and friendship in the real world. Arguably, cyberspace offers new opportunities for individuals to acquaint themselves and develop lasting bonds but hinders the interaction necessary for a group of any size to cohere.

This may be because the absence of place means I need never "run into" anyone from the group again, reducing the incentive to loyalty and against exit.[18] As Robert Axelrod in his classic work on the theory of cooperation writes: "The very possibility of achieving stable mutual cooperation depends upon there being a good chance of a continuing interaction."[19] But in cyberspace the boundaries are open, interaction is relatively anonymous, and therefore there is little incentive to cooperate when disputes arise. The ability to sanction or shame defectors or, conversely, to reward loyalty is further limited in a virtual space. Where collaborators know each other or have some kind of reputational tie in real space, these incentives are preserved. This is why social networks and reputation-based systems proliferate to exploit the trust and intimacy developed offline for online interactions.

Despite an emerging literature on the metaphor of cyberspace as place[20] or virtual frontier, place is, arguably, but a turn of phrase. Let me be clear: There is a there there in cyberspace. We have a sense of being somewhere and we loyally return to websites where we have been before. This is adequate for forming certain individual bonds and emotional attachments but it is *harder* to create the connections for "the body politic" in a disembodied space. The inability to see self and others in relationship to a space problematizes group culture. The social rituals and visual totems that inculcate a culture within the group are also absent. Not only are there no uniforms or explicit manifestations of belonging in a world of disembodied identity, but there is no food. I mean this literally. The ritual of breaking bread (or beer), as a way to cultivate solidarity and belonging, does not exist. There is no substitution for the fellowship of the *Kaffeehaus* in cyberspace.

Not only do people who want to sustain groups have to work harder to maintain their bonds, but also there is no way to cultivate allegiance or attachment to a place. In real space, the group may be defined by the physical space where it meets. Anyone who shows up at church is part of the group. The architecture of the space itself is defining. Cyberspace changes this calculus. It is for this reason that Meetup.com has been so successful. Meetup marries the communications potential of the Internet to the architecture of real space as a way to form and sustain communities of interest. With Meetup, people go on the Internet to find a group in their neighborhood and organize a time to get together in real space with real coffee.

The difficulty of reinforcing attachments is exacerbated by another, related problem. Not only is there no ability to see space and place, but there is also a significant limitation on the ability to see others in the text-based world of the first-generation Net. This blindness liberates people from physical prejudices but it also produces social dislocation that reduces the level of trust.

There is another impediment to group life online. The absence of any connection to "real-world" institutions and power disconnects the social space of cyberspace from what we think of as the public sphere. At present, there are few, if any, institutionalized citizen juries or other consultative mechanisms in cyberspace. The perception is that online groups "don't matter" to real-world politics. Worse yet, typically participation in cyberlife has meant deracination from real-world community. The more time spent in cyberspace, the less time spent in real-world communities, leading to a loss of influence over real-world power and a loss of participation. Even though conversations about policy and money can take place just as easily online as in the corridors of power, online politics (perhaps until the Howard Dean campaign) has been seen as peripheral to democracy. In fact, the abysmal failure of Dean's candidacy only served to reinforce this perception. This is, in part, because the political elite is not computer literate but also, in part, because social groups and the web of civic and social organizations that shape the public sphere cannot yet subsist in the thin atmosphere of today's cyberspace.

The Social Life of Information

Technology poses a similar problem for information and groups. Just as there is lots of disorganized communication, there is also too much data. On the one hand this is a good thing for group formation. New technology enables access to a greater quantity of information, more opinions, more ideas, more stuff. This raises the overall level of knowledge or at least the opportunity to develop knowledge. E-mail, weblog tools, and easy means for linking make it easy to share and cross-reference information. People can draw connections between pieces of information.

On the other hand, too much information leads to the familiar problem of information overload. The absence of a discrete number of centralized information arbiters creates problems of information quality. This, in turn, promotes informational cascades, where the group simply defers to the opinion of one charismatic or powerful member who proposes what is important and relevant. This can contribute to "group think," polarization, and other social dynamics antithetical to the practice of participation.

Ultimately, the problem for the group life of information is that real people need to make sense of abstract information and concepts and translate them into relevant knowledge for use in solving problems and making decisions. Cyberspace is a wonderful repository for vast quantities of information. But our two-dimensional, text-based interfaces, while allowing us to order data chronologically, do not *readily* lend themselves to other forms of presentation and organization. We have a hard time mapping the informational landscape of cyberspace and making sense of it without the visual aids we use to organize informational inputs in real life. In reality, I process information all around me by its size, shape, color, intensity, location, and relationship to other people and places. The virtual world is full of information but, for the most part, I have very limited tools by which to make sense of it. These are social spaces of human interaction but we still receive our information as if we were reading a book.

The contemporary interface of the Internet certainly makes it easier to form new groups but poses challenges to sustain those groups or coordinate their productive work. Beyond simply the cost and difficulty of using new technology, the inability to see people in cyberspace or to have a sense of place and space limits the flourishing of group culture necessary to maintaining a group over time. The overflow of communication and information make it harder to engage in productive and collaborative work. In particular, if we want to engage in participatory groups, which depend upon sharing responsibility and power, the nature of cyberspace itself thwarts the coordination of such forms of collective action. Structures and rules can be "coded into" the architecture of virtual spaces but we, thus far, have had limited experience creating structured environments for group life.

The Political Sociology of the Second-Generation Internet

The *Second Life* tax revolt described at the beginning of this chapter is a good example of emerging collective activism in virtual worlds. All multiplayer games specifically reward and require collaboration as a way to achieve an in-game goal, such as storming a castle or scaling a wall. As subscribers become increasingly invested in these places, when something is not to their liking they are willing not simply to leave, but to join—and join in trying to shape the virtual world they inhabit.

Virtual Worlds and the Physics of Groups

The technology itself manifests many characteristics absent from the first-generation Internet that are conducive to sustaining group life online. Visual technologies, like virtual worlds, put the sidewalks back in. This makes it easier for groups to form. In a virtual world, one encounters others in a space. Avatars can be next to each other without people having to be next to each other. The technology is spatially oriented and has its own geography of space. In a virtual world, unlike a website, I can occupy a plot of "land," build a house there, invite guests over to break bread, drink tea (or unlimited margaritas, for that matter), or form a discussion. While I may be able to meet at a web address, here I can also *see* who is present and in what capacity vis-à-vis the group. These spaces are persistent and exist whether or not I am in the world. This also means I can create a theater for gathering, protest, action, and participation. In *Second Life,* in fact, residents formed a group to protest the use of flying or "teleporting" (*Star Trek*–style) from one location to another and insisted that all subscribers should have to walk from place to place to promote social encounters. This is despite the fact that *Second Life* already requires teleporting between central transportation hubs rather than point-to-point in a world. Though it is a virtual world, *Second Life* is full of sidewalks. The residents, not the company, have built these. People build virtual sidewalks presumably to replicate common features of the real world but also to encourage social interaction in the space.

By reintroducing the concept of space, groups and communities can cohere around specific locations. It may turn out that in the second-generation Internet, community once again comes to be defined by space. In all virtual worlds, groups develop their own themed spaces where they congregate. In *Second Life,* there are areas for World War II fanatics and for skydiving enthusiasts. Sometimes groups construct new landscapes to resemble a particular place they like, including the landscape of another virtual world or game. As in the real world, place becomes relevant to group formation. Unlike the real world, however, there is more freely available and accessible space and users exert more control over how it is designed.

In addition, having to operate in a defined place—even one that is not as resource-limited as the real world—requires that players mediate their differences to the extent necessary to cooperate and cohabit a shared cyberspace. If inhabitants in a virtual world disagree about the architectural design of a new neighbor's house and object to her building a Tudor monstrosity in a modernist, glass neighborhood, there is a wider range of available dispute resolution options in a virtual space. The house can be "cut-and-pasted" into a new neighborhood more easily in pixelated space than in brick-and-mortar space. However, the conceit of the virtual world and the geographical limits imposed by the capacity of the server still require people to get along to the point of living together. The whole idea of the virtual world or the videogame is to engage in collective action. As such, by reintroducing the concept of space, the interface itself promotes the work of groups over the action of individuals.

The place of the virtual world also reintroduces the concept of public space, not in the doctrinal sense of having state-owned "land" or a place of public accommodation with special First Amendment protections but by metaphorically presenting a place for social interaction and conversation. The landscape need not resemble a town square or Main Street or the country fair (though it easily could). In the virtual world, the country fair is everywhere that people can come together and interrelate. Precisely because the space is a social and technical construct, it more explicitly represents the otherwise unarticulated function of space as a locus for social gathering.

In a virtual world, rules and structures can also be programmed into the physics of the game, thereby improving the physics of the group. Virtual worlds are governed by technical internal rules—the electronic *Rechtsstaat*. It is a commonplace to assert that values are embedded in the software, which regulates behavior in accordance with these values. Virtual worlds, in particular, constrain the behavior of avatars within a set of rules programmed by the game's creators or which the creators, increasingly, allow the players to determine and then enforce through the technology or through player norms. The game may impose the payment of taxes, rules of behavior, including when it is permissible to attack other players, and sanctions for infractions against the rules. It is because of this self-governing feature that virtual worlds are especially susceptible, not only to imposing structure on communities, but to allowing groups to decide their own rules.

Virtual Worlds and the Culture of Groups

These new cyberspaces are real-time social environments. Technologically, this is an obvious point but its implications are profound. This cyberspace encourages participation and iterative interaction in a way that could be avoided in the world of the web. Though asynchronous interaction has its deliberative benefits, the option to engage in the *real-time* exchange of ideas remedies the problem with earlier cyber-social interaction. Virtual worlds are designed explicitly for use by groups of people and therefore, unlike earlier video games or even the web, they are not designed to be individualizable services. They are the manifestation of social interaction. What makes them virtual worlds is precisely that people interact here.

EverQuest and *Star Wars Galaxies* are vast communities spread across several servers (and therefore members of each so-called "shard" do not interact directly). Massively multiplayer games, like all real-time communications technologies, foster belonging to a group by allowing for the immediacy of face-to-face social interaction. People go to virtual worlds to seek sociability, interact with others, and participate in a common activity of play or work. As inherently social environments, they have been singled out as ideal test-beds for social and legal experimentation because they emulate society in all its complexity. But they go beyond social scientific experiments in constructing artificial life by offering a space for genuine interaction.

Another and perhaps the most important characteristic of the new cyberspace is the avatar, the simulacrum of self within the game space. Virtual worlds allow subscribers to create individuated characters with unique identities whom they and others can see. Historically, a player saw an avatar in the third person, controlling the character but not inhabiting its gaze. Now most virtual worlds and online games are designed to let participants see through the eyes of the avatar from the first-person perspective.

What is relevant about assuming a body in cyberspace is not the replication of real world physicality. After all, one cannot feel pain or physical sensations through one's avatar (yet). Rather, by acting through avatars players take on a role distinct from, yet related to, their own identity. This makes the experience of participating richer and more experiential than the anonymity of the old frontier. At the same time, avatars can be freed from the constraints of gender, race, and class that may impede participation.

The idea of creating a persona to represent oneself is inimitably connected to the idea of freedom and autonomy. But it realizes democratic values to an even greater degree than is implied merely from the notion of self-directed identity. Creating an avatar is akin to assuming the role of citizen. Avatars are "public" characters, personalities designed to function in a public and social capacity. Avatars think and act as members of a game community rather than as private individuals. Having to construct an avatar in a virtual world not only allows me to see myself but it demands that I design a personage for interaction with others. In this way, I am forced to think about how I want to appear as a member of a community.

By virtue of being physically disembodied from the creator, avatars in the theater of the game space may act in antisocial and even pathological ways—ways in which the "real" person never would—shooting, maiming, and killing in brutal fashion. But the existence of the avatar offers myriad positive, democratic, and participatory possibilities too. Virtual worlds, which emphasize iterative social interaction, may elicit these qualities in ways that first-person shooter video games, such as *Hit Man* or *Grand Theft Auto*, do not. First-person shooters do everything to reinforce my role as a killer. But in simulated social spaces, while I can have fun raining rockets on a parade, I can also assume the identity of group participant and member.

That avatar, like the citizen, can also choose to behave in public-spirited ways that the avatar's creator might not. As a persona, the avatar is a citizen—a legal and moral personage distinct from the private individual—who acts in a social capacity. There is a tremendous tension in the "real world" between the demand to act and think in the public interest as the member of a community and the short-term interest in free-riding and self-serving behavior. Avatars are citizens of the online world, imbued with rights and responsibilities, but also conceived of as social personalities. The construct of the avatar offers new promise to observe and experiment with the notion of public citizenship and public spirit.

More practically, the avatar is a way to distinguish among roles within a group. A character can become associated with a particular function that can be assumed by different people. The game *Neverwinter Nights*[21] uses something called the "Character Vault" to allow players to check out an avatar from the library. The Neverwinter Vault protects players against cheating and the artificial manipulation or leveling of characters (think of someone starting a marathon and then paying Florence "FloJo" Joyner to jump in midstream and finish the race). But groups might use the character vault idea as a way to create and store particular roles to be played within a group. Once one person checks out that role, it is taken. Members of the group can then see the person assuming that role. For example, in a deliberative exercise the moderator can assume a particular avatar (a skin or costume), which can then be passed from person to person in the world so that everyone can easily identify the moderator (or the librarian or the current speaker or the ostracized member). In a deliberative negotiation on a contentious policy issue, different avatars might represent particular stakeholders in the debate.

Avatars can assume socially diverse roles. Avatars can be imbued with physical, social, and economic disabilities and participants can be made to play "with a handicap" as a way to teach empathy and learn the impact of political choices on those of differing ability. Imagine participating in a group where you must assume the persona of someone of a different race or gender. It is one thing to voluntarily pretend to be African American and for others to have to guess at your racial identity. It becomes a different exercise when one is either forced to assume that identity and can project that identity unambiguously to others. I am not talking about socially engineered deliberation experiments—although these become possible in a virtual world—but enabling choices about identity that facilitate a sharing of roles and better decision making. Even more interesting, imagine the use of an avatar to represent a group. The avatar is the physical manifestation and embodiment of the group. Just as we talk about corporations as fictional legal persons, now we can see those persons. Corporations go to court, sue, are sued, issue statements, own assets, make collective decisions. They can act on behalf of and represent the group. The members of the group can control the avatar collectively and look to the avatar to see the group.

Of course, in most virtual worlds avatars can be changed like outfits. This gives rise to the question: If avatar identity is not persistent, does that reduce the probability of cooperation and participation? After all, identity is as fluid in a visual Internet as it is in a text-based one. People sell characters on eBay or in the game's bazaar all the time.[22] Is this a hindrance to deepening group culture?

Consider first that the mutability of avatars is a design choice. It would be just as easy to require a constant avatar to participate in a world. Or, more reasonably, a group might require appearing in that group with an identifiable avatar that is known to the group. Participants have an incentive to be identified within the group and to maintain a constant identity for purposes of that group even if they change it for participation in other groups. Second, the mutability of traits in cyberspace may make people more, rather than less, aware of their tribalism and cause them to strengthen group ties. This may enhance the strength of group culture by encouraging membership. Third, even if hairdos and body shape change, avatars have other identifying characteristics which can be used to encourage membership. In *Second Life*, there is a limited set of last names. The designers chose to require players to take one of a given list of last names as a way to encourage people with like names to interact with each other and share a sense of kinship. These names do not change even though appearance does. Members of a particular group assume special honorifics. In other games, players identify by the race, guild, profession, class, or clan to which they belong (or, in the case of *America's Army*, to a battalion or unit).[23] Increasingly, social networking and reputation systems are being built into virtual worlds to make identity more meaningful and transparent than in real space. The mutability of identity raises the question, which we will address below, of whether it is necessary to have a trusted identifier for an online identity in order to facilitate group life.

When people appear as embodied characters interacting face-to-face they behave better. "Griefing" (as complaining in a video game is known) is known to happen on text-based message boards far more than in the world itself. Through visual and graphical representation, this new technology enables people to see the role they have assumed and to perceive the personae of others. People appear as people rather than as dots. This makes it easier to sense oneself as part of a group. Softimage Behavior software allows users to simulate the behavior of crowds of any conceivable size and to model the complex behavior of groups visually.[24] Arguably, the existence of the avatar combined with real-time, multiplayer interactivity changes the suitability of cyberspace for groups.

Finally, I do not want to overlook the relevance of play to groups. Because they rely on the same technology as video games, virtual worlds conjure a sense of playfulness. They are fun. The visual rhetoric is that of a game. The fact that they allow players to be inventive and participate in a shared fantasy by, let's say, turning off gravity and floating, encourages collective laughter. In real-life meetings, shared laughter creates an ethos of the group. There is a developing "ludic literature"[25] analyzing the culture of play in virtual worlds and video games that suggests that group play strengthens the bonds of group identity. This is not far-fetched at all, especially when we consider that so many of our legal entities are the collective fiction of their members.

Virtual Worlds and the Social Life of Information

The first generation of cyberspace has made knowledge communities—groups organized around information—possible on an unprecedented scale. Millions of people already contribute to creating the gargantuan information storehouse in cyberspace (in 2000, 33.5 terrabytes on the web alone and growing at the rate of 10 percent per month).[26] With visual interfaces and the visual representation of information, people will wield more powerful tools for understanding and communicating information, perceiving the connections between pieces of information, and, perhaps most important, putting that information in a social context.

Visual representation of information is not a new phenomenon by any means. From cave painting to maps we have developed technologies to portray complex information visually. Photo and video are well-worn technologies integrated into the online medium too. But now, visuality is becoming more prevalent and relevant to the interfaces of cyberspace as a mode of expression, not just consumption. Graphical content can be created faster and by anyone with inexpensive tools. Virtual worlds and other visual technologies are emerging that permit multivariate representations of information. Instead of being limited to text, typeface, and position, data is represented through three-dimensional geography, a rich color palette, unlimited forms of style and shape as conveyed across three and even four dimensions (since walking through the world takes time). Like maps, virtual worlds tie color and landscape to information. With visual technologies and virtual worlds, we are moving away from paper-based, chronological representations of information toward the representation of information in physical and graphical form.

Virtual worlds are full of graphical information objects—images on the screen that communicate information. Imagine the difference between a single screen of text describing a legal concept, such as the doctrine of adverse possession, and a three-dimensional interface where a scenario representing adverse possession (e.g., a squatter in a house) is portrayed.[27] Imagine the difference between a list of data, organized by date, and a visual map of the same information showing the connections and relationships between that information, its relevance to the user's query, and the quantity of the information. Visual technologies affect the possibility for the social life of information in three ways. First, the ability to see information as a graphical object permits the wider dissemination and easier apprehension of new information. Second, having information in graphical form facilitates discussion about it. Third, the evolution from video games to virtual worlds enables the collective creation of knowledge by a group rather than the didactic imparting of information.

In a virtual world, as in the real world, information is communicated in many forms, including words and text. Though virtual worlds have their origins in word-based, role-playing games, like MUD1 and LambdaMOO, they have evolved into a visual medium where information can be represented as a graphical object. Possession of a shiny orb may signal a special role within the group. That orb can convey information in so many ways. The color, chromaticness, shape, spacing, size, intensity, and text of an object[28] convey meaning in a visual environment. For example, if a group wants to engage in participatory decision making about a particular issue, each member might deposit either a red or a green sphere in a given place to indicate a position on the issue. While a list of yeas and nays can be tabulated, in a visual environment more options are available. The numbers can still be calculated. But the eye can, in one glance, get a sense of the room. The intensity of the color of the sphere might indicate the intensity of feeling on the issue, with dull colors indicating ambivalence. Its shape might indicate different specific rationales or arguments. A large sphere might signal disagreement with substance while a smaller one might suggest a disagreement as to form. The placement of the sphere—nearer or further away from another sphere—might indicate and be readily perceived as signaling relationships between members in the group. There are myriad new possibilities for conveying information—and manipulating it—in a visual environment that did not previously exist in a text-based cyberspace. This kind of informational toolkit gives groups more flexibility and nuance to do their work.

With information assuming an embodied form, it becomes more readily available and understandable because it is more detailed. This is not to say that visual presentation of information is not just as susceptible of manipulation, abuse, and distortion but, done right, the technology offers ordinary people more effective ways to make sense of complex data. Information objects convey meaning on many levels and with more layers of complexity than text. Graphical representation of information through shape, size, color, sound, and the many variables available for representing information in a visual environment enrich the availability of information for the group. What would be clutter on a website, may be intelligible and meaningful in these new interfaces.

The presence of a visual totem—think of the Golden Calf—makes the information manifest and gets it in front of people. Community can form around an object (like a place) to which people feel a sense of ownership and belonging. The memento strengthens the sense of the group but it also creates a connection to the information. It is the technological equivalent of show and tell. The eye cannot avert its gaze so easily but must, rather, confront the information object and respond to it. This is the idea of "push technology" taken to the next logical level. The mere availability of a piece of data does not mean that people will process it. Creating an audience has been one of the central conundrums of the first-generation Internet. There has been the fear that people are not happening-upon information or confronting it.[29] In a virtual world, the ability to give information physical form may make it more likely that people will perceive it. If a decision or problem is represented in physical form, it is harder for the group to ignore and it gives the group a shared object for reflection and discussion.

More important from the perspective of participation, the "high-density" display of visual information means that control of information is given over to viewers, not to editors, designers, or decorators.[30] The visual interface involves viewers more actively in the processing and interpreting of information. Individuals can interpret what they see but groups can also discuss and deliberate on information objects. A silver sphere might represent a pro argument while a gold sphere might represent a con position. Imagine if participants set themselves the rule of having to assemble equal numbers of each as requirement for participation in a debate. Much can be done with these new tools to easily encourage deliberative practices without imposing costly external constraints.

Third, virtual worlds themselves are the product of collective storytelling[31] and they encourage information creation as a collective activity. "Games," writes designer Franz Lantz, "have more in common with jazz, classical, and all forms of music than they do with say, painting. The important idea is participation, not necessarily improvisation."[32] In massively multiplayer games, "thousands or tens of thousands of people play a game whose effect is to tell a story together, instead of going to the movies and receiving the story as a finished good." The universe of the virtual world is partly the creation of the designer, who creates some of the sets, and partly the collective construct of the players, who breathe life into the frame created by the "game god." Players work together to solve a problem, achieve a goal, such as breaching a castle wall, or defeating a villain. In virtual worlds that function as societies rather than mere game spaces, participants increasingly act as self-governing creators of their own communities. They develop and share information within the world and have at their disposal tools to draw connections with and to information. The game gods supply the infrastructure but participants create the meaning. This requires a high level of collaboration and collective action.

It is because of this collective knowledge building—not because games are being used to teach political subject matter—that virtual worlds are well-suited to enhancing democratic political culture. Visual displays of information foster participatory practices and ways of doing. But we need to pay attention to how we visualize information within virtual worlds to take advantage of the power of these new interfaces.

Imagined Communities: Online Groups, Real-World Power

All new technologies convey a promise of revolutionary change and social betterment. These optimistic myths persist even in the face of counterfactual evidence of the ills of technology or the realization that technology is neutral and it is how we use it that really matters. Today, even after the dotcom disaster, the myth that technology will revolutionize democracy soldiers on. Given the pervasive ills of our representative institutions and the deep sense of malaise about traditional forms of liberal democracy, it is no surprise that we speculate about technology's promise.

Institutional problems render it increasingly difficult to make public decisions congruent with the values of the people being regulated by those decisions. Our institutions are ill-equipped to measure the public interest effectively or to galvanize an expression of public interest. Neither can we rely on the privatized media in an era of sound bytes to communicate the decisions of government or hold government accountable to the people. So we look to technology and the electrification of democracy to save our existing institutions. We have invented a variety of unfulfilled scenarios for "e-democracy" that are descriptively and normatively problematical in part because they focus on ways to make current institutional structures faster without addressing how technology, in fact, might change those structures for the better.

I want to posit an alternative that neither imagines the disappearance of the state nor gloms a deliberative chamber on to its existing structures. Instead, this strategy suggests a different model of consociational democracy premised on the collective action of groups exploiting new technology. It is based on the understanding that visual and social technologies, like virtual worlds, make it possible for people to see the groups to which they belong and to participate in them more effectively by sharing tasks via a computer network. The new computer screens replicate and sometimes improve upon group socialization in real life. Through collective action, whether purely online or enabled by technology offline, groups can make decisions and solve problems.

Civic Cyberspace

In order to move toward a world of more autonomous groups engaged in legitimate collective action that, whether it takes place online or off, has real-world effects, we must first cross the chasm between real-world political power and virtual politics. Right now, there is a pervasive sense that what takes place online exists in a closed system with little impact on real world-power. So the question is: How do we get from here to there? How do we take advantage of virtual worlds to realize a vision of more distributed and more collective decision making?

Let's envision a scenario whereby for every bill that is proposed in Congress (or state legislatures, for that matter) and for every regulation proposed on the Regulatory Agenda of federal agencies, civic fairs are organized in virtual worlds to generate public input and participation. While a federal agency might convene the fair, it is unnecessary to expect that government itself needs to organize all such consultative activities. Rather, in these private online spaces, interest groups and activists can hold events to engender public debate. Virtual worlds, like *Second Life,* can hold citizen participation fairs and solicit the help of interest groups and other civil society actors in organizing meetings, not only for the juries but also for the community of practice interested in issues ranging from transportation, to workers' rights, to clean air. Participants in virtual worlds—in the same way that they blog about public events—can organize their own blogs. Interest groups, who know how to make abstruse legal subjects relevant, can use the space to generate public discussion. In this large yet controlled space, there is room both for the government and for interest groups to organize conversations about policy.

The Internet, in particular place-based virtual worlds, could become the "place to be" to decide matters of policy. There is no reason why these conversations should take place in back-corridors in Washington. To this end, we should experiment with the creation of such virtual "civic fairs" with booths for purveying information in textual and graphical form and assembly areas for interaction and deliberation among real people represented by avatars. The "county fair" environment will signal that the dedicated space is both fun and civic-minded. Interested parties, such as trade associations, activist groups, and scientific experts will be able to rent booths for presentation of information and advocacy. These interest groups are the best organizations to attract people to the fairs. By inviting one group to join, others will follow and will draw in their constituents.

Citizens can walk from booth to booth, learning about a proposed rule or policy and the various positions—not simply from reading information but from talking with other members of the community. People enjoy exploring new environments. They will mill about in the fair, stopping at booths, chatting with "neighbors," talking to experts, and encountering agency officials, some identified by a unique uniform.

Because the environment is persistent, these booths and the information they convey can remain open even when the avatars have gone home. Remember that graphical information objects can distribute themselves. The online fair can operate continuously, without staffing, but it can also become the venue for planned events during which larger groups assemble to give speeches, debate, question panels of experts, interact with models that illustrate relevant data and show the implications of various alternative decisions, and register their views in varying ways.

Since there will be a defined (virtual) geographic space associated with the fair, interested people will know where to go and come back to. There will be spaces that people can "happen upon." Groups will be able to set up locations near the fair to do ongoing advocacy and education. These can be spaces where young people get more involved and where it is possible to cultivate an ongoing community of practice without the resources needed to hold hearings in real space. The same can be done in the blogosphere and be linked to virtual worlds.

We might marry such a proposal for the virtual civic fair to the idea of the citizen jury. For each proposal, a policy jury comprising randomly selected citizens who elect to serve in this capacity as a substitute for doing criminal or civil jury service will be assigned to a group to oversee a policy proposal. Better yet, multiple small-group juries from around the country will be constituted. The staff member at the agency or in Congress responsible for the measure will be accountable to these juries. They will meet in the civic cyberspace fair within the virtual world. Membership in each jury will be identified by a special avatar or color or symbol that will show who the jurors are and to which juries they belong. Other groups will continue to participate, interacting with and trying to influence group members. The participants will use the tools and scripts of a virtual world to visually show competing policy proposals and render their debate visible.

Currently, lawmakers make proposals too late in the game for input to be meaningful; citizens react viscerally and vociferously without the benefit of adequate information or channels to make a difference in policy making. Yet politicians and the public alike worry about how to exploit the Net to create meaningful public consultation. They worry even more about relinquishing power to the public to make its own decisions, organize its own discussion, and build participatory groups of the kind we have seen emerging through such efforts as Meetup and Moveon. If the state takes such groups seriously, policy discussions—whether of congressional bills or agency rule makings—might take place online, encouraging groups to engage in positive and proactive activities. This can take the form of officially sanctioned citizen consultation juries organized both online and off. But, in addition, such citizen participation in lawmaking might be the result of decentralized and self-generating action taking place in the blogosphere and in groups of all kinds. This would be a first step in the transition from consulting the public to engaging the public.

There is much to flesh out if we are to develop a system of civic cyber fairs and citizen juries and use them to connect people by means of the networked screen to groups to create greater political accountability. The details require extensive planning and collective imagination. But it is crucial that we adjust the terms of the contract of governance to allow for more distributed, decentralized, and congruent decision making that is as representative of the reasoned will of the people as technology will permit. Having such civic cyberspaces will not simply democratize lawmaking, but will encourage the citizenry to take responsibility and engage in the practices of public life, including problem solving, conflict resolution, deliberation, and decision making. This does not require either a special day for doing deliberation or another attenuated, representative fourth chamber of government. Instead, the proposal is to take advantage of the strength of groups and the possibilities for using technology to sustain them to make political accountability and transparency an everyday practice. If we care about the future of our democracy, we need to do more to explore the way new technologies make it possible for groups—small and large—to take action and, as a result, to wield power in the virtual world and, in so doing, to wield power in the real world.

NOTES

1. James Surowiecki, *The Wisdom of Crowds: Why the Many Are Smarter Than the Few and How Collective Wisdom Shapes Business, Economies, Societies and Nations* (New York: Doubleday, 2004).

2. Fundrace.org is a project of I-Beam, an interactive art and technology gallery in New York. See http://www.fundrace.org.

3. The Michael Moore videoconference took place on June 28, 2004. Thanks to Paul Marino for participating and providing a description of what took place. *See* Byron York, "Michael Moore, MoveOn, and *Fahrenheit 9/11*," *National Review*

Online, *available at* http://www.nationalreview.com/york/york200406290902.asp (June 29, 2004) (last accessed August 19, 2004).

4. Surowiecki, note 1, *supra*. (Surowiecki explains how and why groups make better business decisions).

5. Yochai Benkler, "Coase's Penguin, or Linux and the Nature of the Firm," 112 *Yale L.J.* 369 (2002): 396 (describing the production of economic and cultural value by groups).

6. Institute for Information Law and Policy, Cairns Project, *available at* http://www.nyls.edu/cairns. (Cairns is an online tool developed by the author to study collective action).

7. For a more thorough exposition of groups and democracy, see Beth Simone Noveck, A "Democracy of Groups," *First Monday*, vol. 10, no. 11, at http://firstmonday.org/issues/issue10_11/noveck/ (November 7, 2005).

8. David R. Johnson, Susan P. Crawford, and John G. Palfrey, "The Accountable Net: Peer Production of Internet Governance," *Virginia J. of Law and Tech.* (April 2004), *available at* http://ssrn.com/abstract=529022 (describing emergent decision making).

9. John Seely Brown and Paul Duguid, *The Social Life of Information* (Cambridge: Harvard Business School Press, 2000) (arguing that information and individuals are always part of social networks).

10. Lawrence Lessig, *Code and Other Laws of Cyberspace* (New York: Basic Books, 2000). *See also* Elizabeth Reid, "Hierarchy and Power: Social Control in Cyberspace" *in* Marc A. Smith and Peter Kollock, eds., *Communities in Cyberspace*, 107–134 (London: Routledge, 1999).

11. According to SourceForge, most open-source projects are actually in the early stages of development and it is unclear how many will be completed. See SourceForge at http://sourceforge.net/index.php.

12. For example, AmericaSpeaks, a Washington, D.C., based nonprofit committed to organizing deliberative town hall events, had its greatest success with Listening to the City, where the deliberation of six hundred people led to the scuttling of the proposed designs for the World Trade Center site. Their work was reactive. The group did not create new proposals. Listening to the City, *at* http://www.americaspeaks.org/projects/listeningnyc.html.

13. Beth Simone Noveck, "Designing Deliberative Democracy in Cyberspace: The Role of the Cyber-Lawyer," 9 *B.U.J. of Sci. and Tech. L.* 1–71 (2003); Michael Froomkin, "Habermas@discourse.net: Toward a Critical Theory of Cyberspace," 116 *Harv. L. Rev.* 749 (2003).

14. The Rotisserie Software or H2O project homepage *at* http://h2o.law.harvard.edu/index.jsp.

15. The Wiki Encyclopedia *at* http://en.wikipedia.org/wiki/Main_Page.

16. Beth Simone Noveck, "The Electronic Revolution in Rulemaking," 53 *Emory*

L.J. 1 (2004) (discussing technological innovations for managing the conversation of citizen participation).

17. Noah D. Zatz, "Sidewalks in Cyberspace: Making Space for Public Forums in the Electronic Environment," 12 *Harv. J. Law & Tech* 149 (1998).

18. Albert O. Hirschman, *Exit, Voice and Loyalty: Responses to Decline in Firms, Organizations, and States* (Cambridge: Harvard University Press, 1970). *See also, e.g.,* David R. Johnson & David G. Post, "Law and Borders—The Rise of Law in Cyberspace," 48 *Stan. L. Rev.* 1367 (1996); David G. Post, "Anarchy, State, and the Internet: An Essay on Law-Making in Cyberspace," 1995 *J. Online L.* art 3, *at* http://www.wm.edu/law/publications/jol/articles/post.shtml.

19. Robert Axelrod, *The Evolution of Cooperation* (New York: Basic Books, 1984), 16.

20. Dan Hunter, "Cyberspace as Place and the Tragedy of the Digital Anti-Commons," 91 *Cal. L. Rev.* 439 (2003); *See also* Mark A. Lemley, "Place in Cyber-space," 91 *Cal. L. Rev.* 521 (2003); Alfred C. Yen, "Western Frontier or Feudal Society? Metaphors and Perceptions of Cyberspace," 17 *Berkeley Tech. L.J.* 1207 (2002).

21. *Neverwinter Nights* is set in a huge medieval fantasy world of Dungeons and Dragons. http://nwn.bioware.com/about/description.html (last visited August 11, 2004).

22. On a given day, eBay showed thirty-two avatars for sale. http://search.ebay.com/avatar_Video-Games_W0QQsofocusZbsQQsbrftog Z1QQfromZR10QQsacategoryZ1249Q26catrefQ3DC6QQsotrZ2QQcoaction ZcompareQQcopagenumZ1QqcoentrypageZsearch. Julian Dibbell describes his experiment trading avatars and digital property in his weblog, *Play Money,* avail-able at http://www.juliandibbell.com/playmoney/index.html (the experiment concluded on April 15, 2004) (last visited August 11, 2004).

23. *See* Zhan Li, *The Potential of America's Army as Civilian Public Sphere* (2004) (unpublished Master's Thesis, Massachusetts Institute of Technology) *available at* http://www.gamasutra.com/education/theses/20040725/li_01.shtml (login required). (contains inventory of battle units in America's Army).

24. Product information, *available at* http://www.softimage.com/products/behavior/v1/ (last visited August 19, 2004).

25. Johan Huizinga, *Homo Ludens: A Study in the Play-Elements in Culture* (Boston: Beacon Press, 1938); Jesper Juul, "The Game, the Player, the World: Looking for a Heart of Gameness," presented at the Level Up conference in Utrecht, November 4–6, 2003 (transcript *available at* http://www.jesperjuul.dk/text/gameplayerworld); Constance Steinkuehler, "The Literary Practices of Mas-sively Multiplayer Online Games," paper presented at the Annual Meeting of the American Educational Research Association, San Diego, Calif. (2004); Katie Salen and Eric Zimmerman, *Rules of Play* (Cambridge: MIT Press, 2003); Betsy Book,

"These Bodies Are *Free,* So Get One *Now!:* Advertising and Branding in Social Virtual Worlds," *available at* http://papers.ssrn.com/sol3/papers.cfm?abstract_id=536422 (last accessed August 17, 2004).

26. Bernardo A. Huberman, *The Laws of the Web: Patterns in the Ecology of Information* (Cambridge: MIT Press, 2001), 1.

27. This proposal was made by Susan Crawford. Susan Crawford's Homepage, *at* http://scrawford.blogware.com/.

28. Peter Gärdenfors, *Conceptual Spaces: The Geometry of Thought* (Cambridge: MIT Press, 2004), 1–15 (theory of conceptual representations as a bridge between the symbolic and connectionist approaches).

29. Cass Sunstein, *Republic.Com* (Princeton: Princeton University Press, 2001), 3–23 (chapter entitled "The Daily Me").

30. Edward Tufte, *Envisioning Information* (Chesire, Conn.: Graphics Press, 1990), 50.

31. Darren Werschler-Henry and Marc Surman, *CommonSpace: Beyond Virtual Community* (Indianapolis: Prentice Hall, 2001), 43.

32. Frank Lantz, "Entry 10," *in* Amy Scholder and Eric Zimmerman, eds., *Re:play: Game Design and Game Culture* (New York: Peter Lang, 2003).

About the Contributors

JACK M. BALKIN is Knight Professor of Constitutional Law and the First Amendment at Yale Law School, and the founder and director of Yale's Information Society Project. His work ranges over many fields, from constitutional theory to cultural evolution, from law and cyberspace to law and music. His books include *Cultural Software: A Theory of Ideology* (Yale Univ. Press, 1998); *The Laws of Change: I Ching and the Philosophy of Life* (Schocken, 2002); *Processes of Constitutional Decisionmaking* (Aspen, 5th ed., 2006 with Brest, Levinson, Amar, and Siegel); *What Brown v. Board of Education Should Have Said* (NYU Press, 2001), and *What Roe v. Wade Should Have Said* (NYU Press, 2005). He writes political and legal commentary at the weblog Balkinization (http://balkin.blogspot.com).

RICHARD A. BARTLE cowrote the first virtual world, MUD ("Multi-User Dungeon"), in 1978, thus being at the forefront of the online gaming industry from its very inception. A former university lecturer in Artificial Intelligence and current Visiting Professor of Computer Game Design at the University of Essex, he is an influential writer on all aspects of virtual-world design and development. As an independent consultant, he has worked with almost every major online gaming company in the United Kingdom and the United States over the past twenty years. Richard lives with his wife, Gail, and their two children, Jennifer and Madeleine, in a village just outside Colchester, England. He is the author of *Designing Virtual Worlds* (2003).

YOCHAI BENKLER is Professor of Law at Yale Law School. His research focuses on the effects of laws that regulate information production and exchange on the distribution of control over information flows, knowledge, and culture in the digital environment. His particular focus has been on the neglected role of commons-based approaches toward the management of resources in the digitally networked environment. He has written about the economics and political theory of rules governing telecommunications infrastructure, with a special emphasis on wireless communications, rules governing private control over information, in particular intellectual property, and of relevant aspects of U.S. constitutional law. He is the author of *The Wealth of Networks* (Yale Univ. Press, 2006).

CAROLINE BRADLEY is Professor of Law at the University of Miami Law School. She began her academic career in 1986 as a lecturer in law at the London School of Economics and Political Science. She obtained her LL.M. (first class) from Jesus College, Cambridge in 1984. Professor Bradley joined the University of Miami Law School faculty in 1992 and teaches courses on European Community law, international finance, and business associations. Her research interests are in comparative corporate law, financial regulation, and legal harmonization.

EDWARD CASTRONOVA is Associate Professor of Telecommunications at Indiana University. He obtained a B.S. in International Affairs from Georgetown University in 1985 and a Ph.D. in Economics from the University of Wisconsin-Madison in 1991. He has taught public policy and political science at the University of Rochester and economics at California State University, Fullerton. Professor Castronova's essay, "Virtual Worlds" is the most-downloaded economics paper at the Social Science Research Network. He is the author of *Synthetic Worlds: The Business and Culture of Online Games* (Univ. of Chicago Press, 2005).

SUSAN P. CRAWFORD is Assistant Professor of Law at Cardozo Law School, teaching cyberlaw and intellectual property law. In 2005 she was elected to the board of ICANN. Crawford received her B.A. (summa cum laude, Phi Beta Kappa) and J.D. from Yale University. She served as a clerk for Judge Raymond J. Dearie of the U.S. District Court for the Eastern District of New York, and was a partner at Wilmer, Cutler & Pickering (Washington, D.C.) until the end of 2002, when she left that firm to enter the legal academy. Susan writes about digital copyright issues and Internet governance. She has also published many online essays about ICANN (most coauthored with David R. Johnson), and maintains a website and blog at http://scrawford.blogware.com.

JULIAN DIBBELL, author and journalist, has, in the course of over a decade of writing and publishing, established himself as one of digital culture's most thoughtful and accessible observers. He is the author of two books on virtual worlds, *My Tiny Life* (Henry Holt, 1999) and the forthcoming *Play Money* (Basic, 2006), and has written essays and articles on hackers, computer viruses, online communities, encryption technologies, music pirates, and the heady cultural, political, and philosophical questions that tie these and other digital-age phenomena together. Currently a contributing editor for *Wired* magazine, he lives in South Bend, Indiana.

A. MICHAEL FROOMKIN is a Professor at the University of Miami School of Law in Coral Gables, Florida, specializing in Internet Law and Administrative Law. He is a member of the Royal Institute of International Affairs in London and serves on the advisory board of the BNA Electronic Information Policy & Law Report and on the Editorial Board of Information, Communication & Society. He is also a founder editor of ICANNWatch.org. Professor Froomkin writes primarily about electronic commerce, electronic cash, privacy, Internet governance, the regulation of cryptography, and U.S. constitutional law.

JAMES GRIMMELMANN is Adjunct Professor of Law at New York Law School and a fellow of the Information Society Project at Yale Law School. He received his J.D. in 2005 from Yale Law School, where he was Editor-in-Chief of LawMeme, and a member of the *Yale Law Journal*. He holds an A.B. in computer science from Harvard College. He has worked as a programmer for Microsoft and as a legal intern for Creative Commons and the Electronic Frontier Foundation. He clerked for Judge Maryanne Trump Barry on the United States Court of Appeals for the Third Circuit. He studies the law of technology with the goal of helping lawyers and computer technologists speak intelligibly to each other. He has written and blogged about intellectual property, virtual worlds, the legal regulation of search engines, electronic commerce, problems of online privacy, and the use of software as a regulator. He has been blogging since 2000 at laboratorium.net. His home page is at james.grimmelmann.net.

DAN HUNTER is the Robert F. Irwin IV Term Assistant Professor of Legal Studies at the Wharton School, University of Pennsylvania, where he teaches Electronic Commerce Law and Cyberlaw. He regularly publishes on issues dealing with the intersection between computers and law, including papers dealing with the regulation of the Internet, the use of artificial intelligence in law, and high technology aspects of intellectual property. He is the coauthor of *Building Intelligent Legal Information Systems,* published by Kluwer. He has been editor or guest editor of a number of research journals, including *Journal of Law and Information Science, Computers and Law,* and *International Journal of Applied Expert Systems.*

DAVID R. JOHNSON is a graduate of Yale College (B.A. 1967, summa cum laude) and Yale Law School (J.D. 1972). In addition, he completed a year of postgraduate study at University College, Oxford (1968). Following graduation from law school, he clerked for Judge Malcolm R. Wilkey of the U.S. Court of Appeals for the District of Columbia. Mr. Johnson joined Wilmer, Cutler & Pickering in 1973 and became a partner in 1980. He recently retired as a partner of WCP and is devoting substantial time to the development of new types of "graphical groupware" software products. His previous legal practice focused primarily on the emerging area of electronic commerce, including counseling on issues relating to privacy, domain names, and Internet governance issues, jurisdiction, copyright, taxation, electronic contracting, encryption, defamation, ISP and OSP liability, regulation, and other intellectual property matters. He helped to write the Electronic Communications Privacy Act, was involved in discussions leading to the Framework for Global Electronic Commerce, and has been active in the introduction of personal computers in law practice. Currently, he is a Visiting Professor at New York Law School where he teaches Cyberlaw.

RAPH KOSTER is an MMORPG designer and currently the creative director at Sony Online Entertainment. He was the lead designer for *Ultima Online* and its first expansion *Ultimate Online: The Second Age* and served as the creative director for *Star Wars Galaxies.* He also helped create and write a text-based Multi-User Dungeon called LegendMUD. He is the author of *A Theory of Fun for Game Design* (Oreilly & Associates Inc., 2004). He writes and speaks frequently on online game and community issues, and maintains a website of writings at http://www.legendmud.org/raph/.

F. GREGORY LASTOWKA is a Professor at Rutgers School of Law, Camden. He was an attorney in the intellectual property litigation group at Dechert LLP in Philadelphia from 2001–4. He has published several articles in legal and popular journals on the application of intellectual property laws to new media. Professor Lastowka is a graduate of Yale University (1991) and a returned Peace Corps volunteer (Turkmenistan 1994 to 1996). While serving in Turkmenistan, he cowrote the first Turkmen-English Dictionary. He later attended the University of Virginia School of Law (J.D., 2000), where he was a Hardy Cross Dillard Scholar, an articles editor of the *Virginia Law Review,* and was elected to the Order of the Coif. Following law school, he clerked for the Honorable Walter K. Stapleton of the U.S. Court of Appeals for the Third Circuit.

BETH SIMONE NOVECK is the founder of the State of Play annual conference on law and virtual worlds and director of the State of Play Academy, a center for learning and scholarship within the virtual world. She is an Associate Professor of Law at New York Law School, where she heads the Institute for Information Law and Policy and the Democracy Design Workshop, an interdisciplinary "do tank" dedicated to deepening democratic practice through technology design (http://dotank.nyls.edu). Professor Noveck teaches in the areas of e-government and e-democracy, intellectual property, and constitutional law. She concentrates her writing on law and technology with a focus on the intersection between technology and the design of legal and political institutions. Beth Noveck is the creator of civic and social software applications, including Unchat, Cairns, the Gallery, and Democracy Island. A graduate of Harvard University and Yale Law School, she did graduate work at the University of Oxford and earned a doctorate at the University of Innsbruck with the support of a Fulbright. She is a fellow of the Information Society Project at Yale Law School.

CORY ONDREJKA is the Vice President of Product Development for Linden Lab, the creators of *Second Life.* He joined Linden Lab in November 2000 and brought an extensive background in software development and project management. Most recently, Mr. Ondrejka served as project leader and lead programmer for Pacific Coast Power and Light's Nintendo 64 title, "Road Rash." He also served as lead programmer for Acclaim Coin-Operated Entertainment's first internal coin-op title. Prior to Acclaim, he worked on Department of Defense electronic warfare software projects for Lockheed Sanders. While an officer in the U.S. Navy, he worked at the National Security Agency and graduated from the Navy Nuclear Power School. Mr. Ondrejka is a graduate of the U.S. Naval Academy, where he was a presidential "Thousand Points of Light" recipient and became the first person ever to earn Bachelor's of Science degrees in two technical majors: Weapons and Systems Engineering, and computer science.

TRACY SPAIGHT has been an avid observer of and participant in multiuser dungeons and online role-playing games for more than a decade. In 2002, he was awarded media grants from the Texas Council for the Humanities and the Texas Commission on the Arts to begin work on a feature-length documentary film for television broadcast and theatrical release called *Real People, Virtual Worlds*. The project has morphed into a collaboration with British photojournalist Robbie Cooper, whose *Alter Ego* seeks to document global gaming culture in photographs and essays. Tracy recently joined Rapid Reality as Vice President for Research and Development, where he is also the lead designer on a MMORPG set in medieval Africa. Tracy has held fellowships from the National Science Foundation, the Russell Sage Foundation, and the Deutsche Akademische Austausdienst. He has published several articles on the history of science in publications like *Sky & Telescope, Rittenhouse, Science Technology & Human Values*, and the *Journal for the History of Astronomy*.

TAL ZARSKY is a Lecturer at the University of Haifa Faculty of Law where he teaches Contracts, Advanced Property, Cyberlaw, and Telecommunications Law and Policy. He writes on issues of law, privacy, data mining, and technology. Professor Zarsky holds a J.S.D. and an LL.M. from Columbia Law School, and received his B.A/LL.B. degree (summa cum laude) in Law and Psychology from the Hebrew University of Jerusalem. He is a fellow of the Information Society Project at Yale Law School.

Acknowledgments

This book arose out of a conference held at New York Law School on November 13–15, 2003, entitled State of Play, which became the first of a series of conferences of the same name. The original State of Play I conference was cosponsored by New York Law School's Institution for Information Law and Policy and Yale Law School's Information Society Project. The editors would like to thank everyone involved in the preparation and execution of the conference, including in particular Chun Li, who proved indispensable in making it a reality. State of Play is a registered trademark of New York Law School.

The editors would also like to acknowledge the following previous publications from which chapters in this book were drawn.

Chapter 2: F. Gregory Lastowka and Dan Hunter, "The Laws of the Virtual Worlds," 92 *Cal. L. Rev.* 1 (2004), excerpted and reprinted with permission of the authors and the *California Law Review.*

Chapter 3: Richard Bartle, "Virtual Worldliness," 49 *N.Y.L. Sch. L. Rev.* 19 (2004); chapter. Reprinted with permission of the author and *New York Law School Law Review.*

Chapter 5: Edward Castronova, "The Right to Play," 49 *N.Y.L. Sch. L. Rev.* 185 (2004). Reprinted with permission of the author and *New York Law School Law Review.*

Chapter 6: Jack M. Balkin, "Virtual Liberty: Freedom to Design and Freedom to Play in Virtual Worlds," 90 *Va. L. Rev.* 2043 (2004). Excerpted and reprinted with permission of the author and *Virginia Law Review.* Jack M. Balkin, "Law and Liberty in Virtual Worlds" 49 *N.Y.L. Sch. L. Rev.* (2004). Excerpted and reprinted with permission of the author and *New York Law School Law Review.*

Chapter 7: F. Gregory Lastowka and Dan Hunter, "Virtual Crimes," 49 *N.Y.L. Sch. L. Rev.* 293 (2004). Reprinted with permission of the authors and *New York Law School Law Review.*

Chapter 10: Cory Ondrejka, "Escaping the Guilded Cage: User Created Content and Building the Metaverse," 49 *N.Y. L. Sch. L. Rev.* 81 (2004). Reprinted with permission of the author and *New York Law School Law Review.*

Chapter 12: Tracy Spaight, "Who Killed Miss Norway?" *Salon,* April 14, 2003. An online version remains in the *Salon* archives at http://www.salon.com. Reprinted with permission.

Chapter 13: Susan P. Crawford, "Who's in Charge of Who I Am? Identity and Law On-Line," 49 *N.Y.L. Sch. L. Rev.* 211 (2004). Reprinted with permission of the authors and *New York Law School Law Review.*

Chapter 14: Tal Z. Zarsky, "Information Privacy in Virtual Worlds: Identifying Unique Concerns beyond the Online and Offline Worlds," 49 *N.Y.L. Sch. L. Rev.* 231 (2004). Reprinted with permission of the author and *New York Law School Law Review.*

Chapter 15: Caroline Bradley and A. Michael Froomkin, "Virtual Worlds, Real Rules," 49 *N.Y.L. Sch. L. Rev.* 103 (2004). Excerpted and reprinted with permission of the authors and *New York Law School Law Review.*

Chapter 16: David R. Johnson, "How Online Games May Change the Law and Legally Significant Institutions," 49 *N.Y.L. Sch. L. Rev.* 51 (2004). Reprinted with permission of the author and *New York Law School Law Review.*

Chapter 17: Beth Simone Noveck, "A Democracy of Groups," *First Monday* (November 2005), vol. 10, no. 11. Reprinted with permission of the author.

Case List

ALA v. Pataki, 969 F.Supp 160 (SDNY 1997), 136n12

Am. Amusement Mach. Ass'n v. Kendrick, 244 F.34d 572, 577-78 (7th Cir. 2001), 113n7

Amalgamated Food Employees Union Local 590 v. Logan Valley Plaza, Inc., 391 U.S. 308, 325 (1968), 114n20

America's Best Family Showplace v. City of New York, 536 F. Supp. 170, 174 (E.D.N.Y. 1982), 113n7

Bd. of Dirs. of Rotary Club of Duarte, 481 U.S. 537, 546-47 (1987), 115n32

Black Snow v. Mythic, 139, 143, 145

Blumenthal v. Drudge, 992 F. Supp. 44, 49-52 (D.D.C. 1998), 116n42

Boy Scouts of America v. Dale, 105-106, 115n31, 115n33

Carparts Distribution Ctr., Inc. v. Automotive Wholesalers Assoc. of New England, Inc., 37 F.3d 12, 18-20 (1st Cir 1994), 115n31

Cyber Promotions Inc. v. American Online, Inc., 948 F.Supp. 436, 441-44 (E.D.Pa.1996), 214n16

Green v. America Online, 318 F.3d 465, 472 (3d Cir. 2003), 214n16

Hackbart v. Cincinnati Bengals, Inc., 601 F.2d 516 (10th Cir. 1979), cert. denied, 444 U.S. 931 (1979), 114n12, 128, 135n5

Hudgens v. NLRB, 424 U.S. 507, 518-521 (1976), 114n24

Interactive Digital Software Ass'n v. St Louis County, 329 F.3d 945 (8th Cir. 2003), 113n7

James v. Meow Media, Inc., 300 F.3d 683 (6th Cir. 2002), 113n7

Joseph Burstyn, Inc. v. Wilson, 343 U.S. 495, 501 (1952), 113n6

Kremen v. Cohen, 337 F.3d 1024, 1030 (9th Cir. 2003), 135n3

Lloyd Corp. v. Tanner, 407 U.S. 551, 563-564 (1972), 114n24, 115n26

Marsh v. Alabama, 98-99, 114n20, 114n21

Mutual Film Corp. v. Industrial Comm., 236 U.S. 230, 243-45 (1915), 113n5

New Jersey Coalition Against War in the Middle East v. J.M.B. Realty Corp., 650 A.2d 757, 775 (N.J. 1994), 115n25

Noah v. AOL Time Warner, Inc., 261 F. Supp 2d 532, 544-45 (E.D. Va. 2004), 115n30, 115n31, 214n16

STATUTES

Index